AT BALTHAZAR

The New York Brasserie
at the Center of the World

REGGIE NADELSON

✳ ✳ ✳

Recipes by
Balthazar Executive Chef
SHANE McBRIDE

Photographs by
PETER NELSON

GALLERY BOOKS

NEW YORK   LONDON   TORONTO   SYDNEY   NEW DELHI

G

Gallery Books
An Imprint of Simon & Schuster, Inc.
1230 Avenue of the Americas
New York, NY 10020

First Gallery Books hardcover edition April 2017

GALLERY BOOKS and colophon are registered
trademarks of Simon & Schuster, Inc.

For information about special discounts for bulk purchases,
please contact Simon & Schuster Special Sales at
1-866-506-1949 or business@simonandschuster.com.

The Simon & Schuster Speakers Bureau can bring authors to your live event.
For more information or to book an event, contact the Simon & Schuster Speakers
Bureau at 1-866-248-3049 or visit our website at www.simonspeakers.com.

Interior design by Matteo Bologna

Manufactured in the United States of America

1 3 5 7 9 10 8 6 4 2

Library of Congress Cataloging-in-Publication Data

Names: Nadelson, Reggie, author. | McBride, Shane,
writer of supplementary text.
Title: At Balthazar : the New York brasserie at the center of the
world / Reggie Nadelson ; with new recipes by Balthazar executive chef
Shane McBride ; photographs by Peter Nelson.
Description: New York : Gallery Books, [2017]
Identifiers: LCCN 2016024701| ISBN 9781501116773 (hardcover : alk. paper) |
ISBN 9781501116780 (pbk. : alk. paper)
Subjects: LCSH: Balthazar (Restaurant : New York, N.Y.) | Cooking, French. |
LCGFT: Cookbooks.
Classification: LCC TX945.5.B35 N33 2017 | DDC 641/5944—dc23
LC record available at https://lccn.loc.gov/2016024701

ISBN 978-1-5011-1677-3
ISBN 978-1-5011-1679-7 (ebook)

 *TO DICK ROBINSON*

Thanks

Half a dozen years ago, I first approached Keith McNally about doing a book. The owner of Balthazar, Keith would always rather talk about the theater or cast-iron architecture or Soviet Constructivism than about his restaurant or himself, but in 2014 we met for coffee. He mentioned that he was a fan of English history. I said I was pretty good on the subject.

Keith smiled and said, "Who was the first Tudor king?"

I fell for it. "Henry VIII, of course," I said.

"Henry VII," said Keith. "Do your book."

He promised complete access to whatever I needed. He more than kept his word. He never interfered, not once, though occasionally when I'd run into him, winding me up a little, he'd say, "Aren't you done yet? What *are* you writing?"

※ ※ ※

Give me such shows—give me the streets of Manhattan!

—Walt Whitman

Contents

Breakfast at Balthazar

When I was a kid growing up in Greenwich Village in the 1950s, we sometimes ate out at Longchamps on Twelfth Street and Fifth Avenue, a couple of blocks from where we lived. I loved eating out. I loved restaurants. Longchamps was pink, it had natty Art Deco furniture, and it was French. There was French onion soup au gratin and a maître d' in a tux. His name was Mr. Naigish.

There were years when we had Thanksgiving at Longchamps. This gave my father quite a bit of pleasure. He invited the family. He paid. My pop, who wore bow ties and drank martinis, sometimes ordered wine as well. I'm sure it both impressed and pissed off his brothers—my uncles were rye-drinking kind of men, rye in the old sense, not rye made by hipsters in little hats—who had to trek in from Flatbush, from ancestral Brooklyn.

What's more, Mr. Naigish addressed my parents by name. This was my first inkling that to be a regular, to be known at a neighborhood restaurant, even regarded as friends, made you special. Over at the Steak Joint on Greenwich Avenue, Dan Stampler called my parents Sally and Sam. This was the thing I was crazy about, this feeling you were an insider in a singular little society.

I was a fat, smart, nosy little girl, and God knows I liked the food, but I loved the people: the uptown crowd in suits and minks, slumming in the Village; local families out for spaghetti and meatballs; the artists, writers, and musicians arguing at coffee shops over immense slabs of pie and coffee. Even more interesting were the people who worked at restaurants, out front or behind the scenes: the singing waiters at Asti's on Twelfth Street; the occasional real Frenchman at Charles French Restaurant; the one-armed waiter at Frank's Pizzeria on Bleecker Street, his empty shirt sleeve pinned back, who tossed the pies with the brio of a juggler on *The Ed Sullivan Show*.

Then there were the waitresses at Schrafft's where my mother took me on special occasions for ham and Swiss on toasted cheese bread served by these plain Irish girls in hairnets and black uniforms. Some of them had been hired just off the boats, my mother said. It sounded like a kind of spooky religious order. I longed to ask about their lives, these women far away from home. Where did they live? Who were they?

At the Coach House—it was located in an actual old coaching house on Waverly Place—black waiters in white gloves served dinner. The idea was that you were dining on all-American food in some theme park little version of another age, perhaps down south. It was unusual, too, in a city where if you went out to eat you generally ate French or Italian or maybe blintzes at Ratner's. The fried chicken, the corn bread made in special black iron molds, and the black bean soup were all delicious. The owner, Mr. Leon Lianides, was imposing and, unless you were quite famous, a little intimidating. Still, everyone else was very nice, very gracious. I always wondered, though, if after they finished work, when the waiters took off their white gloves, they also retired their smiles for the night.

* * *

Longchamps, the Steak Joint, Charles, the Grand Ticino, the Cookery, the Sea Fare, all gone now. My parents are gone; the restaurants, gone. The bars, too. Bradley's, the Cedar on University Place, where Jack Kerouac, it was said, pissed in the ashtray. As kids, we went trick-or-treating at the Cedar because instead of candy, you always got cash.

What I took with me from childhood was that sense of a different world where you might be admitted or at least given a glimpse. Anytime a maître d' hugged me or a waiter called out my name or a bartender offered me one on the house, I felt I was in; I had arrived.

The truth is, I guess, I've always been on the lookout for a place where I could embed myself: a local bar, a restaurant, a coffee shop. Maybe it's simply that lifelong yearning for community, the driving force in the life of a lonely only child.

* * *

"Top of the goddamn morning to you," said the good-looking young guy at the door as I stumbled into Balthazar around eight most days. James Weichert, the young guy, was always in a loud Hawaiian shirt, an impish grin on his face.

"My shirt was not Hawaiian, it was Comme des Garçons," James says now.

At first I ate alone in the bar area, read the paper, and chatted to James. I had been assigned a piece about boats for the *Financial Times*. I hate boats. It turned out that James, though, was an enthusiastic sailor who had just joined the gay and lesbian Knickerbocker Sailing Association in the hope of meeting a nice guy he could settle down with and who also loved boats.

"You should meet some of the other regulars," he said one morning.

So it was James who introduced me to Steven Zwerling and

Rona Middleberg. Soon, I was eating breakfast with them every day, hurrying to get out of the house.

"Breakfast is about mortality," Steven Zwerling said. Almost every morning, perhaps to stave off his sense of finite time, he ordered the same thing—two oatmeal scones, two blueberry jams.

Steve, who worked for the Ford Foundation then, was king of the morning, boss of Balthazar breakfasts. Of breakfast, he said, "It's the most biological of meals. The fast is broken, of course, but also it comes upon many of us who are only half emerged from sleep and all its demands. We drag ourselves over to Balthazar. The coffee that arrives to make everything better . . . We distract each other with stories, occasional frustration, even rage at the rest of the world, a couple of useful insights, a little compassion and understanding. And laughing."

Erudite, funny, mournful, and very tall, Steve was a repository of New York stories. He had met—or seen—everyone: Jackie Robinson, the Rosenbergs laid out in their caskets at a funeral parlor in Brooklyn, Fidel Castro. When Castro visited Columbia University in 1958, Steven, a student then, rushed out of the crowd to shake Fidel's hand. Fidel was very tall, too, and handsome.

Steven was married to Rona Middleberg. Rona always sat facing the front door and could thus check out everyone who came in. Small, beautiful, musical, with long brown hair and a soft manner that belied her skepticism and stainless steel business brilliance, she seemed to run half of NYU. Rona liked a pain au chocolat in the morning, though she could be persuaded to share a sticky bun from time to time.

Breakfast—the communal breakfast at Balthazar—really came together in the aftermath of 9/11 when the whole city, especially downtown Manhattan, leaned in toward itself for comfort. For months, the large black cloud hung over the hole in the ground where the World Trade Center had been. I could see it from my place in SoHo. When I'd left town on September 9, the Twin Towers were there. I came home a week later, and they were gone, evaporated, disappeared, turned to dust. The smell never went away. At Balthazar within a few days of the attack, people hurried in, looking for some kind of solace, or at least coffee. "Have one on us," one of the managers said to everyone who entered. "We're glad to see you." Code for *Glad you're alive.*

Those mornings it was never crowded, though you might see an artist slumped over his bowl of café au lait, up unnaturally early, having stumbled in looking for caffeine.

We became a gang. An ad hoc group of people—writers, teachers, a performance artist, a Wall Street lawyer who occasionally appeared in very tight spandex bike shorts—we referred to ourselves (ironically, of course—this was Manhattan, after all) as the "Balthazaristas." I published a piece called "Breakfast at Balthazar" in the *FT Magazine.* Friends began calling up, asking delicately if they could come by, as if we were a secret cult, the Skull and Bones of Spring Street.

Most days by eight-thirty we were in place, tables 81 and 82 pushed together, plenty of room in case David Easton showed up. An august interior designer, David was always beautifully dressed, usually wanting a glass of red wine even at eight in the morning, often with a very funny, very dirty joke to make us laugh. He'd drink up and be off to Charlottesville or Aspen.

We had our own share of celebrity spottings: Jon Stewart with his then young family; Mel Brooks, who came and sat with us for a little while and made us laugh so hard we gagged on the sticky buns; Nigella Lawson, who popped in for a hefty slice or two of fruit focaccia. She was a girl who loved to eat. Once she said to me, "Those diets that say you can have one cookie, do you think they mean one bag of cookies?"

* * *

We talked. Argued. Bitched. A bit bored one year, we complained that there was no matzo during Passover, though none of us was the tiniest bit observant. The staff produced matzo. Rona said she made a great matzo brei and was allowed into the kitchen to make it. The rest of us were as envious as if she'd been awarded a backstage pass to a rock concert. We had always been curious about the unseen life at Balthazar.

Over the months and then years, we kept talking, no subject forbidden: new jobs, family feuds, old loves, vacations, the Yankees, cancer. There was much discussion of disease; colonoscopies were a favorite topic. At first we felt this was because we were all, one way or the other, neurotic New York Jews. Then, one day, Maria Aitken, the English actor and director, popped in for a croissant and stayed to tell us the story of her colonoscopy, and how she failed to understand the pain until she heard herself from a distance, moaning like a cow.

Mostly what I remember about those years of breakfast at Balthazar, though, were the jokes, the uncontrollable laughter.

For years I could barely stand to miss a breakfast. And then, like everything, it changed. The breakfast menu grew. Packs of alien financial types began appearing. James left and got his MBA. Steven and Rona spent more time in Florida to be close to Steve's mother, who died at a hundred and seven. Until she hit a hundred, she often came to breakfast with us.

Suddenly Balthazar was going on twenty. Like all long-running love affairs, breakfast at Balthazar became habit. There were the inevitable irritations: What to do about someone who suddenly started showing up regularly and whom we did not really like? Should we all pay our own checks instead of each picking it up in turn? Was the table too crowded? Were we laughing less?

But those mornings, with the sun coming through the windows, Balthazar was at its most tranquil. The old French mirrors, the pewter surface of the long bar, the wood, the white-and-black tile floors gave you a sense of *dépaysement*—I don't think this has a true translation, this French word for feeling you're far away in another country. It wasn't France, but who cared?

Adam Gopnik, the author and *New Yorker* writer, said, "Balthazar is an elaborate re-creation of an imaginary place, not a fake but a delicate hybrid, a product of this city, of New York as much as Paris." A country of the mind, Balthazar was a restaurant that reminded me of my childhood dreams of New York.

In the end, breakfast at Balthazar, and Balthazar itself, was, for me, about the fulfillment of that terrible longing for community. I thought it might last forever.

"It's just breakfast," Rona said one morning. Nobody believed her.

PART
ONE
EARLY

CHAPTER 1

CURTAIN UP

efore dawn, long before the doors at Balthazar opened for
breakfast, the cleaners were at work, and through the big
windows on Spring Street I watched them wiping down the
red banquettes, shining the glass and brass, sloshing water across
the black-and-white-tiled floors and mopping it up. A woman in a
green sweatshirt with a sparkly Eiffel Tower on it, her head down,
intent on her work, polished the mahogany bar. She ran her cloth
over it. Then she did it all over again, pausing to turn to a guy in
sweatpants. I couldn't hear what they were saying. I could see their
mouths moving as they called out to one another—but what about?
On the other side of the window they were inaudible to me, in the
same way they were invisible to most of the daytime world, to the
city itself, these people who worked in the dark and disappeared to
another job at dawn.

Balthazar looked like an empty theater, the play over—or not yet
begun—everyone gone except the cleaning crew, these mostly unseen workers who, like stagehands, had come in at two in the morning and would be gone by daylight.

Ghosts. Massiel Pagan, who had been our waiter—both men
and women at Balthazar were called waiters—for years, told me she

was certain that Balthazar was haunted. Massi was a sharp young woman; hardworking, ready to crack a joke, she indulged us with extra portions of toast and did not suffer fools . . . or ghosts. But she heard them. Early one morning when she had been almost alone in the restaurant, she heard these ghosts calling her name from downstairs. She went down. The ghosts had disappeared. But they had known Massiel's name.

My alarm had gone off at five. I was due to meet Balthazar's executive chef, Shane McBride, at five-thirty. It was cold. I slammed shut the kitchen window, turned on the radio. Rain was coming. Cold rain. Wet fog.

I made a cup of instant. From my kitchen window, I could see the back of a little building with tiny dormer windows set high up. The front of it faced Spring Street. In it were the remnants of a well where, on the last day of 1799, Gulielma Sands's body was found. Her suitor, Levi Weeks, was accused of the crime. Weeks got off, but then, he was very well connected. Acting in his defense had been Alexander Hamilton and Aaron Burr. It was the first celebrity murder trial of the nineteenth century.

After I saw the musical *Hamilton*, I could not get it out of my head that Hamilton and Aaron Burr had been here. On my block, a few yards from my house, the pair of them, working a case that made all the papers. I never looked out from my kitchen without thinking of them.

Poor dead Hamilton; poor Aaron Burr, his reputation ruined. But in 1800, they had been here, two middle-aged lawyers on Spring Street, past their glory days but still as alive and contentious as the guys in tasseled loafers down on the courthouse steps, guys who might have climbed on a stool later at Balthazar's bar in search of a good stiff drink.

• • •

I took a shower, yanked on some clothes, closed the door, got the elevator, and left the building. Nobody at all was on Greene Street.

In the building across from mine, only the owls were lit. The woman over there kept some kind of plastic owls in her window, and recently she had added light-up ducks, or chickens, some sort of fowl. The other windows were dark.

For the first time, I was going in to Balthazar to get a look at what made it tick—the kitchens, the guts of the place, the staff in the restaurant, of course, but also the people behind the scenes. For years now, I'd been doing this, getting up, walking to Balthazar, but only for breakfast and not at this godforsaken hour. Not when even the garbage trucks that came twice, three times a night, had come and gone.

On the other side of my street was a shop that sold strange Japanese clothes worn by bald white mannequins. I liked the idea that they had just finished a night out at the clubs and were only now settling down to their day job in the windows.

Greene Street was empty. And beautiful. Even when it was much more desolate, even a half century ago when it was run-down and broken, it always had the bones of a great beauty.

Early in the morning, SoHo had the feel of a tiny hamlet, a little late-nineteenth-century principality, a low-rise square mile that seemed private in the dark, sheltered against the traffic, the high-rises, even the city itself.

I loved the way SoHo looked with only the streetlights for illumination, when it seemed almost unchanged for decades. The little, tightly packed grid was lined with cast-iron buildings, all of them four or five stories, most painted in pale colors—white, cream, light gray—and with massive windows. Most were decorated with elegant lintels and pediments and slender columns, opulent enough to satisfy the prosperous silk and dry goods merchants who commissioned them in the 1870s and 1880s.

Henry Fernbach, a German Jewish architect who had come to New York as a young man, made Greene Street. On my block between Prince and Spring Streets, he designed the lovely cast-iron buildings, including my own at number 95; built in 1881, it was neo-Grecian with Corinthian columns, curly leaves sprouting at the top. Most sumptuous of all was 114–120. It had been the grand Manhattan branch of Frederick Loeser's Brooklyn department store; now it was occupied by Louis Vuitton. A nice symmetry, I thought.

South on Greene Street, my block empty of tourists, shoppers, UPS men, and FedEx men. No construction workers were turning one more building into a condo with wildly skyrocketing prices, no city workers digging up pipes.

The streets here still flood in March or April, the ancient springs still run deep underground. In 2012, when Superstorm Sandy hit, SoHo lost all its power for a week and Balthazar's basement flooded knee-high.

Behind its preening shop fronts, beneath the apartments and condos, like much of New York, SoHo was broken. The cobblestones were chipped like bad teeth. New York was not a twenty-first-century city; downtown here it was barely of the twentieth.

Mornings, early like this, the quiet always seemed unnatural, this lack of noise like a thick layer of insulation suffocating the city. New York this silent always seemed like a little death.

But New York was safe now. Apart from a rash of shoplifting in my neighborhood, the kind where guys ran into Burberry and snatched a hundred key rings—key rings seemed a dull and poor catch for serious thieves—there wasn't much crime. I had lived through the crack epidemic, though, and in the predawn dark, a faint sense of menace lingered. When I heard footsteps behind me, I began to jog, but of course it was only a man from down the block with his enormous shaggy yellow mutt.

I hurried. I was late. The chef was coming in to meet me. A diffident man, he had seemed a little steely about the whole idea. This might be an adventure for me, but to him it just meant getting in early.

Heading for Broadway, I passed number 119, where my friend Lynne, who is an artist, has lived for more than fifty years. On the ground floor was the Kardashian shop, and the mannequins there had perky nipples. On weekends, young girls hurried inside and came out with designer water bottles. Across the street from it, Donald Judd's house was a museum now, and you could book a tour of this little theme park of art.

I ran across Spring to Broadway and stopped to look up over Lady Foot Locker where there was only a tiny remnant—a little piece of window frame—of the St. Nicholas Hotel, which, built in 1853 and torn down thirty years later, had been the grandest hotel in the history of New York City. The fabulous hotel, the fancy furniture and crystal chandeliers, and now it was only a fragment over Lady Foot Locker.

All this history, all this *stuff*, and four minutes, a fifth-of-a-mile walk, from my house to Balthazar. Balthazar had marked its territory in SoHo, *as* SoHo; it gave the neighborhood a destination, pushed up the prices and the glamour, it dragged SoHo east across Broadway.

A yellow truck was just pulling in from New Jersey, where Balthazar's breads and morning pastries were made. Bright light flooded the restaurant, and I could see Shane McBride, the chef, huddled with Erin and Katy. There was the smell of smoke. Something was wrong.

Overnight, an electrical fire had sparked behind the wall of the men's room downstairs. This resulted in a cloud of thick acrid black smoke, followed by the alarm, the fire engines, and the firefighters who put it out and had, in the process, cracked a porcelain urinal and torn out most of a wall.

Katy Wagner, that night's manager, had closed up the restaurant around two and settled down with some paperwork when she smelled the smoke. She called 911; she called Erin.

"Good morning." I was a little nervy and therefore too cheery, too chipper. That it was a good morning was something that had not occurred to Erin Wendt. Keys in hand, she had driven in from New Jersey, probably breaking the speed limits in two states. No time that morning to make breakfast, as she almost always did for her four kids—blueberry pancakes for the two boys, chocolate chip for the two girls—or to say good-bye to her wife.

"Jesus," Erin said. "Shit always happens here."

Erin, who had been Balthazar's general manger for years, had risen in the ranks to become deputy director of operations for Keith McNally's company, which included seven restaurants and a bakery, but Balthazar was her baby. When the acting GM had suddenly quit, Erin came back. So she was doing two jobs, but it was better like this because after fifteen years—after working in the bakery and the restaurant as a waiter, as a manager—she knew all of it, knew every new host who came in late, which dishwasher had a family problem. Erin had hired most of them. She also kept track of every glass that broke, the price of pork, the improvements on the garbage disposal, all of it.

Balthazar was open to customers from seven-thirty in the morning until one or, on weekends, two a.m., and anyway, nobody was ever actually thrown out. With the cleaners working overnight, this meant it operated on a twenty-four-hour schedule, and no matter when a problem came up, Erin was there in person, or on the phone, worrying about it, fixing it; it was always hard for her to let go of even the tiniest day-to-day requirement. Even now, her eyes flicked toward the ceiling; she had noticed a light fixture with a dim bulb.

A husky, pretty woman in her early forties, black hair, pink cheeks, Erin had improbable dimples when she laughed. She was not, however, laughing, not now, not right this minute. In cargo pants and a pink-and-white-striped shirt, Erin tugged at her pearl earring and conferred with Krzysztof Spychalski about the replacement of piping and the porcelain urinal in the men's room.

For a moment, the idea of paying for new copper pipes was pissing her off mightily. But after a brief exchange with Spychalski that included some ribald remarks, Erin did laugh. Settled back into her usual can-do attitude. Fifteen thousand things to do that day to keep the machine oiled.

The two of them had worked together for more than a dozen years, and Polish Kris, as he was affectionately known, was a calm man. Bearded, good-looking, Kris was soft-spoken with a faint Polish accent, and he could make anything. He had done fine woodwork back in Poland but was currently on Keith McNally's staff as the overlord of fixing stuff and was also working as project manager at one of McNally's new restaurants. He had seven of them now.

Kris told Erin she was right about the size of copper pipes, and Erin, pleased, said, "The stuff I know, I could open a contracting business."

"It's OK, I'm on it," said Kris. To me he said, "The truth is I'm here to solve the problems. With me, Keith is nice. Always, always. He never yells at me. I think I am only one," Kris added, grinning, his well-seasoned charm showing.

Somebody smelled smoke again. There was a brief frenzy, a little flurry of activity. Then everyone went to work. No big deal after all, not for these people who, as a community, had lived through 9/11, the murder of one of their own, the 2003 blackout, and Superstorm Sandy.

By six, Katy Wagner was leaning on the bar, drinking coffee out of a paper cup, checking the day's staff schedules with Bruce Rabanit, the manager this morning.

Dark-haired, with a mobile face that lent itself to the stand-up comedy she did off duty, Katy ran the training at Balthazar. She was a desperately hardworking woman, one of a gang of staffers who went out after work—more in the early days—to SoHo bars. Rumors were that very late at night Katy liked dancing on certain bars, that once in a while she even took her top off. Maybe just rumors.

Everyone liked Katy; everyone worried about her. But for sure she was a lifer at Balthazar. Until suddenly, not long after I saw her that early morning, she quit. Exhausted. Overwhelmed. A woman who had been obsessed with always getting it right, and then she'd had it. "She'll be back," somebody said. "Everybody always comes back." Soon after Katy left Balthazar, Puck Fair closed.

A pair of breakfast waiters sat in one of the wooden booths near the bar, refilling salt and pepper shakers. This was one of the jobs waiters did, this and filling up little pots with ketchup and mustard before dinner. They had already been downstairs in the mysterious catacombs under the restaurant, had changed into their work clothes: black pants and tie, white shirt, bistro apron.

In her black dress and white apron—some of the women referred to them as their "French maid's costumes"—Amari Williams, her apron tied crisply around her waist, was sorting through little glass pots of Bonne Maman jam: apricot, blueberry, strawberry. The staff manual required that waiters know the jam flavors by heart.

At the bar, a good-looking guy with an Irish face was examining a plastic box, checking the fruit—oranges, limes, lemons—for the day ahead. He looked at the soda stream, nodded at the barback, who was setting down a crate of water he'd brought up from storage in the cellar. It was only 6:39 by the old clock over the front door, and already the day was full on.

"Let's go," said Shane. "Five-thirty a.m. to three p.m. is really the heartbeat here, it's why I wanted to get you in early. In the morning, all the deliveries come in," he added. "All the storage, the walk-ins fill up, the food prep is in full swing, lunch—the first big meal of the day—is getting under way. The first thing I do is go to the kitchen, check on my breakfast guys. I generally do a walk-through of the whole place."

At forty-two, Shane was a stocky good-looking man with the reddish-blond hair of his Celtic ancestors. He was drinking iced tea from a plastic thirty-six-ounce cup he had in one hand; with the other, he held open a swing door. I followed him into Balthazar's kitchen.

All those years I had eaten breakfast at Balthazar—and not just breakfast—I had wondered exactly what went on in the kitchens, back of house, out of sight, below stairs, behind those swing doors. Now, I was in! I was in! This idea of getting beneath the surface had been on the horizon so long, and then suddenly I was there; like Wordsworth, I had crossed the Alps.

The kitchen was improbably small, about fifteen feet by twenty-six, and it smelled richly of bacon. Bacon on the stove caught my eye. More was sizzling in a pan. Shane had a fistful of bacon strips, and he said, "Smell that!" and offered me some. I ate a couple of strips; he ate the rest, a blissful expression flashing across his face. A trained French chef, he was nonetheless a southerner and smitten with the pig. On his left arm was a tattoo of a butcher's pig; on his right, four stars, and the outline of a fifth. Like most chefs he was waiting for the big five.

"This is bacon from Tennessee. This is going to go on my soft-shell crab BLT next season. There's no exquisite recherché stuff that gets made here," said Shane. "These guys are making good food for people to eat. It's just about cooking."

The guys were doing a sort of prep and precook for breakfast: bacon on, sausages on, eggs ready for boiling and scrambling, piles of bread for toast, batter for the pancakes. To keep up with orders, you had to be ready; speed was everything. In the mornings, the kitchen was at its calmest, a chamber group much more than the frenetic rock and roll of the evening shift.

Shane said, "Morning." The five cooks called out, "*Hola. Hola, Chef.*" Intent on their work, these quiet men in white jackets passed along an occasional comment in Spanish—family, politics, baseball—to their mates. Shane shook hands with Cesar Guzman, a sous chef from El Salvador; he had an almost perfectly round face, like a full moon. That day, Cesar was in charge. He had a faraway look. Maybe he was daydreaming of summer, when he liked to barbecue all kinds of meat, he said, especially venison, in his backyard.

Cesar's favorite dish was the Wednesday special, the salmon coulibiac, an elaborate Russian dish of salmon and hard-boiled egg, spinach, mushrooms, dill, rice, butter, and crème fraîche baked in a shell of rich puff pastry. Very rich. It was one of those complex dishes that was invented in Russia in the early twentieth century—a dish the aristocrats gobbled up just before the revolution—and then imported to Paris by Escoffier. One day I watched Cesar make the dish and when he spread the pastry over the whole confection it was like a couture dressmaker fitting a garment with exquisite precision.

Like many of the men in the kitchen, Cesar had been at Balthazar from the beginning. Before the beginning. "Cesar painted the walls," Shane told me. "Twenty years ago."

Twenty years in the febrile world of New York restaurants made Balthazar a pretty old pup. It was an institution now, a fixture in the city landscape. Adam Gopnik, who writes as well as anyone about restaurants and much else for the *New Yorker*, said, "The thing that strikes me, and it's greatly to Keith's credit, is that New York is such a fickle place, where restaurants go into fashion and then out of it so rapidly. That he's kept this place going now for, what, twenty years? That's kind of astonishing."

Balthazar served around half a million meals a year, give or take. After twenty years, Balthazar was crowded almost around the clock, and took in roughly $25 million a year. The statistics were mind-numbing. Still, Balthazar's longevity and success couldn't be explained merely by the numbers; to simply run the stats was, in a sense, meaningless, like explaining Shakespeare to a dog. What really made it tick was the staff, the waiters, the cooks, the prep guys and porters, the bartenders and barbacks. Erin Wendt had been around for a fair number of those years.

Pleased she had figured out a cheap price for the copper piping, Erin pushed through the swing doors into the kitchen. One of the cooks gestured to her. He wanted to tell her that he thanked the company for his recent promotion. She replied in Spanish. It was the lingua franca of New York restaurants. Almost everybody was Hispanic; many of them did not speak much English. I never went into the Balthazar kitchens without thinking what a long trek it had been for many of the staff coming from a Mexican town, or the Dominican Republic, or Bolivia, to Spring Street.

Following my gaze, Erin clocked that I was lost. "Look, the kitchen is broken down into six stations: fry, grill, sauté/meat, fish, hot appetizers, and garde-manger—that's salads and cold appetizers." She rattled them off, pointing to each in turn.

On the same level with the restaurant, this kitchen was where as many as 1,500 meals a day were produced. From first breakfast orders at seven-thirty—a plain boiled egg, eggs en cocotte baked in cream and thyme in little ramekins, waffles with warm fruit syrup— until one or two in the morning, when the last drinker called for a cheeseburger and frites, it all happened in this improbably small kitchen. With a stainless steel worktable in the middle, blackened stoves against the wall, and a pass-through on one side that led out the back and then down to the prep kitchens, somehow it served its purpose.

During meals, waiters in the restaurant took the orders, punched them into a computer, and pressed "Fire." In the kitchen, a sous chef printed out each order. The guys in the kitchen cooked the food. A runner picked up the plates to carry them out to the guests; the sous chef stuck the printout on a spike. All day, every meal, the spike filled up with paper. These paper remnants of every dish, every meal, throughout eighteen hours, were the record of a day at Balthazar.

"Goddamn, this is awesome," Erin said. There were rare moments when Erin seemed to stand back and remind herself about the scale of things and how the Balthazar machine ticked over and maybe how—just once in a while—pleased she was to be its chief engineer.

Behind the kitchen was a minute area with a large sink where the dishwashers worked. Hard to see how so many people squeezed into this claustrophobic area. As the day went on, it got as jammed up as New York's side streets at rush hour: waiters pouring ketchup from huge containers into tiny stainless steel pots; runners and bussers scraping plates into the garbage cans; bakery people looking for a stash of fresh baguettes in a minuscule cupboard. At the back of Balthazar, there wasn't a square inch to spare.

"You coming?" said Shane, still in his snazzy Barbour jacket, drinking his tea and shaking the plastic cup so the ice cubes clinked around in it. It was a nervy gesture, like an adolescent tapping his foot.

I followed him down a flight of metal stairs into the basement and into an area at the bottom of the stairs pretty much directly under the kitchen but much bigger. In this prep kitchen where I found myself, the floor was still damp. A short man was pushing a mop across the far side of the room.

Overhead, strong fluorescents drenched the room with hard light. Against one wall were two enormous stoves; on one was a row of tomatoes, soft, juicy skins puckered, ready for peeling. Next to the stoves was a freestanding cylindrical machine about six feet high.

"It's called a steam kettle. We cook small people in it," he said. Shane then looked at me quizzically, noting my expression, maybe thinking I was so stupid about the workings of a professional kitchen I might have believed him. "Actually," he said, "it's used for big batches of chicken and veal stock."

In the center of the room was a long stainless steel table and another one pushed against the right-hand wall. Five guys in white jackets were at work, baseball caps or scarves on their heads, heads down, eyes focused on their work. This was the room where most of the food was prepared. Apart from an occasional comment in Spanish and the clatter of a knife, there wasn't much noise.

I tried not to skid across the damp floor.

The men went on slicing, dicing, mincing, peeling. It wasn't seven yet, but they'd been in for a while—easily an hour—and the prep was in full swing. From the time they came in early in the morning, the prep guys cut onions for soup, onions to caramelize for breakfast potatoes; they peeled shallots, cleaned and cut asparagus; they snapped the tips off skinny French beans, and diced carrots. Mounds of green were piled on the table along with red and yellow peppers. The men were fast and they were good.

"The same guy has been cutting the onions like this for going on twenty years," Shane said. "This is a tough and sometimes shitty business, so to do it you have to love it at some level."

Leaning in over their work, intent on it, wielding those knives with such skill, the prep cooks resembled a pack of surgeons in an operating room. At the table against the wall, a cook was making béarnaise sauce. I looked around for a cookbook, even a scrap of paper with a recipe, but there weren't any, not that I could see.

"There's definitely recipes written, but most of these guys have been making the same stuff—vinaigrette for the frisée lardons—from the beginning. A lot of them have little books with the recipes, we had a master book, but I can't remember anyone looking at it," Shane said. "They were making the Maître d'Hôtel butter yesterday same as today, they know it's thyme, parsley, garlic, shallots. It's weighed out in an aluminum barquette—that's what they're called—and those are the recipes. And they're kind of just handed down from person to person. Like in a family."

Shane shook hands with some of the guys working at the table then headed for his office a few yards from the prep room. On the way there we passed a kind of rolling cart about six feet high, made up of metal shelves, and on the shelves were the fresh morning pastries that had come in the yellow bakery truck. Croissants. Apple galettes. Sticky buns studded with pecans.

"Help yourself," said Shane. I got hold of a sticky bun and put it surreptitiously in my purse. "It's OK," he said, clearly a man who noticed everything. "You don't have to hide it." His expression indicated I was behaving like a kid who had stolen cookies from the cookie jar. He helped himself to an almond croissant.

I followed Shane into the chef's office. It was only a few feet from where the men were operating on the veg.

Books leaned against one another on some rickety bookshelves in Shane's cramped office. On one shelf there was also a bottle of port, a jar of nuts, a few broken food blenders. A blue bike hung upside down over Shane's desk. There was no window, no light except from an overhead fixture.

"I get in, I eat donuts, I have a tea, I look at porn," he said, turning his computer on and producing a mock yawn. "Just kidding."

At first, Shane wasn't easy to read; I got the feeling if he didn't like you, you'd know it. But he was surprisingly straight with me, answered all my questions, including the invasive and sometimes, when it came to cooking, naïve—well, not naïve, idiotic. Apparently, he hated bullshit. "I'm just a cracker from the South," he liked saying.

Shane has only the faintest hint of a Florida accent, but then, he grew up in West Palm Beach.

"Not exactly a bastion of rednecks," I said.

"Not really," he said. Anyway, it would have been a mistake, thinking of Shane McBride as unsophisticated. He was the executive chef at four of Keith McNally's restaurants, some of the city's best. This took deep confidence and tremendous talent, also balls and a kind of obsessive unwillingness to give in to fatigue after even a ninety-hour week. He had worked ninety hours at one job on his way up the restaurant ladder, a climb that could destroy body and soul. But the competition was ferocious and part of the game was showing off your machismo, your prowess, as well as your cooking chops. As a result of the crazy schedule, Shane got so sick he still suffered from asthma and bronchitis.

The "cracker" business, this line of Shane's about being a bourbon-loving good old boy—though he really did love a good bourbon—was his way of telling you how much he hated pretension in the food business.

There's plenty of it in New York, too, where people discuss food and restaurants as if these were life and death, and maybe they are, maybe the greedy pursuit of what we eat is a way to deflect reality, a displacement activity, a way to suspend all thoughts of death.

Making great food, though, was far from the only remit of the modern executive chef. Food prices were constantly exploding. Balthazar often did 7,700 covers a week, more than 10,000 around Christmas.

Every morning, Shane looked at the stats from the night before—customers, food, money—and to see if anyone had asked for something special, or sent a dish back to the kitchen, or expressed delight, or got pissed off.

Budgets and food portions were often on Shane's mind. Unless he had a meeting or there was an emergency like the overnight fire that had brought him in before dawn this morning, he usually showed up at nine-thirty or ten. Plenty of nights he didn't get home until twelve or fourteen hours later.

He tossed his iced tea container into the trash. With a distracted air, Shane banged around in his locker at the back of the little room, looking for his chef's jacket and pants. When Erin appeared in the open door, he was wearing only a T-shirt and some big green shorts printed with beer mugs. Erin started laughing, big belly laughs, and they kidded around and mugged for my camera and bitched and complained. This was a tough business—tough, hard, and relentless— which resulted in a lot of joking and plenty of expletives.

Shane's phone rang. There was a problem. Shane apologized. "Can you come back a little later?" he said.

Outside the chef's office to my left was a hallway. Against the wall were potatoes in orange net sacks and cardboard boxes marked GPOD that contained more potatoes. The walls were painted gray, and a little of the paint was peeling; the light came from those overhead fluorescents.

A voice behind me said, "It's big. It's big down here."

It was Erin. "People are pretty surprised when I tell them this is a whole city block, that it runs underground from Broadway to Crosby Street," she said. "Come on."

She turned left. I followed. Along the wall opposite the potatoes were doors to the walk-ins where food was stored. In one was the meat; sometimes there was a couple grand's worth inside, so the meat fridge was locked every night at seven.

Erin opened another door, another little room in the magic kingdom of food. A blast of icy air. Air with only the faintest whiff—more of a whisper, in fact—of the sea. "Fish," said Erin. "Beautiful fish." I followed her inside the room-size fridge. On the shelves, fish and seafood were stored in boxes and crates. Oysters, trout, shrimp, skate, black sea bass, scallops—those big fleshy sea diver scallops the color of cream with a hint of pink. Red lobsters, too, and sacks of clams. "This is the freshest fish in the city," Erin said.

In another room were the milk, eggs, cheese. With a kind of awe, Erin said, "Last Friday we bought 120 dozen eggs just for Saturday and Sunday brunch." Her phone rang. "Hey," said Erin, "give me a few. OK. Have a look around."

More corridors, more gray walls with peeling paint, the same ugly light. I followed the corridors. There were no windows in this underground world, no daylight in the endless catacombs that led from the prep rooms all the way, a whole block, to the back, the farthest end, where delivery bikes were stashed.

The freight elevator that usually brought goods down from Balthazar's back entrance on Crosby Street had a canvas pull to lift and lower the door. Some of these old elevators remained in SoHo, even in the residential buildings. It reminded me of the time when there had been artists in SoHo, some of them squatting in lofts. Back in the 1980s, even the '90s, when you went visiting, you yelled up from the street, somebody threw down keys, you went in and worked that freight elevator.

From time to time I passed somebody sloshing a pail of water over the floor, then mopping it up. It looked shabby down here. Still it was almost impossibly clean in spite of the tangle of rooms and closets, corridors and odd spaces where people worked.

Thinking I was back near Shane's office, I bumbled into a room with a sign that indicated the boiler. I went back out to the corridor. A man pushing a handcart loaded with crates of asparagus looked up at me briefly and kept going. I was lost. Once I had driven to the farthest reaches of Brooklyn out by the ocean, to little communities where I had never been. There is a short story by Thomas Wolfe called "Only the Dead Know Brooklyn." It captures wonderfully the emotions of a new visitor trying to work out the subway system, knowing he has not a chance in hell of getting it right. It was how I felt now in this immense underground. I turned around and threaded my way forward.

Off one corridor were rooms where I saw crates of wine; in one was a wine fridge that included a Corton-Charlemagne that would run you 2,200 bucks in the restaurant. I kept going, through an area lined with gray metal staff lockers, one with a sticker for Greenpeace, to what appeared to be a staff area, tables shoved together. At one of them a young guy sat staring at his phone and drinking from a Starbucks coffee carton.

There were rooms with cartons of dishes, napkins, aprons, glass, cutlery; rooms with coffee, peanut oil for the fries, and bottled water. Through a door I could see a big laundry room. A woman was folding napkins. Waiters' jackets hung on a metal rack. A man with sleek black hair stood, shirtless, at an ironing board.

I passed a man tucked in a corner making chicken liver mousse and another rolling out fresh pasta. I stumbled into a large room then where a man with a nice face, a white jacket, and white flat-cap was cracking eggs with one hand into a large bowl. Later I would get to know him as Mark Tasker, the chief baker.

Mark's room had that singular overwhelming smell of pastry baking, pastry heavy with butter and sugar. Glazed hazelnuts were piled in a little pyramid on a table and I could almost taste them, nutty, crackly, sweet. Mark put down the egg in his hand, took pity on me, and directed me back to the chef's office.

Down here in this maze of rooms and corridors, in the kitchens and storage facilities, the prep rooms, the cubby holes where somebody made agnolotti and somebody else fresh banana ice cream, was the beating heart of Balthazar. Without it there would be no restaurant upstairs. Everything I saw fed its bloodstream. It was like a body laid bare; you could see the innards, the organs, the lymph and marrow. To a newcomer, it looked impossibly chaotic. Nothing seemed to connect. I was as lost as I'd been once on a movie set where I didn't know anyone or anything, and all I managed to do was trip over bundles of cable and into a shot.

Setting out here was like starting a new language. For a moment, when I found myself in a space where there was nothing at all, just a room with gray walls, I felt that one day somebody would find my whitened bones here, my skeletal fingers clutching the sad remains of a sticky bun. The twelve-story building where Balthazar occupied part of the ground floor had been put up in 1903. In the building's underground where I was, the sound of the boiler, a generator, a disposal system, the freight elevator, the innards of the restaurant itself, seemed to groan and whimper.

"Hey!"

Erin had found me.

On her way back to her office—her cave, she called it—she greeted Dwight, the regular delivery guy from Hunts Point Market in the Bronx. Anne Winniger, who did the flowers, had just come in from the market. In her arms was an enormous bundle of stock, lilies and overblown roses; some of the petals fell onto the floor; the too-sweet scent of the stock trailed behind Anne.

The striking thing about Erin was that she knew her way around Balthazar, upstairs and down, and could have walked it blindfolded. To keep Balthazar ticking over, not counting Anne Winniger or Polish Kris, not including the executives who looked after all of McNally's restaurants, it took 246 people, give or take. It took one executive chef, two assistant general mangers, seven managers, four maître d's, ten hosts, one wine director, one wine assistant, the cellar master, ten bartenders, three barbacks, forty-nine waiters, fourteen runners, forty-seven bussers, six sous chefs, one pastry chef, twenty-five line cooks, fifteen prep cooks, eight raw bar prep cooks, six stewards, fifteen porters, thirteen dishwashers, not to mention the staff in the adjoining bakery.

It was a big machine, and it required a fastidious sense of organization and an almost impossible consistency, so that no guest would ever be disappointed.

We stood outside her tiny office, and Erin said, "The chicken we serve is the same chicken we served in 1999." Erin, who could remember details from decades earlier, was a natural-born storyteller.

"Sure, in those early days, it was sex, drugs, and rock and roll." Erin laughed at the memories, at a time in the late 1990s when she didn't get up at five in the morning, when everyone shopped at the Salvation Army shop on Spring Street. When they all felt invested in food and wine and were taking cheese classes and thinking about opening their own places. "We were young and single, and it was before New York became Disneyland," Erin said. "Harvey Keitel sat on the bench outside smoking, every actor, Broadway, off Broadway, was coming in." Different times.

There was money in the city. A downturn, a crash in the fall of 1997, was a hitch; it didn't last. The economy bounced back. Good times were available.

"We were kids. We worked like crazy and then partied all night. If you worked at Balthazar in the early days, you lived in a bubble," Erin said. "Everyone smoked. I don't think the words 'human resources' existed, and the majority of people who were working here lived in little shithole apartments, and you probably didn't like your roommate, but nobody stayed in their apartment, and you got paid in cash, got off at twelve-thirty or one in the morning, went to Blue Ribbon and ate and got shit-faced, and you still managed to get it done. The waiters would come in perfectly pressed, perfectly coiffed."

Did Erin sigh? Was she missing the old days when there was a seat-of-the-pants ethos about Balthazar, and Keith McNally was always around; when meetings took place in the restaurant, and I'd see them in the back corner, staff members huddled with Keith, figuring out what had gone wrong and what was working?

One of the prep cooks had a question for Erin. She nodded briskly. It was time for her to go, to begin the assault on the little Everest of tasks that went on and on throughout every day. There were a thousand moveable parts in the Balthazar machine, and many of them were human: waiters, dishwashers, cooks. The need for replacement wineglasses, or a new calendar over the bar—this was a kind you could only get from certain Parisian shops—these were Erin's business, and so was the way the napkins were folded. And everything would begin all over again the next morning, like a play that was always the same and always different.

We started upstairs to the restaurant. Erin climbed ahead of me, still talking. She looked at her watch. It was ten after seven. A long day ahead. "Everything that happens all through the day builds towards dinner," she said. "Everything."

CHAPTER 2

BUILDING BALTHAZAR

Upstairs, the restaurant was calm and beautiful, the hectic activity below hidden from view. I remembered seeing Balthazar when it had opened in 1997. I'd been outside looking in. April 1997. Filthy snow still clung to the pavement from a freak storm on April first, but it was a mild spring night. Cars, taxis, limos were in gridlock, horns blaring while residents leaned out of loft buildings and screamed: "Shut the fuck up."

At 80 Spring Street, something was happening.

There were huge glass windows that spilled yellow light onto the pavement, a seeming mirage on what had been a desolate stretch of Spring Street. Paparazzi had replaced hookers and crack dealers. A gorgeous, loud, juiced-up crowd pressed forward, swarming the door. A whiff of excitement, ambition, and desire was palpable. On the red awning overhead, blocky gold letters read: BALTHAZAR.

Did I press my face against the window? Only in memory, but if I had, I would have seen the mirrors, the flowers, the black-and-white-tiled floor, the sexy rosy lighting that makes everyone gorgeous.

Waiters swooped around the tables like dancers, their white

bistro aprons tied tight around their fabulous bodies, attending to the glittering customers made up of movie stars, models, and artists moving as if on a stage, in a sleek choreography of pleasure and privilege. This was a party. The front door was ajar, and you could hear, you could feel, the palpable throb of excitement, music, laughter, and fame.

Now, at seven in the morning, the same space was almost empty and I could see it for itself. The large room, the high tin ceilings, made it feel spacious but not cavernous; there was nothing minimalist about Balthazar—but it was opulent, not oppressive like some of the other vast SoHo spaces. The walls had been lacquered a sort of gilded yellow and the patina was richer than it had been twenty years ago, as if the colors had been strained through cigarettes and beer and Champagne.

Red banquettes and booths ran along the walls and in the middle of the room, and just above them were sconces in the shape of flowers made of opaque glass. Near the front windows were freestanding tables, set now with crisp white paper. Huge bouquets of flowers, those full-blown magenta roses and creamy hydrangeas, stood on the backs of the banquettes.

The long mahogany bar, the twenty-seven-foot pewter top, the glass shelves against the wall behind it shone with rows of glasses and bottles, some containing amber Cognacs and burnished single malts. At either end a pair of caryatids—those sculpted half-naked classical ladies beloved by the Belle Époque—seemed to hold up the ceiling.

At the back of the room: the oyster stand. Over it, a mirror where the specials had been written in white, as they would have been in a Paris brasserie. On two other walls, more mirrors hung tilted slightly so the room could preen, could show itself off in the antique glass with its golden reflection.

During the day, in sunlight, the mirrors reflected the room and everyone in it with a brilliant energy. At night, lights turned down, the looking glass showed the room itself as if lit by a thousand candles.

When Keith McNally opened Balthazar in 1997, Rudy Giuliani was New York's mayor and would be reelected in the fall because crime was down in the city and Giuliani had not yet gone nuts about sex shops in Times Square or the 1999 Chris Ofili exhibit at the Brooklyn Museum that featured a painting with the Virgin Mary and some elephant dung. Bill Clinton was still President, and when Tony Blair became Prime Minister that spring there were parties all over London. In August, Princess Diana was killed in a Paris car crash, Elton John's "Candle in the Wind" was number one on both sides of the Atlantic. The Spice Girls, *Titanic*, Puff Daddy were big, Tiger Woods won the Masters, Dario Fo the Nobel Prize in literature.

It was also the decade when downtown Manhattan was said to be almost unbearably cool, with SoHo at its very center. If, in truth, artists were beginning to leave, looking to the Lower East Side and Brooklyn for cheaper space, it still had the glow, the magnetic pull. The bit of SoHo along Spring Street east of Broadway was ragged then and could boast of an urban edge; at number 80, before Balthazar took it over, there were a few little ramshackle shops, a leather warehouse, and a tannery; a low note of cow often drifted on the morning air.

Even before work began on Balthazar, Kris Spychalski—Polish Kris—was planning to make a dress for his wife and had dropped into the warehouse to pick up some leather. "It was incredible," he said. "Bolts of leather, remnants, scraps, sheets of leather in brown, tan, black, dyed a strange hot pink, all of it piled on racks twelve feet high along the walls and against the partitions that divided the space and shook when you walked."

Months went by; inside the warehouse work began on what would be Balthazar. Locals tried to peer in but paper covered the windows, and workers who came and went refused to talk.

"I used to go to a notary at 80 Spring, and one day there was brown paper in the windows," Michele Oka Doner told me. Michele, who was a sculptor and artist, was the first person I ever knew who had a loft where she worked and lived. Later, I'd see her flying—or seeming to fly—through the neighborhood. Very tall, with the posture and demeanor of a grande dame, or perhaps an Isadora Duncan dancer, she was usually dressed by Morgane Le Fay in fluid, flowing art clothes; some of her coats sailed like great wings behind her. (Le Fay was the first great couture shop in SoHo.) Even when Michele was working on a piece of sculpture with a blowtorch in her hand, she looked strikingly regal. She and Fred, her husband, are still regulars at Balthazar. She remembers before it opened.

"I saw that brown paper, I put my head in," Michele recalled. "I asked a guy what was going on, and he said they were making a restaurant. I asked whose it was, and he said Keith McNally, you know, from Odeon and Lucky Strike, and of course I knew Keith. 'What kind of restaurant?' I said. 'A French restaurant.' 'Well, tell Keith to remember they should serve the locals,' I said to him. Keith did. He understood the neighborhood, and Balthazar grounded SoHo."

Keith's pal Lorne Michaels told me he, too, had seen the place when it was pretty much still a wreck, just a ramshackle old warehouse with nothing much going for it. When the brown paper came down, when Balthazar opened, he was knocked out. It put him in mind of that George S. Kaufman line, he said. "If God had the money, this is how he would do it."

"*Poyekhali*" is a wonderful Russian expression that means "Let's go!" "*Andiamo!*" "*Allez!*" It also implies a spur-of-the-moment daring, a raffish, seat-of-the-pants kind of willingness to risk it, an instinctive decision to just go for broke. "*Poyekhali*" takes its real potency from the fact that, when he was already in the capsule waiting for liftoff, just before he became the first man to fly into space, this is what Yuri Gagarin said: "*Poyekhali!*" Every time I talked to somebody about how Balthazar was dreamed up, funded, and built, I'd think of it: *Poyekhali.*

"We didn't know anything," Ian McPheely, the designer, told me. "You've heard of the sketch on a napkin? That's how we did Balthazar. Or Keith would bring in some little blurry photos of Paris and a sketch. I had never seen a brasserie." So right up until they got to work, not two years before Balthazar opened, Keith McNally had only an idea, a possible location in a leather warehouse at 80 Spring Street, and a backer with enough faith in him that, on the basis of a little sketch on a napkin, wrote a check for two million bucks.

At seven-thirty, as he did most mornings when he was working, Bruce Rabanit, one of Balthazar's three managers, unlocked the front door. Among the first customers through the door was Dick Robinson. He settled into the smallest booth near the bar—Dick was always aware that others might need the larger booths—and ordered café au lait in a bowl and a couple of soft-boiled eggs. It was Dick who had written the check.

I'd gotten to know Dick over the years during those breakfasts at Balthazar. And I'd run into him on Broadway near Prince outside the Scholastic Building. Once in a while we had brunch together and ate too much bacon.

A charming man with a gentle, almost shy manner and an impish smile, Dick was a sweet guy and a shrewd businessman; the CEO of Scholastic Press, he had built it into a two-billion-dollar operation that published the Harry Potter books and the Hunger Games series. Child literacy had long been his passion, and over the years he had co-opted a wide range of young celebrities including Taylor Swift and Usher to work on it with him.

He loved books and had done his graduate work at Cambridge with the legendary critic F. R. Leavis. For a while as a very young man in the 1950s, Dick had also been a bit of an anarchist who admired the Beat poets and was, briefly, a college dropout.

One morning when we were having coffee together, he described for me his erratic path in and out of Harvard that reads like a pulp picaresque, with jobs in lumber mills and as a switchman on the Rock Island Line, and working construction alongside guys who had been given cushy jobs, perhaps by their shady relatives; a scene straight out of *The Sopranos*.

Everyone at Balthazar liked Dick Robinson.

Henry Ly, one of the bussers, brought water. Dick shook his hand. Henry greeted him with his usual diffidence. I asked Henry how his kids were. "I have three now," he said. His oldest girl was sixteen; I remembered when she was born.

At Balthazar, there was always a lot of hand-shaking, of managers, waiters, bussers greeting regular guests; sometimes there was cheek-kissing, too, and customers inquiring about Henry's baby or Nicole's trip home to see her mother in France.

"But why take the chance on Keith?" I asked Dick as he drank his coffee. Why gamble on Keith, whom he knew only from Martha's Vineyard?

Dick said he was living in SoHo at the time, and with Silicon Alley gearing up, he saw the potential for a big restaurant in the area. And then, too, he had been happy as a young man in Paris in the brasseries that seemed a wonderful amalgam of literary salon and tavern, of intellectual and artistic ferment.

Originally, it was Dick Robinson who had called Keith, not the other way around. He had a little building on Mercer Street and had been thinking about it as a restaurant. Keith looked at it, but it was only 2,500 square feet and he was thinking of something bigger. Much bigger.

Dick said, "Then Keith called me and said, 'I'd like to show you something.' And he showed me the space that was to be Balthazar. He said, 'Well, what do you think of this?'"

Keith told Dick a bit about what he was planning. Dick thought it was brilliant. He knew that Keith had done Odeon and Lucky Strike, and he figured—as he generally did—that instinct was probably a better bet in business than crunching numbers.

"I said I thought it was great, and Keith said, 'Well, fine, why don't you be my partner?' The idea was that we'd split it—he had the expertise, I'd do the money," said Dick, ordering his second bowl of café au lait. So he wrote the check in the summer of 1996.

I asked Dick if he'd hung around much during the time Balthazar was under construction, those fifteen months when there was brown paper up in the window. "Once in a while I'd come over and take a look at it," he said. "And that was that."

Poyekhali.

I had always wondered why, apart from the big windows on Spring Street, there weren't any others at Balthazar. When I walked around the corner to Crosby Street, I noticed something I'd never seen before: there had been windows here along the east-facing wall of the restaurant, but they had been boarded up, which, it turned out, was Keith McNally's idea.

Balthazar's designer Ian McPheely told me that everybody thought Keith was nuts. In New York City, light is so precious nobody in living memory had ever done this. But in Balthazar, Keith wanted a restaurant that was a world to itself, where the real view was of the room, and where you were cocooned in a seductive sanctuary, exported for a few hours to a different place where, as Ian said, "You could be anywhere, except you're not, you're in Balthazar."

No view here. The idea of a restaurant that is about a view always seems pretty overrated at best; you can't eat a view or talk to it or seduce it. Balthazar was always about the life going on inside, the theater, the choreography of customer and staff, the business of food and drink, of gossip and status and laughter. Not so different from what Brillat-Savarin described in a Paris restaurant a couple of hundred years ago.

I wrote a screenplay once (it was truly terrible) in which when I couldn't figure where and how to set a scene, I'd send the characters to eat and drink in various venues, one of them a bar in the shape of a pineapple. The director commented that these people appeared to spend an awful lot of time eating. It was true. It was all that I knew.

In New York where apartments are small, everyone in a hurry, private life often takes place in public places, as often as not in restaurants. Restaurants, cafés, bars, diners, coffee shops, taverns, brasseries; this where we meet each other, seduce each other, where friendships and deals are made, marriages sealed, breakups negotiated, where we celebrate; these are places for serious conversation and casual gossip, for come-ons and brush-offs, and all over a beer, a bottle of wine, a cup of coffee, a burger and fries.

You go to drown your sorrows, read a book, think about writing a novel, or leaving your job. No surprise that in so many great urban movies there are so many restaurants, or clubs, or cafés. I think of the scene in *Goodfellas* at the Copacabana; of the diner in *Diner*; or the bar in *Star Wars*; or the seedy Viennese nightclub in *The Third Man*. Rick's Café Américain in *Casablanca* and Maxim's in *Gigi* and Freddy's Barbecue Joint in *House of Cards*. Nobody in any of them cares about a view.

At Balthazar even the front windows that look out on Spring Street are frosted partway up—there's not much to see anyway— and on them are printed some of the offerings: DEGUSTATION DE LIQUEURS; SPECIALTES DE BIÈRES; PLATEAUX DE HUÎTRES.

Ian McPheely had never seen a brasserie when he started work on Balthazar. Born in Canada, he attended Washington University in St. Louis and Chicago's Art Institute. He had planned on a life as a fine artist. To make a living he painted houses. "Lots of houses," he said.

He struck me as a man who could build a hut for himself on a desert island and worry about the proportions and the design. I can imagine him, a sucker for detail, worrying about the exact relationship of the door to the height of the hut, and agonizing over the blank spaces in between. The space between objects was as important to him as the objects themselves, in much the way, I think, that for certain playwrights the silences are as meaningful as the dialogue.

Like so many designers and architects, Ian wasn't particularly chatty, at least not at first. Only when he warmed up to the subject did the enthusiasm for his work show, and the more he talked, the more you saw how it consumed him. "We didn't even have a budget," Ian said over coffee in the corner of the Balthazar bar. "We had no idea how much it was going to cost or how long it would take."

When he described the process of building Balthazar, it was as if he and his crew had been kids, students, people who were willing to take a flier. They gutted the place and then they stood around looking at it. "We'd just draw it, we had a really great lead carpenter in Joe Hammerstein, and I remember sitting with him in front of the bar and saying, 'OK, what are we going to do?'"

What they did was lay it out on a piece of paper, rip it up, do it again, three more times, four more times, until finally Ian, or maybe it was Keith, said, "This is it. Let's go. Get it to a carpenter and say, 'Do this.'"

Ian and the crew began setting up a workshop in the basement in 1996. Everything came out of that shop: the ceiling, the wainscoting, the bar, the frames for the mirrors, as well as the banquettes and pretty much everything else. It was a motley team of artists, writers, and musicians, all moonlighting as builders and carpenters to make ends meet and because they loved "building stuff," as Ian put it. "It was a lot of fun. There were also still generations of real craftsmen back then, this still existed in New York. And there was a wonderful camaraderie."

They worked late. There was no time to go home at night and do drawings, and there were no computer programs you could use at the time. When he started on Balthazar, Ian had, in fact, only just gotten his first computer, which he used to print out work schedules and not much else. His day began in Brooklyn at dawn back then, so he could pick up building supplies early enough to make the trip over the bridge before six-thirty a.m., a ten-minute journey that, if you waited until eight, would be an hour and a half. He always arrived with drawings and handed them out to the crew, who were already unloading materials from trucks at the curb. As I listened to his account, I realized how much he loved recalling this crazy episode, this piece of work, when his crew made it up as they went along.

It made me think of old rockers recalling their salad days in a garage band. There was a sheer pleasure in what seemed like ancient history, in a handmade thing as you would never do now, not when computers instantly spit out hundreds of copies of architectural plans of robotic perfection.

I envied them all. As a solitary writer, I had yearned for a community, a gang of collegial workers making something good. It was my fantasy, of course. In these stories of builders and rockers, there were rarely any women except as groupies.

Still, it was a lovely idea, all those young artists, writers, musicians, arriving on Spring Street at dawn, wrestling with how you made up a restaurant, how you really just invented it out of thin air. The story became a kind of myth, this notion that Keith built Balthazar based simply on intuition, on what his gut told him.

There has always been a certain English attitude that good and great and interesting things—art, music, inventions, ideas—rarely come out of corporations or business schools, but from instinct. Out of passion or inspiration or taste or just a knack, a particular kind of savvy. God knows it's hyperbolic when you're talking about a restaurant, but when I thought about the way Balthazar was built pretty much without a plan, it reminded me of this. Keith McNally did not have an MBA. He had not eaten in a restaurant until he was sixteen. The words "hospitality industry" would probably make him gag.

At Balthazar one afternoon, I found myself sitting at the bar alongside an Englishman I knew and who said he was close to Keith and had been for a long time. He told me that most of the stuff at Balthazar was definitely old. He swore that the floor tiles were old, that the bar was an antique. "Trust me," he said, sinking into the glass of white wine in front of him on the bar. This was a smart guy, and I'd known him a long time, and then of course there was the patina! The mirrors! The ancient zinc bar!

It was part of the lore, the mythology of McNally, that he was a wizard. He could turn a new restaurant old, could burnish a place, could make it glow so you would believe it had been there for a century. I had believed it. *How old*, I had thought; *how lovely was this patina, how fine these antiques.* The sheer ambiance. The ancient tin ceiling and those walls so yellowed with the residue of a million cigarettes. You walked into Balthazar, and it took you over, this illusion of age, of history.

Legend was that the bar at Balthazar had come from a Wyoming auction house. That it was a hundred years old, had perhaps been taken from a saloon where Butch and Sundance (or Newman and Redford) drank. More likely that the real Sundance actually had a drink not far away when, before the doomed trip to Bolivia, he and Etta stayed at Mrs. Thompson's Boarding House on East Fourteenth Street.

"It actually came from an old dive bar in Harlem that was closing down," Ian said. "Keith, or one of his sources—and he has plenty— found it, he bought it, thought we could reuse it. It was completely rotted away, and when you picked it up it just fell apart. We took the components and re-created the bar. Keith found somebody in Paris who could cast a twenty-seven-foot-long pewter top. Pretty much everything else was fabricated here, in the basement in our workshop."

Even the caryatids, the carved ladies on either side of the bar, had been made to order. Fin de siècle Europe was partial to these sculpted bare-breasted women—they were based loosely on a Greek and Roman tradition—who held up ceilings in place of columns. Ian remembered the pictures that Keith had produced of caryatids somewhere in Paris. One of his carpenters who was also a sculptor had re-created them. Including the breasts.

I wondered if there had been models, and Polish Kris laughed. "One of the waitresses, as I recall," he said. "I don't remember which one."

It was the drawing of the bar that had convinced Dick Robinson.

"I remember," said Dick, "Keith just showed me an impressionist detail of the kind of bar he had in mind with mirrors and bottles that looked like something from Toulouse-Lautrec and nineteenth-century Paris, particularly the glass. He drew that little picture, and that was it; that was the thing that sold me."

I loved the idea of Keith McNally standing in the middle of the room as the mirrors were hung, directing the angle at which they were tilted for the greatest effect, for the best way they would reflect the action. He had always wanted to make movies and this would be his best production.

"The right tilt is about eighty-four degrees," said Kris Spychalski. Reflected in them, Balthazar was, from the start, a pretty sumptuous babe, showing herself off to her adoring admirers, who could also look at themselves and everyone else in the room.

The mirrors, some old, some specially aged, arrived in pieces from everywhere. "It was like a crossword puzzle, putting them together," Kris said. Like so many other elements, I realized, Balthazar was made up of a billion bright bits coming together perfectly.

Kris was good at making things and remaking them, and like so many at Balthazar who came from around the world, his story had been about politics and fate. In Kraków, where he grew up, he had a woodworking business. He was in Vienna in 1981, looking for materials, when General Jaruzelski declared martial law in Poland, and the borders were sealed and communications cut. Kris was reluctant to go home, if he could get back at all. So he caught a flight to New York. He remembered looking out from the old TWA terminal, and when he went outside, the first thing he felt was the humidity of a New York summer. The second thing was that he fell in love with New York. He settled in Greenpoint in Brooklyn, the traditional Polish neighborhood, and started working for Keith McNally.

"Nobody could imagine this space as a restaurant except Keith, who is a visionary," said Kris. "I was into modernism, he wanted curves and old stuff and patinaed stuff, and I saw how brilliant it was."

When it came to the mirrors, said Kris, "Keith and everyone brought in about a hundred eighty distressed mirrors, or pieces of mirrors, and I put them on the floor and assembled them."

Still, the mirrors would not look right, the restaurant would be duller, the customers less gorgeous, if it weren't for the gilded lighting. This is what gives you the delicious sense that you have been lit by God, or at least Vittorio Storaro.

Ian claims it was incandescent light that produced the illusion of a thousand candles, gave the room a natural beauty, "like sitting around a campfire."

Clearly a practical man, Ian seemed a meticulous designer who, devoted to the tiniest detail, was downright passionate about the lighting. The object of it was to create an equal bath of light throughout the room. The equidistant points of warm light would be at face height because if it were higher you'd be in the shadow. On the wall just at the end of the bar, he put the light box with about thirty settings that could be changed throughout the day and night. Ian got it perfectly right, but he knew problems were coming, and they arrived in the form of the government ban on incandescent lighting. The little lights in the flower-shaped sconces on the wall were small enough that these would be all right. But for the rest, when I saw him, he said, "We're in the process of changing, but LED and fluorescent are ugly forms of lighting, and LED doesn't really save that much energy."

He'd been thinking about these problems for fifteen years, he said, and was now working with a form of neon called cold cathode, designing new colors with an Italian company; you needed two of them to make up for the incandescent lights.

"There's phosphorescent powder inside the cathodes," Ian told me. "It's tickled by a wave of electricity, and the color changes." It is, he said, delighted as if by a magic trick, "like lightning bugs rubbing their hind legs together to make a spark."

Lightning bugs!

It took more than lights, though, to get Balthazar running.

I met Judi Wong at Café Cluny in the West Village, which she owns with Lynn Wagenknecht, Keith McNally's ex-wife.

A slim, stylish dark-haired woman with big glasses, Judi had been involved with the Odeon and was in at the beginning of Balthazar, and she remembers how it was in SoHo. "You'd run into people doing things in other restaurants, and they knew about jobs and what was going on at the galleries and who was sleeping with whom," said Judi.

Judi was part of the SoHo scene. She worked at Jerry's on Prince Street, and then went to Kin Khao and to Kelley and Ping on Greene. "I was kind of a SoHo person, a downtown person," said Judi, who, along with Niels Koizumi, was one of the general managers when

Balthazar opened. "We hired all these, like, proper French waiters to be captains, and they knew so much about service and wine. But Keith trusted me, which is really, really amazing. You know, I was just a little girl from Canada."

Judi told me it was as if every ounce of Keith's energy went into making things perfect. For six months before the opening, there were endless meetings. "Before it opened, every square inch of that place was touched by Keith."

Whenever Judi Wong goes back to Balthazar, it is, she told me, like coming home: "In the restaurant business, people come and go constantly. To be able to keep a core family group there is a testament to the top. It comes from the top. From Keith."

When I next saw Ian McPheely, he was worrying about the walls. Keith was not happy with the color. Something had happened over the years and the quality of the patina at Balthazar had changed. It was off, it was too dark. Paint wasn't the problem because there wasn't much paint on the walls. Ian had tinted the plaster and glazed it over to add dimension. "You get the depth," he said. "The walls kind of radiate because the light's going in and bouncing back out."

It was in these details and his obsession with them that Ian had connected almost viscerally with Keith. That, and the constant upkeep. "It's like a great ship," said Ian. "Keeping a huge restaurant in order is like keeping a great ship afloat, the detail is everything, the work never ends; sometimes I see the cleaning crews coming in very late—the early morning, in fact—and as they swarm the restaurant, the kitchens, sloshing water over the kitchen floors and scrubbing the glass and brass, it reminds me of a crowd of sailors endlessly pushing back against decay and rust." Ian added, "But the joy of Balthazar, in design terms, is that it is itself." The tin ceiling was bought in sheets. The pretty flower-like sconces on the walls were found in Paris, but refabricated in New York.

"Everything is real," said Ian. "There's no plywood, no veneers, it's all dimensional, and what happens when you use dimensional materials is, as it gets older, it looks better and better. There's the process of accretion and the process of burnishing. But if you use only veneers, it gets chipped off and looks terrible."

This stopped me dead. It hurt my head. Balthazar was not old, but it was *real*. Had the stuff been antique but made of cheap material and cheesy construction, if the materials and furnishings were old but crappy, would it have been less righteous? Would designers have seen through it? Would it have made for a superficial copy of a Parisian brasserie that did not have the patina, only the veneer? Authentic? Original? Did this new construction so finely made make it all better? Good? Real? And still there had been my drunken Englishman insisting it actually *was* old. Only Umberto Eco, who understood the theory of the theme park better than anyone, could have dissected this, and he was dead.

Of all the design elements at Balthazar, it was the bar that caught Adam Gopnik's eye the night we had dinner together. "As we're sitting here, I'm looking at the wall of liquor and wine bottles above the bar. I can't think of anything quite like that in Paris," he said. "The scale of it, floor to ceiling, the expanse of it is deeply New York, even though it comes out of an entirely French idiom of display and, indeed, of wine drinking."

Adam thought for a moment and added, "There's obviously elements of both New York and Paris, but it's a Parisian style that's been exploded outward and upward to become something entirely New York. There's really no place like this in Paris, but it's nonetheless an entirely Parisian place. That's the paradox and the fantasy of it."

BOOZE AND GAS

At the far end of the bar the woman who came in every morning ordered her usual tequila and lime. She sat on a stool. James Norris—most people called him Jimmy—the bartender with the Irish face, made her cocktail. She drank it. Then Jimmy, clearly aware of the woman's habits, shook up an espresso in a cocktail shaker and poured it over rocks for her.

A couple was eating breakfast at the bar, too. The man, in a pink polo shirt and jeans, sat on a stool, smothered his scone in butter and blueberry jam, ate it, ordered another one. He spread his copy of the *Times* on the bar and glanced at it while he ate. The woman beside him, who wore a long black coat, set her coffee cup down and asked Jimmy about his son's First Communion. He showed her a couple of photos in his iPhone. Asked if she wanted her usual second cup or maybe something else for a change.

Before eight-thirty during the week, there were still locals who stopped by and sat slumped over their papers and phones, sucking up enough caffeine to get themselves started for the day ahead. This time in the morning, you could go about your own business and nobody would bother you. After a while, more customers usually filed in; today there was a trio of young women who sat down at the bar, ordered breakfast, and began laughing at nothing in particular. The restaurant filled up.

An octet of business types, young and bulky with muscle, the computers over their shoulders yanking at their suit coats, was standing around the front desk. Julia handed menus to Asbury, the host for the morning, and he showed the guys to a large table near the front window.

Julia Mintz was unflappable. At the front desk, she was taking calls, checking the reservation list, dealing with customers. She was twenty-five, pretty, and very astute, and she loved the work. Seating charts were like math, and Julia loved math and had gone to Wesleyan to study physics. Then she switched to classics. She graduated unsure what to do. Her mother suggested a stint at Balthazar. Her parents, who lived in Greenwich Village, were regulars.

Julia had started as a host, had put in her time showing customers to tables, helping out the maître d' until she became one herself. She worked in the morning and at lunch, and she was very good at what she did.

There were always a few children of regulars working at Balthazar, and it reinforced the sense that Balthazar was a family. If some were the children of privilege, nonetheless, those who cut it were tough and self-possessed enough to deal with irritable customers and long hours, sore feet and late nights. Some, like Julia, had been eating out in New York restaurants from the time they were little and were not easily intimidated.

"There's really only one rule," said Julia. "You never ask the customer if they have a reservation. It's just against the ethos here, it's so off-putting. So I just smile and say, 'How can I help you?'"

At the bar, a few guys climbed up on stools, ordered the full English breakfast.

It didn't take long for the plates to arrive, loaded with bacon and eggs, sausage and beans and hash browns, tomato, mushrooms, and fried bread. This stuff was as good as what you got at the traditional English caff, or almost as good; nothing ever quite matched up to the basic greasy spoon over there, the kind beloved by taxi drivers and knowing tourists. Something about the baked beans: heavy, greasy, delicious.

The guys ate and waited for the bartender to make their drinks; Jimmy made a Bloody Mary spicy enough to blow your head off, and this was what they had come for, to ease them into the day or help with a hangover. Liquor was the lifeblood of a restaurant; it was essential, where the real profit lay. This reminded me what Richard Lewis, Balthazar's architect, had said.

The two essentials to get a restaurant running, he told me, were "booze and gas." These required licenses and permissions, and getting these in New York City meant navigating a bureaucracy comprehensible only to the initiated.

I went to visit Richard Lewis, and I had the feeling I'd been there before. In the building, one of the old apartment houses way up on Central Park West and 103rd, you could have been visiting some elderly Jewish relatives. It was an easy walk to Central Park, where people sat on benches and walked their dogs or their babies. Some pigeons flew over my head.

A born New Yorker, Richard was a compact man who looked like an architect, had that self-contained air of people who can make things and make things work, who knew his way around space and straight lines. His office was in the penthouse on Central Park West where he lived.

Through a door I saw a room where a row of young architects sat quietly at drafting tables, and then we went on into the living room where I looked greedily at the wraparound view, in which the whole city appeared framed by the window.

Richard Lewis seemed a cool customer, a disciplined man in black clothing who calmly took account of all the personalities and obsessions at play in the making of Balthazar. Ian McPheely, the fine artist turned designer, always sweated the lighting; Keith himself pondered the color of the walls. Nothing at all about Balthazar was standard, Richard told me. In its way this business of the exquisite possibilities of the details became an art form in its own right.

Said Richard, "Ian had a lot of sources. Keith personally had to see everything, and he's very particular about every finish. The finishes might be very subtly different, and he might reject all of them because they just weren't right."

Art was fine and good, and it produced the beautiful results that made Balthazar such a knockout, but building it required an architect who could deal with permissions and licenses, who could figure out the space for the storefront bakery, the means of communication from the upstairs kitchen to the work space below, who could see to and oversee the electricity, the gas lines. A restaurant needed plumbing, exhaust venting, and drainage, and these needed an architect who could work with a mechanical engineer. Everything depended on the menu you were planning and on that cooking equipment. This part of the work was not improv.

"I was the go-to guy for doing bakeries," said Richard. "Keith wanted bread baked in a traditional French way; he needed big bread ovens installed in the basement of an old building. I was about the only architect in New York who knew how to do bread factories just at the time people were making bread for the first time, especially in those kind of baking ovens."

The planning had begun in 1995, when McNally rented part of the cellar at 80 Spring for kitchens and a prep area. Because Balthazar was going to serve food and booze, rezoning was required. Worse still, the entrance was not wheelchair accessible. As a result, the entire floor was built on a platform about two feet off the ground.

I listened to Richard and thought, *Who in his right mind would open a restaurant?* Even twenty years ago when it was comparatively easy, when things downtown were still pretty loose, and the city did not require so much in the way of health and safety, nonetheless, an architect needed not only talent and cash—plenty of cash—but a profound, flexible, shrewd understanding of the city's byways. This Richard Lewis had. He talked to me about community boards, about the maze of building codes and possible variances and waivers, about the methods of negotiating permits, all the things that made New York hell for builders and restaurant owners.

And that was central to Richard's expertise, the filing of plans, the knowledge he had of the way New York City worked, the exquisitely, painfully detailed requirements of community boards and the Landmarks Commission.

In 1973, Landmarks had saved SoHo.

Before the New York City Landmarks Law was passed in 1965, a heartbreaking number of great New York buildings had been torn down: the Singer Building, the old Waldorf Astoria, Wanamaker's department store. But when Penn Station went, there was a real public outcry.

I remember the old Penn Station: when I was little, my father often took me to look at the fabulous pink marble edifice modeled on the Roman Baths of Caracalla; it was a train station that had made even the dullest commute seem a great journey.

Subsequently, when the city's building czars, led by Robert Moses, went after Grand Central Station, the destruction of New York came to a screeching halt, the protest led by Jackie Kennedy. This was followed by the Landmarks bill, and in 1973, the "Cast Iron District"—as SoHo was called—was saved by all of this; saved, too, by the artists who took up arms against Moses, who had intended to drive a highway through downtown Manhattan from the East River bridges to the Holland Tunnel.

Moses's plan had been to tear SoHo down and push the highway straight through Greenwich Village.

This being New York, there is, of course, a whole contingent of die-hards who feel the Landmarks Law is a ridiculous, even evil interference with the destiny of the city. New York's fate, they say, is change. If there had been a Landmarks Law a hundred years ago, some crummy buildings would not have been knocked down to make way for the wonderful structures that replaced them, and we would have become a city held forever in a suspension of nostalgia.

Still, in Landmarks, SoHo had a weapon, and we used it. By the time Balthazar was in the cards, developers had descended on SoHo in droves and the residents had about had it with the bars and restaurants and condos and fancy stores. Even now, whenever I hear the words "community board," I get cold sweat on the back of my neck. My stomach lurches. I remember all the meetings with the Community Board, all the protests we held, all the block associations—ours was called Gang Greene—and I think about Spy Bar.

For a while you could get away with pretty much anything in SoHo, so long as you didn't touch the façades of the buildings. Landmarks issues were related only to the exteriors and a foot or so of depth from the outside wall in. Spy Bar, two doors down from my building on Greene Street, got away with murder because nobody touched the façade of the cast-iron building.

All night long, drunks stumbled out at two, three, four a.m., and some wandered to the pay phone across the street—no cells in those still-primitive times—to phone ... who knew? Their pimps? Their girlfriends? Their drug dealers? Hard to say. Worse still, taxis lined up until five in the morning, waiting for customers, honking ceaselessly until dawn. I had a friend then who was a detective with the NYPD, and he suggested dropping rotten fruit on the cabs or, better still, putting tacks on the street. I thought he was kidding but I wasn't entirely sure. So I went with the fruit. People said it was childish, but it was deeply satisfying throwing rotten fruit out the window onto cars; and sometimes, with luck, you got a shrieking clubgoer at five in the morning.

Eventually, after several agonizing years, Spy Bar shut down, but it made some locals feel that even one more restaurant or bar would sink the neighborhood.

And so news of a new, and very big, restaurant over on Spring Street gave us empathy for our neighbors. SoHo was at the tipping point. Commerce was taking over. Art was done for, we all said. People were pissed off.

After Katrina, a friend in New Orleans who was visiting New York said, "The difference between us is, in New Orleans, we feel you have to beg for the city to do something, tip your hat, say please, tug that forelock. In New York, you think it's your birthright, and you yell and demand what you want. You don't always get what you want, as the man said, but you make the noise." We made noise.

"If you want to fuck over a club or restaurant that's threatening to open on your block, you go testify at your community board and also at the liquor license hearings," Richard said. "If you're too close to a school, a church, if the community board just doesn't like you, or you have a restaurant that has a bad reputation, they're all strikes against you."

According to Richard, Keith McNally was very shrewd about people in the community—essential in the public relations offensive to get community board approval. When he discovered this, Richard was relieved. "Keith would make compromises," he said. "He'd say, 'OK, I'm willing to close at eleven at night.' Or whatever it took." The way Richard remembered it, though he was unsure of the exact details, Keith even invited a Catholic priest he knew in Ireland to come to New York and testify to his character. Apocryphal or not, it says something about at least the perception of McNally's urban smarts.

In the end, Keith got pretty much what he wanted, Richard said. He got the booze and the gas; he got the permissions. Richard added,

"He was very charming, very savvy." Keith McNally, everyone agreed, was a consummate politician who somehow, often mysteriously, made sure everything that went down was hunky-dory.

In the morning, especially when it was almost empty, you could really hear the music at Balthazar. Verdi, I thought that morning; the morning playlists were almost always classical: Mozart, Haydn, a bit of opera.

Some silvery Vivaldi came on the sound system next. Keith had chosen all the music, had made up the playlists himself, and years ago I often saw him at Tower Records on Fourth Street and Broadway, leafing through albums or cassettes, lost in the music.

Putting together the playlists was something Keith McNally relished. His close friend William Miller told me Keith had started doing this in the 1980s at Odeon, his first restaurant. It took Keith months of research and editing, said William, who had worked briefly at Odeon. He recalled that "the restaurant filled with the sounds of Frank Sinatra singing 'Fly Me to the Moon' or 'Someone to Watch Over Me' on one of Keith's brilliant and painstakingly compiled music tracks. He made a unique and incredible collection of reel-to-reel tapes that he could use at different times of day to subtly change the mood of the restaurant. It was a kind of art form that he used over and over."

Keith had done it at Odeon and again at Balthazar, and this was not Pandora or some robotic selection of tracks, the modern equivalent of elevator Muzak. This was specific, music chosen by one guy— Keith McNally—according to his tastes to suit different moods and times of day and even the light at Balthazar.

CHAPTER 4

PRACTICAL MAGIC

When José Luis saw that my cappuccino that morning was in a small glass, he shook his head in mock despair and snatched it away. He was back before long with a huge frothy iced cap in a glass that usually contained lager and placed it in front of me with a grin. "Lady?" he said. "Better?" It was better. José Luis Juarez was one of Balthazar's great bussers; nothing escaped him.

It was the bussers like José Luis who made the restaurant run, kept it in shape, saw everything, knew it all, didn't speak much. When Keith McNally opened Balthazar in London, he sent some of them over to show the Brits how it was done. An ex-manager told me how devoted Keith was to the bussers who, in turn, "would run in front of a bus for McNally."

By nine, some of the bussers had already been in for hours. Early in the morning, after the cleaners had gone, they checked everything in the restaurant, alert to every detail.

Like set dressers on a film, they examined the way things were arranged, polished every glass, and then did it again. If there was a speck of dust, one of them was on it, wiping down the red banquettes. They set out cutlery and glasses, but only after examining the glasses to see if they needed polishing. During meals it was their job to slice huge loaves of bread, put it in baskets, serve it; it was their job to pour water and serve the coffee.

There were no busboys at Balthazar; male or female, they were all bussers. Traditionally they'd been men, but there were a few women now, among them Ante Diopp. Ante, who was from Senegal, had started in the ladies' bathroom, working for a company contracted to supply attendants. But the attendants were let go when a customer complained in print about their presence. McNally told *First We Feast*, a restaurant and food blog, that although he was looking forward to "standing at Balthazar's urinal without another man staring at me, I'll very much miss my bathroom attendants. They've been absolutely wonderful people to work with."

I had liked the women in the ladies' room, handing out towels or peppermints, though I figured it must be really tough on them, stuck downstairs all day, no windows, no daylight, some people leaving lousy tips or none at all. But then Keith offered these people jobs in the restaurants, and Ante had been among them.

Ante was, a manager told me, among the best bussers they'd ever had. That morning while I was drinking my coffee, she appeared with a pile of fresh napkins from the laundry run by Sau Cheng, who is married to Wong Cheng, another of the bussers. (Everybody calls them Mr. and Mrs. Koon, and nobody seems to know how they got the name.)

It was said that Mr. Koon often worked six days a week and would have worked seven if permitted, and that he owned several buildings in Chinatown. "Keith completely trusts Koon," a former waiter told me. "If it should come to a dispute between a customer and one of the staff, he may well call Koon and ask what happened."

The best estimate is that there are around 24,000 restaurants in New York if you count the boroughs, ten thousand of them in Manhattan alone. Eric Ripert, the chef-owner of Le Bernardin—arguably the best French restaurant in the country—told me that he'd eat at Balthazar every day if he could. He told me he was crazy about the food but also the style, the esprit, the soul of the place, and part of it was what he called the "magic trick," the changing of the paper tablecloth, the sleight of hand, the deft way in which the bussers whisked the old paper away and set the new one.

"This is an art," Ripert said. "It was the first time that I've seen a restaurant that does it in front of you, that's saying, 'We're going to show you what we're doing,' instead of hiding it. 'This is part of the process. This is how we clean up and take away the dirty paper and put down a new one,' and it's like an entire show basically in front of your eyes." The changing of the paper tablecloth was always the bussers' great moment. In other words: practical magic.

I was sitting in my regular booth, over by the bar, where there were three and a half booths made out of slatted wood. At another table was Emily Mortimer, the actor. Every time the front door opened she started, and I wondered, *Who is she waiting for?*

The toasted baguette I was eating was crunchy; slathered with butter and apricot jam, it was delicious. I was eating it happily and drinking coffee, watching the action, eavesdropping on the table behind me a little, when a few minutes later, José Luis ran over again, this time with a bowl of ice and an urgent need to see if I wanted more coffee. "You want something, lady, you want more coffee, more water, more butter? I want you to be happy, lady." José Luis was avuncular and in charge.

Hair slicked back, with a pencil mustache, José Luis resembled a renegade Zapatista, or perhaps an actor from a remake of *Viva Zapata!*. You might say, "How are you?" And he'd reply, "Maybe one more cappuccino?" Or he might tell you, in response to your query about his health, "Very good. I am very lucky. I have everything."

Or "Life is good. Maybe we are going on vacation to Disney World soon." I could never work out whether he was kidding around or just happy. But I always thought he was aware he was playing a kind of role.

José Luis almost always laughed and shook hands and kissed the ladies if they were regulars, if he knew them well, on the cheek. Two cheeks. Over the years I had come to the conclusion that José Luis really was a brilliant actor. In his public life at Balthazar, there were no problems. José Luis was all smiles. I always failed to get a sad tale out of him or a history of tough times.

For years I had tried to get him to tell me his whole story, to talk about his life in Mexico and the—possibly brutal—trip to America, but that was his private business, and there was no reason for him to tell me about it. Maybe it was because of my lack of Spanish; maybe it was that his happiness was invested in being, in seeming, happy. "My wife, she is a very good cook," he said one morning, patting his stomach. "Mexican food," he said. His wife cooked Mexican, he told me one day, which was very good, except for chicken parm, which was his favorite.

"José Luis, how come you're working on Thanksgiving, Christmas, every weekend?" I said once, concerned that he was looking a little peaky.

"Mexican people, we have big parties, we drink tequila. You need extra money. White people, they drink water, white wine—you have money, you buy good tequila. Ah, life is good, ah, tequila, Cuervo, the best, you have money in your pocket, you buy the best, you don't have money, you don't buy."

"I know, I know, but, José Luis, when can I come visit you, when are you going to invite me to your house, to one of your parties?"

What, exactly, would I have accomplished by visiting José Luis's house? It was a hack's arrogance, imagining you could understand other lives this way, by simply going for a single visit. Wasn't it? It would have been an awkward invasion of José Luis's life, still more so to publish any of it, and he, a fiercely competent, protective family man, knew it. And so we stayed in our familiar roles.

"Big parties. Parties, you need money for this—how are you, you need ice? You need one more cappuccino?"

I began feeling we were in a curtain-raiser by Beckett.

But José Luis and my friend Steve Zwerling had a special thing between them, and one morning when Steve was at breakfast and asking after his family, José Luis suddenly looked very weary. For a moment a shadow crossed his face. He said how hard it sometimes was—he was fifty-three. His son, Jorge, who had worked at Balthazar for four years, was almost done with college. "It will be better for him. He'll be in IT. Me, maybe I'll end my days here. Maybe I'll die here, at Balthazar," José Luis said, and crossed himself.

"So, how's life, José Luis?"

"Life is good, lady. You want one more cappuccino?"

Facing the kitchen doors, I was in an excellent place from which to watch the action. I could see the runners coming out, trays loaded.

Ranfis Felix brought me a plate of scrambled eggs. No matter how early it was, he was always smiling; a tall young man with a chin beard and an inexhaustibly cheerful disposition, his origins were in Puerto Rico. "Good morning, good morning," he said, reaching behind his back to pull a pepper mill out from the waist of his apron. "Some fresh pepper?" he said. I nodded.

Ranfis's brother, Aneri, had worked at Balthazar, too, but last summer he graduated from the Police Academy. After the ceremony, the family celebrated at Balthazar. "It was nice, we had drinks, we had ceviche," Ranfis told me. "Except my brother. He was in full uniform and he couldn't drink." Ranfis laughed. He hoped to follow his brother, and he smiled wider at the thought that he would someday become a cop with the NYPD. "No bacon today?" he asked now. I gave in. He went to the kitchen and got me an order of bacon. "Almost burned, right? The way you like it?" he said. Then he was off, back to the kitchen to collect more plates of food for the customers who were, the morning rush on, streaming in, filling up the tables.

The runners were a special breed; somewhere between waiter and busser, they brought the food from the kitchen to the customer, always sure-footed, always certain of which dish was for which customer even at a table for eight. When Balthazar was crowded, the runners could weave through the tables fast, like Olympic hurdlers, never dropping a loaded plate or a tray.

I liked thinking of the runners as those messengers in Shakespeare—*Antony and Cleopatra* is full of them—minor characters but indispensable, the guys who bring the news about action offstage. *Madam, he is married to Octavia.* The bacon will be here in a minute, lady.

By nine-thirty, the businessmen had gone. The smell of freshly made coffee floated my way. Joan Jonas was at the next booth, reading the *Times.* A performance artist, she has led the field since the 1960s and a couple of years ago Joan was a star at the Venice Biennale. We nodded in the way New Yorkers do, chatting fondly for a minute or two but without any requirement for an intimate exchange, not at this hour.

Far fewer locals lingered all morning the way we used to. Few people had the time to sit around and tell jokes for three or four hours, though rarely was anybody ever turned out of Balthazar unless they were falling-down drunk or abusive, and those things didn't happen in the morning—rarely even at night. Recalling those four-hour breakfasts at Balthazar made me wistful.

I got some money out of my pocket to pay the check. Erin came up from her office in the underground world of Balthazar, and she thanked José Luis for polishing the woodwork earlier. I followed her gaze as she looked over the room, the bar, and wondered again how she managed.

"I don't need a lot of sleep," Erin said in answer to my question. "I lie awake planning at night." Her phone rang. She took a call from Pat LaFrieda, the butcher who supplies all of Balthazar's meat, and discussed the price of some piece of beef over which she expressed mock outrage and ordered it.

Erin got up then and hurried to the front of the restaurant to greet Roberta Delice—the wonderfully named chief executive of McNally's operations. With Keith in London, Roberta was his woman at the front, and she was in charge of pretty much everything at all of his restaurants.

When Roberta showed up at Balthazar—she had come over from the McNally offices a block away—the staff paid attention; the faint frisson of attention to power was palpable.

Near the door, their faces set in pleasant expressions, Roberta and Erin stood talking. It all looked extremely civil, but I would have loved to eavesdrop. From where I sat I had no idea if they were merely discussing the overnight fire in the men's room, or if there was some intriguing bit of strife inside the Balthazar family, some altercation, a low rumble of discord that might turn into a major blowup, a cause célèbre, grist for the culinary gossip mill!

To inquire would have been imprudent; it might have messed with my access. So I tamped down my imagination as best I could for the moment and stuffed my mouth with more bacon.

CHAPTER 5

HELL'S HUNDRED ACRES

Beyond Balthazar's front windows, I could see people hurrying to the 6 train. SoHo was awake. The dog walkers were out, and so were the joggers. Parents led their children by the hand to school. There were plenty of toddlers in SoHo now, plenty of pups, too.

Across the street was the Museum of Modern Art Store, and opposite it, Sur La Table, but this part of Spring Street was not especially distinguished by fancy shops. There was a branch of Chipotle where Shane sometimes got his lunch, and a pop-up sneaker store that had popped up so many years earlier I figured nobody else wanted the space or could afford the rent. The last remaining newsstand was gone; a tiny branch of Baked by Melissa had appeared selling those teeny killer sweet cupcakes in scarily psychedelic colors from a window in the wall.

At the curb, the Asian soda-can lady was in the process of adding a few more empty soda cans from the garbage to one of the enormous black plastic bags where she kept her treasure. One bag at each end of a long pole, she carried it across her shoulders like a Chinese water carrier in an old print. Nobody paid her any attention except for a four-year-old boy in a bright green hoodie who pointed at her and giggled and whose mother shut him up and dragged him to the subway.

On the corner another of the regulars was sitting, a homeless guy who occupied the same place every day. His cardboard sign declared his sad state and his embarrassment at being in it. Increasingly there were homeless men on every street in SoHo; a few women, too. In recent years the homeless seemed to have multiplied. Somebody on almost every corner.

These days, they marked out their turf with sleeping bags and shopping carts, and they had elaborate signs they had created, many of them with detailed biographies. One man who had made his home behind street-level scaffolding had posted a series of signs concerning his past, his life as a veteran, what he needed, and why. We were in the age of competitive begging, it seemed. I might have thought the whole thing humorous; it wasn't. It was desperate. Homelessness was getting worse, New York's mayor doing nothing.

From time to time a lady, very thin and old, sat on her walker at the corner of Spring and Broadway, a few yards from Balthazar, asking for money and weeping, tears sprouting from her rheumy eyes and falling down her ancient face. Over at Dean & DeLuca on the corner of Prince Street, tourists emerging from the store with bags of fig-scented vinegar and truffled cheese and sandwiches that went for fifteen bucks seemed miffed by the presence of the homeless guy outside; this was not what they had been expecting in the dazzling shopping mall that was SoHo.

I had not seen my favorite panhandler for a while now, the cheerful man who often requested money for the "United Negro Pastrami Fund." One of my neighbors had tried to help him. We had also tried to get him a spot with ACE, the organization that provides the homeless with jobs cleaning the streets, but our guy didn't want in. He said, good-naturedly, that he drank and he liked drinking and he had a bed with an aunt somewhere in New Jersey. So I usually gave him a couple of bucks, and he smiled and went on his way.

Real estate drove the city north from the eighteenth century onward. The greedy, self-satisfied city fathers, those entitled Knickerbockers who lived close to Trinity Church, considered they had a right to do as they liked; like every generation in the city, they lay awake nights dreaming about real estate. Even in the eighteenth century they knew that in New York, this was where the moola was.

What they saw, looking up Manhattan Island, was not the paradise of stream and forest, hill and valley, meadow and lake that had greeted the first settlers. They did not care much about the fields where you could lie down and eat wild strawberries or streams where oysters were big as plates. What they saw were buildings. Buildings on neat plots spanning the whole length of the island. Buildings, bricks and mortar, would make you rich. For this they imposed a strict grid and they knew what they were doing.

The imposition of this system of streets, the making of parcels of land of equal size, was a developer's dream. Streets could be easily paved. Houses could be built fast and cheap. Transportation would flow, and, oh Lord, big, big money would be made. The system of right-angle streets was pushed uptown across the whole island. Trees were cut down, hills crushed flat, ponds filled in.

The new New Yorker looked north and reveled in it. Broadway was paved up to Astor Place. The gentry built their spiffy new houses along Broadway, and the big stores—Tiffany, Lord & Taylor, Arnold Constable—followed. So did the grand hotels and pleasure gardens.

After about thirty years, which seemed to be a life cycle in New York neighborhoods, the nobs moved north again. The area around SoHo was perfect now for the prosperous merchants, the mercantile men who dealt in silk and cotton and dry goods. The cast-iron warehouses they commissioned, lavish with decoration, seemed to suit the new post–Civil War businessmen, pleased with their rising fortunes and plump from dinners at Delmonico's.

These guys wanted bragging rights. They wanted buildings that showed off their status. Cast iron, easily forged in nearby foundries, including one on Broome Street, was light and easy to work with and cheaper to shape than masonry; it made for elegant façades. Neoclassical styles were popular; so were variations on French and Italian period styles. For interior space, cast iron could also be used in the making of columns to hold up the high ceilings of the vast loft spaces and for frames for the large windows. Where workers had toiled in dark airless hovels, now they worked in airy well-lit loft space.

SoHo and bits of Lower Broadway still look remarkably like they did toward the last quarter of the nineteenth century. The great lesson in understanding New York and its particular beauty—and this has been said a thousand times but is worth saying again—is to look up. Up is where the builders put the best decorations: the lacy wrought iron balconies on Ernest Flagg's Beaux Arts Little Singer Building near Prince Street; the ninety-two keystone arches and intricate friezes on the E. V. Haughwout Building near Broome.

In its day, the Haughwout Emporium, which featured the world's first Otis passenger elevator, made and sold cut glass, mirrors, and chandeliers, and among its clients were Abraham Lincoln and the Russian czar. Whenever the spectacle of contemporary SoHo as a shopping mall gets me down, I try to remember this is just what the Cast Iron District was built for long before it became an artists' refuge. The Haughwout was forgotten for decades; now there's a sign in the Prince Street subway station noting its presence as a great New York landmark. But you have to look up to see its glories.

To discover the secrets of Paris, to get away from its gorgeous and grandiose monuments, you have to play tourist as Peeping Tom. You look not up but through—through a gate into a hidden courtyard, into the inviting gloom of a tiny café, through a ground-floor window where a concierge sits half veiled by the net curtains. In

London, you scramble down a tiny mews or into a hidden square with a gated garden to get away from the imperialism of the Mall or the impeccable Regency crescents. In New York, you look up, and not just at the skyline.

In the way of these things, by the 1920s and 1930s when the textile business began moving south, many of the buildings in what became SoHo were either abandoned or used for sweatshops, or a bakery, or the gas stations that gave it the name Gasoline Alley. Even by the early 1960s when artists had begun moving in, it was still a pretty desolate place, a lost New York. The square mile of low-lying buildings was almost hidden from view by the rest of the city, and the buildings themselves, covered in graffiti, were a patchwork of water stains and bruises from all the fires that raged at night. You had to look hard to see the essential beauty.

Lynn Hechtman, my friend on Spring Street who lived over the Dash shop, where the mannequins had nipples, remembered those days. "You also had what people called the bums. But we never considered them bums. They were the guys that helped the local truckers load and unload. There was Dirty Eddie, who lived in a box, basically he was a nice guy who would always let you know where your kids were, that he had seen one of them pass on the way from school. Then there was one who was schizophrenic, I'm pretty sure. But he was a poet and a Harvard graduate. And he would write things on the walls that were incredible, really beautiful pieces."

Lynn and Marty Hechtman, her late husband, were both artists. They arrived in SoHo in 1963. "It was different then," she said, nostalgic for those prelapsarian times of artists and writers, and of community. "We all knew each other."

Late at night, Marty Hechtman usually took their dog out for a walk. More than once, Lynn told me, he saw sparks fly up from a cast-iron building; in those days the buildings were not fire-proofed. When it overheats, cast iron explodes. And if, for instance, somebody at the candy factory had left a pot boiling on an open flame, and it threw off sparks, they often fell on bundles of rags and newspaper stored in the warehouses, the fires fed off it, and flames shot up into the greasy night sky.

Whenever Marty saw the satanic orange flames, he'd run to the firehouse. The engines rattled through the night over the cobblestones; locals put their heads out of their windows; people crowded the streets; working men and artists who drank at Fanelli's emerged from the bar, beer glasses in hand, everyone watching the show. These fires, common for decades, gave the area its name: Hell's Hundred Acres.

Before SoHo, nobody had thought of setting up domestic life in old industrial buildings or commercial spaces. The artists came first, looking for space and light, and the lofts they took over provided both, but also a template for a radical change in the way people lived.

In 1977, Art Spiegelman moved in on Greene Street with his French girlfriend, Françoise Mouly. (They're married now, Françoise is the Art Editor at the *New Yorker*, and they have a grown son and daughter.) At first, Art was not entirely happy. "There was a mattress on the floor for a bed, a table made of a door on two sawhorses, and a broken car seat for a couch," he says with wry good humor. "I grew up in Rego Park dreaming of downtown, sure, but what I dreamed of was the Village, a place with bookshops and jazz and men with goatees."

Instead of the mellow Greenwich Village he had dreamed of—the Village of my own childhood—Art found himself in a huge loft in a cast-iron building scrawled over with graffiti. The artists didn't care. It was shabby but cheap. There was plenty of space. Shopping for diapers or toilet paper wasn't always easy, but you could party all night and nobody cared how loud you were.

A new way of life came into vogue: what had been a warehouse, a tannery, a foundry, a manufacturing plant, each of them now seemed to have seductive potential as a home. Immense windows, interior columns, even the pipes along the ceiling—a whole new grammar of residential life emerged. There followed an explosion of what was called "loft living."

SoHo—the acronym for "south of Houston Street," the reality and the idea—also revealed that the industrial past and its buildings were not just for residential use; stunning restaurants, innovative galleries and shops, alternative work spaces, even schools, took shape in brand-new ways. The concept redeemed abandoned neighborhoods in almost every major city. The idea of the urban acronym itself was a developer's dream because you could label even a crappy neighborhood this way and suggest that it took after SoHo and was therefore desirable and had panache. You could raise the rents.

In lower Manhattan alone, each new area developed faster than the one before. Tribeca—the triangle below Canal Street—was next; artists, but also Wall Street guys playing at the haute boho life, moved into buildings there that had once been occupied by the butter-and-egg men who served local markets. NoHo, north of Houston Street, with its big old buildings along Lafayette, was prime territory for condos. In Nolita—north of Little Italy—a few Italian butchers hung on, and there was still the annual Feast of San Gennaro. Otherwise, it quickly became a sort of SoHo light. There was no stopping it.

I moved to SoHo in 1986. Although I had lived most of my life in Greenwich Village, I only became seriously conscious of SoHo—a few blocks to the south—when I saw *Manhattan*. It must have been around 1979.

In the picture, they go for a walk, Woody and Mariel and Diane Keaton and Michael Murphy, discussing the negative capability of a white cube and dropping names—Gustav Mahler, Carl Jung, Isak Dinesen, Nabokov, Fitzgerald, Lenny Bruce—and they pass the first incarnation of the Castelli Gallery on West Broadway.

Then Woody and Mariel are shopping in the old Dean & DeLuca on Prince Street, and they're selecting exquisite items one at a time, and we're all laughing because it's a sort of museum of food, a white-washed shop with interior columns featuring exquisitely packaged food and a dancer with a ponytail selling fruit, but not grapes from Chile. Grapes were politically incorrect, I think.

In SoHo, in this coolest neighborhood of art galleries and art openings and art and arty people, it was a sign of things to come—this brand-new style, all this food as art objet—but most of all what struck me was that the SoHo zeitgeist was already familiar enough that Woody was laughing at its pretensions and we were laughing with him.

It seems odd to me now that I hardly knew SoHo before I moved here in 1986. I was living only a block up from Houston Street, its northern border, but it was another country. The Village, where I had grown up, was a neighborhood of bookshops, cafés, jazz clubs, folkies, radical politics. My high school friends (we dressed only in black) hung out at the Fat Black Pussycat on Third Street and squirreled away pint bottles of bourbon.

It was the Greenwich Village of Art Spiegelman's teenage dreams: guys with goatees playing bongos in Washington Square and pretty girls in black tights; Miles Davis at the Vanguard and Dylan at Gerde's Folk City; James Baldwin and Ginsberg and Kerouac at the White Horse Tavern; E. E. Cummings in Patchin Place and Joe Gould at Minetta; Ionesco and Albee at the Cherry Lane Theater; Eubie Blake at nearly a hundred playing piano at the Cookery.

By the late 1970s, the Village was a long-settled world of apartment buildings, brownstones, and walk-ups; of progressive schools, artists' studios, and Italian restaurants. In the time-honored New York tradition, people had been saying it was over for a long time. Artists had begun moving to the Lower East Side, to the Bowery, and also to this place called SoHo.

By then I was living on Bleecker Street near NYU and Washington Square, among academics and students and the remainder of the old bohemian world; I rarely looked south. Crossing Houston, I entered an area I hardly knew existed. It was as if Houston Street was a gate that led to a secret place, a little hamlet a mile square that ran from Canal to Houston, Crosby to West Broadway, a tightly packed grid of blocks, each with buildings almost all five or six stories, most of them the cast-iron buildings that gave the neighborhood its singular status.

Once upon a time, you could ask yourself—as Woody Allen put it—"There is no question that there is an unseen world. The problem is, how far is it from midtown and how late is it open?" When I moved to SoHo, it was filling up with bars and restaurants. Soon the galleries were moving out and in their place came the recherché shops like Moss on Greene Street. Bookshops came and then went. As the designer fashion brands arrived, people who had been predicting the decline and fall of the neighborhood for years sighed. The artists had gone. The real estate was skyrocketing.

"It's so over," people said. In the *New York Times*, Yukie Ohta, who grew up in SoHo, was described as the "memory keeper"; assembling a museum in her building's basement, Ohta had gathered smell jars with remnants from the leather factories and bakeries of her SoHo childhood.

To some, Balthazar was the beginning of the end, the last straw. "When Balthazar opened, I just thought, *What else can they do to us?*" said cartoonist Art Spiegelman, bemoaning the old days in the time-honored New York way in which violent change and desperate nostalgia are permanent twins.

For others, like Michele Oka Doner, the SoHo artist who lives on Mercer Street, "Balthazar grounded the neighborhood. Keith always had a layer of a certain je ne sais quoi. It was our canteen. In the early days, anyhow, we knew everybody there. Geoffrey Holder, the great dancer, would come and sit at a table with a big glass of beer and some ice because he wasn't supposed to drink, and the ice made the beer last longer." Michele, who has lived in the same loft since 1981, stopped for a moment, then said, "Balthazar gave SoHo a destination."

"We had a very good run," said Michele as we stood chatting on Spring Street. I had left Balthazar around nine-thirty in the morning, gone to the drugstore, and run into her. She was much more philosophical about SoHo—her dominion—than I was. Things changed. It was implicit in the nature of the city, as if some kind of sculptor was constantly chipping at it, changing it, the art never finished.

Michele gathered her coat around her. "I'm sure to the truckers, and the button manufacturers, the bakers and the last of the ironworkers at the foundries, the word 'SoHo' signaled the end of the world they understood. Something is always displacing something else. Natural process. Look at the Left Bank of Paris. Sartre is no longer at the cafés with fellow intellectuals. The pleasure temples of consumerism dominate the globe."

This gave me a sort of no-exit feeling. It happens from time to time when I can't see how it can get worse, and then it gets worse and Nike builds a huge ugly glass high-rise on the corner of Prince and Broadway that has nothing to do with SoHo's cast-iron past or anything else. Sneakers. The world silting up with sneakers.

Whatever happened to Food, to Jerry's, to the newsstands and the galleries and the artists? Whenever I find myself mooning around about the end of things, when I feel the onset of New York nostalgia, before it bites me on the ass and I start regretting everything and behaving like some grumpy old woman dwelling in an imaginary past, I remind myself that change, commerce, and money have always been the very soul of New York City.

This is a city where art has always pushed up real estate prices and shopping trumps art, where the rich push out the poor, where the discovery of a new kind of habitation—from the apartment house to the loft building—is prey to the real estate agent's rhetoric; it has always been like this. Everybody always complaining, all of us

crouched in the past, scared of the future and prophesying the apoc-
alypse. At the end of the nineteenth century the city was so jammed
with traffic and therefore so many horses, it was reckoned that New
York would literally drown in horse shit.

According to Pete Hamill, the great New York journalist and
writer, nostalgia has always accompanied change. Speed and nostalgia, he writes, have driven this city of immigrants. Tear it down. Regret the loss. There has always been that regret for what's been lost.
It comes on us as soon as the wrecking ball smashes a building. The
minute we see even the crummiest tenement bite the dust, we wail
and weep at the loss, and then move on. New Yorkers have always
loved standing around on the sidewalk, watching the wrecking ball
and kibitzing the workers.

The past is always disappearing, of course, and Michele had made
her peace with this. Balthazar had made SoHo better for her and
for me.

"From our place on Mercer Street to Balthazar, it's ninety-four
steps." Michele paused. "Let's go get something to eat," she said.
"You think there's still some croissants left at Balthazar?" We walked
together to 80 Spring.

Balthazar is actually part of 524 Broadway, a large, eleven-story
building constructed by Arthur H. Bowditch of granite, terra-cotta,
and limestone in 1903. Cast iron had been dumped in favor of steel.
Steel meant you could build big and high, and that changed New
York. The building's entrance is on Broadway and it runs through to
Crosby Street, with Balthazar on the north side of it, facing Spring
Street. After a hundred years, it is still owned by the Propp family.

Morris Propp was a Jewish immigrant who built the first great
business that sold electric Christmas tree lights. 524 Broadway was
home to merchants dealing in silk, lace, silver, and jewelry and, eventually, to Propp's lighting business.

Mornings when I was out before it got light, there were times

I'd see skinny young guys in black with hats running from the train. I would think of Mr. Propp, a young pious Jew, perhaps hurrying from the Lower East Side, working himself to the bone, doing odd jobs, peddling this and that to save the money to start his business. There were scores of skinny young guys in hats in SoHo all the time now; most were hipsters in stingy brim fedoras, of course, but I saw Mr. Propp in them, or his ghost.

I called Rodney Propp, Morris's grandson—who still owns the building—and he told me a little about his grandfather.

Morris Propp was born in nineteenth-century Belarus, which was then part of Russia. Escaping poverty and pogroms, he went to Hamburg, got a ship there, and arrived in New York in 1884. He lived on the Lower East Side and worked as a peddler; worked like a dog, his grandson told me, seventeen, eighteen hours a day. He saved up. Eventually he moved into 524 Broadway, where he opened the company that sold electric Christmas tree lights. He made a success of it and bought the whole building.

Mr. Propp's story raised some of my own ghosts. I never knew my grandparents, but my paternal grandfather must have been another of those skinny, tired, overworked young Jews, hurrying from the Lower East Side, from Forsyth or Eldridge or Rivington, one of the streets where families were crammed into tenements.

In his book *How the Other Half Lives*, Jacob Riis published photographs and wrote about this world of the Lower East Side when it was the most densely populated area in the world. I read it, and the reality was stifling and terrible, but no book, no visit to the Tenement Museum on Orchard Street, could take me to the immigrant world where my father was born in 1903. My father was the last of six brothers, and I was a late child. Rivington Street, where he was born, was not quite a mile from SoHo, but there was no way for me to cross it.

My father came from a generation that protected its children from the bad stuff. I never asked and now he was dead and I regretted it. He always joked around that he planned on writing the Forsyth Street Saga; when we went for lox at Russ & Daughters he told me he had known old Mr. Russ, who had no sons and gave his appetizing store to his daughter. The Lower East Side had throbbed with left-wing politics when my father was young and he joined in because, he said, it was rumored "that the lefty girls were faster." My pop rarely told the harsh stories except once, when he described a family with six or maybe seven kids; the parents too poor to feed all of them, they had to pick which child would not survive and give it a rag dipped in sugar to suck to keep it from crying.

Ten minutes from Balthazar. In the dark mornings on the empty streets, the ghosts, and maybe the golem, still congregated.

At least a million and a half Eastern European Yiddish-speaking Jews arrived in America between 1880 and 1914, fleeing the pogroms, poverty, and the draft that made young men cannon fodder for the Russian army. They came from the immense ghetto for Jews known as the Pale of Settlement, which stretched down from the Baltics through parts of Poland, Ukraine, Belarus, and western Russia.

Some Russian or Belarusian phoned me at home one night claiming he was a Nadelson and was making a family tree, and I was going to hang up because I'd had plenty of these calls, but he said, "Stop." He wasn't lying; he knew all the names. He told me the name of our ancestral home and I wrote it down: Slutsk.

In 2008 I found myself in Minsk, the capital of Belarus. Slutsk was only forty kilometers away, and I got a cab to take me.

A provincial city, it had clearly been bombed flat during the war and rebuilt in the Soviet style—concrete boxes, shabby shops, bad roads.

At the shabby Jewish end of the cemetery, where chickens and pigs wandered across the graves, I found a few of my relatives. My grandfather's twin brother had stayed in Russia; these Nadelsons must have been his offspring. Here in this miserable place under a couple of crumbling headstones. ISRAEL NADELSON, one read. A few survivors among the long weeds. It was silent, except for the pig. Damp, too. I thought I should cry, or pray, maybe, but I wasn't a believer and I couldn't cry. I picked up a stone and put it in my coat pocket.

Slutsk had been a thriving Jewish center once upon a time, before the pogroms, the revolution, the war. World War II saw four thousand Jews slaughtered in two days in October 1941. It was known as the Slutsk Affair. People asked me all the time if I "felt" Russian. I never did. All I felt was gratitude that my ancestors, driven by fear, had the guts to get the hell out.

What did this place have to do with me? With its pogroms and misery, its obsessive religiosity, its superstition; with its need for an authoritarian leader, czar, commissar, it had always felt alien. It did produce Pushkin. Tolstoy. Dostoyevsky. Chekhov. They're on my bookshelf. I see Tchaikovsky's *The Nutcracker* every year.

I had always liked to joke that my people came from *Fiddler on the Roof* without the jokes; after I went to Slutsk, I didn't feel like joking.

Those who could had piled their goods onto wheelbarrows and walked away—like my grandparents, like Mr. Propp—to Hamburg and its chaotic port, where they got a boat for New York. A million and a half Jews; Morris Propp in 1884, my grandfather in 1899.

Morris Propp's family continued to work out of the building on Broadway until, in 1960, Seymour, one of the sons, was tied up and forced at gunpoint to hand over the combination to the safe. The family held on to the building but moved its business uptown.

In 1996, Rodney Propp, Morris's grandson, rented the premises of the ground floor of 524 Broadway/80 Spring—what would become Balthazar—to Keith McNally. Rodney said, "The raw spaces were literally filled from floor to ceiling with bolts of leather and leather scraps. To Keith McNally's credit, he was able to visualize what the space was and what it could be, to dream of a restaurant called Balthazar."

So much about downtown had gone into the making of Balthazar the building, the men who had built it, the immigrants who worked there then and now. Downtown was never just about style and cool or changing tastes or about celebrity or real estate. For me, it was my home; I'd been born here. I haven't got many nationalist feelings, I think nationalism mostly produces the horrors of war and massacre. Except for New York, the city of immigrants, especially the little bit of it that is downtown Manhattan.

I am always sorry that my pop died before Balthazar opened. He wore a beret all of his long life; he liked a good martini; he would have loved it, would have made himself at home. Making cracks about the chicken liver mousse ("What's wrong with chopped liver?!"), he would nonetheless have loved sitting at the bar over a couple of drinks, shooting the breeze with Jimmy, tucking into the steak au poivre. He liked a good time. Once he advised me that he felt the only kind of man worth knowing was one with joie de vivre.

CARAMELIZED BANANA PEANUT TARTINE

Yield: Serves 1

I love sweet things for breakfast and this is plenty sweet.
With ice-cold grapefruit juice and very strong espresso,
it will get you up and out, a spring in your step!

INGREDIENTS

1 slice of country-style bread

3 tablespoons Nutella

1 whole banana, sliced into thin, coin-like pieces

regular granulated sugar

2 tablespoons peanuts, chopped and toasted

2 mint leaves, finely chopped into a chiffonade (stack the mint leaves, roll them, and slice into long, thin strips)

INSTRUCTIONS:

Toast the bread.

Once the bread slice is toasted, spread it with an even layer of Nutella.

Arrange the banana slices so they overlap like fish scales on top of the Nutella layer.

Dust the banana with granulated sugar and caramelize very carefully with a hand-held brûlée torch. If you do not own a torch, you may use the broiler of your oven set on low, watching carefully to ensure that it does not over-caramelize or burn.

Garnish with the chopped peanuts and finish with the mint chiffonade.

BOILED EGG WITH "SOLDIERS" FOR ONE

With a few of the recipes, as with this, I just liked hearing Chef Shane McBride talk them through. This is the classic boiled egg, a favorite at Balthazar. Add a platter of extra-crispy bacon, and there's nothing better.

"Get a hen, yeah? Open a farm, raise chickens, free-range chickens. At Balthazar, we use a great farm upstate in Sullivan County. Go local for eggs.

"If you have a green market in your town, support it. Support the people that grow 'range-free' chickens and their eggs. They're just better. If you buy eggs at a green market, or the way that we buy them, they were harvested that morning or the night before. So you get a better shelf life, you get a better flavor, and they usually have that nice yellow yolk that's just indicative of what they eat and their exercise.

"We've got a good egg. You need a pot of boiling water, a timer—a digital timer helps, or your cell phone timer—and a toaster, and your favorite white bread. I think this is the easiest way you can do it. Pretty much get your pot of water going, a little bit of salt in that water, just a pinch, and you drop in your room-temperature egg; that way it won't crack while it's boiling. That's what happens when you put a cold egg in—they crack. So use room-temperature eggs, boiling water. The second you drop the egg into the water, set your timer for five minutes.

"Halfway through [the five minutes], put your toast in the toaster and toast it. Butter it as soon as it's toasted, cut into strips. Put the egg in an egg cup on the plate with the soldiers stacked up around it. This makes it easier to dip the soldiers into the egg when you crack it open."

CANNELÉ

Yield: Makes 12 individual cannelés

Cannelés are little baked custards with a dark crust. They are best eaten cool, but within several hours of being baked before the crust softens, for maximum contrast between the creamy inside and dark, caramelized, crunchy outside. They make a decadent breakfast item but are good anytime.

INGREDIENTS

15 ounces of whole milk

½ cup granulated sugar

1 teaspoon lemon or orange zest

¼ to ½ of a vanilla bean, split, scraped, and seeded

2 large eggs

2 yolks

3 tablespoons butter

3 tablespoons water

½ teaspoon lemon juice

2 tablespoons dark rum

¾ cup and 1 tablespoon pastry flour

14 tablespoons powdered sugar

INGREDIENTS FOR COATING MOLDS:

2 ounces each of butter and food-grade beeswax

SPECIAL EQUIPMENT:

12 large copper cannelé molds (silicone molds, while perhaps acceptable, do not produce the same quality)

whisk and heatproof spatula

optional: immersion blender or blender

INSTRUCTIONS:

One or two days before you plan to bake and serve the cannelé, prepare the batter. You will not get the best results if your batter is too fresh.

Put milk and granulated sugar in a small saucepan. Add zest. Split and scrape part of a vanilla bean, adding both the seeds and bean to the milk. (Reserve remaining vanilla for another use.) Bring to a simmer and turn off heat, cover, and set aside for the flavors to infuse into the milk for 20 to 30 minutes.

Meanwhile, break eggs and yolks into a clean bowl and whisk to thoroughly combine. Measure out water, butter, lemon juice, and rum into a container. Sift flour and powdered sugar into a separate bowl (or quart container if using an immersion blender).

Have all ingredients measured and your bowls handy before you continue.

Reheat milk to a boil while stirring and whisk some or all into eggs. Then return everything immediately to the pot, set over medium heat, and stir continuously (keeping the empty bowl handy!) until the mixture thickens noticeably. It must not boil, as doing so would make it curdle. As soon as it begins to thicken, quickly pour back into the bowl used for the eggs, along with the butter, juice, and rum. Whisk to combine, melting the butter and releasing the heat. Cool before adding the remaining dry ingredients. You can immerse the bowl into an ice bath to cool more quickly. Remove the piece(s) of vanilla bean before continuing.

Blend in the flour and powdered sugar. You may use a blender—we prefer an immersion blender. Just put everything into a deep one-quart container and give it a whirl before covering and refrigerating overnight. Of course you can also use a whisk, but be sure to get all the flour lumps combined (you may need to press it through a sieve). Refrigerate for at least one day. Batter will keep for about three days.

T O   B A K E :

Combine butter and beeswax in a small pot and heat very gently, stirring to melt. The mixture must not smoke and is very flammable, so be careful. You may set it in another container of simmering water if you prefer. Heat copper cannelé molds until they are hot to the touch, then fill with wax/butter mixture and invert quickly to drain on a rack. Chill the molds. The aim is to get a thin coating, which will help the cannelés release from the molds and give them a desired shine and crunch once they have cooled. The molds will "behave" better once seasoned by a few bakes.

Fill the chilled molds *no more than* I centimeter from the top. It is really important to underfill, as the batter has a tendency to soufflé up initially and the cannelés can get hung up on the rim, causing the bottoms to lift out of the mold (not a good thing).

Place on a baking sheet (one that won't warp), leaving space for airflow in between the molds. Bake at 365°F for 60 to 70 minutes. You can invert one to check the color after 50 to 60 minutes, popping it back into the mold to continue baking if it's not dark enough, with no ill effects. We like these to be a deep caramelized mahogany color.

TO DRINK:

Rebecca Banks, Balthazar's wine and booze director, suggests some delicious things to drink with the various dishes. (It's like having your own private sommelier.) She says there is always a good reason to drink at breakfast, suggesting Champagne or a nice crémant such as NV Les Hautes Terres Crémant de Limoux Joséphine (made in the Champagne style, but from the region of Limoux in the Languedoc).

For the Caramelized Banana Peanut Tartine: Nutella is chocolaty and nutty, so choose a sparkling Burgundy red, like NV Bourgogne Rouge Brut Parigot. It's dry but earthy with mushroomy aromas and flavors that would be fun with Nutella! Why not?!

PART
TWO

LATE MORNING

CHAPTER 6

DAVE CHANG'S BREAKFAST WITH OYSTERS

D ave Chang sometimes dropped by Balthazar for a late breakfast, ate eggs, and when he had time, stayed on for some oysters. Too long, he said, laughing, because he always wanted, in addition, the whole plateau de fruits de mers with the shrimp, periwinkles, crab, lobster. Sometimes he ordered a bowl of French onion soup, too; on a cold morning it seemed a fine idea, especially with the enormous crust of gooey, crispy cheese.

At thirty-eight, Dave—his assistant called him Dave, so I figured it was what he preferred—was, of course, the superstar chef and owner of Momofuku, almost certainly the hippest restaurant of his generation. With a burgeoning empire, he had restaurants opening all over New York and across the world. He loved Balthazar, he told me. For him and his friends, it was a grand institution, what Le Cirque and La Côte Basque had been to the previous generation. Only better and with no bullshit.

Chang's comparison of Balthazar to those uptown joints, the

restaurants of an ancient New York regime, startled me. Le Cirque! La Côte Basque! Here were restaurants that had been in the gossip pages seemingly long ago, restaurants where skinny society babes, the X-Rays of *Bonfire of the Vanities*, gathered to munch a tomato for lunch. Truman Capote wrote a piece called "La Côte Basque" about his uptown lady friends and their secrets.

It all seemed of another age, part of a vanished once-upon-a-time New York, and the idea that Balthazar had now replaced these bastions of society as a grand institution made me feel old.

I took a little comfort from Chang's "no bullshit" qualifier, but there was no question that Balthazar was now in middle age. A vital, celebratory, diverse age, apparently, according to Chang. Then he laid down a thumbnail sociological sketch of Balthazar for me, how he saw it at various times of day with an ever-changing cast.

"Early breakfast is the real power breakfast," Chang said. "Ten to twelve is a random assortment of New Yorkers, of creative types and locals. Lunch you get still more diversity, and then there's three to five, again eclectic, plus tourists, and so on. New Yorkers come back from nine 'til eleven." This was a pretty accurate rundown. Chang went on. "It was always one of those rare places that couldn't be anywhere else except New York, it's a perfect storm of New York, of SoHo and shopping, commerce, creativity, sensibility, but as a result sometimes the food is underrated. It's been so great for so many years, from Riad [one of the original chefs] to Shane, and consistency is so damn hard to do."

Consistency. The requirement in a restaurant to do each dish exactly the same as the last time and do it every day, every week, forever. Once I'd thought it might be fun to decorate cakes or bake fruit tarts, but when I understood each one had to be the same as the last, that there was no room for dramatic culinary improv in a restaurant, I gave the idea up fast.

To be honest, I had expected Chang to be a self-satisfied celebrity chef, in part because it was generally almost impossible to get in to Momofuku, and everyone always made a big deal about it. But at least in talking about Balthazar, he was an amiable guy. Mention of Balthazar seemed to warm up a lot of New York chefs. Mario Batali was another of its fans. I'd even seen Anthony Bourdain quoted as saying he hated brunch as a rule, but he liked it at Balthazar, and Bourdain did not seem the kind of guy who said things just to be kind or to ingratiate himself.

Brasseries were always about hanging out, and for this the chefs loved Balthazar, loved sitting around over oysters and wine. They often went to Balthazar after the James Beard Awards dinner. They stayed very late. They drank plenty.

Dave Chang, if he had the time, could have lingered all morning over oysters, which was interesting because his own clientele, the Momofuku generation, preferred small plates, common tables, quick service. "It's a short attention span generation, and this is what they want," Adam Gopnik said. "Some of the food is wonderful. I think this generation that loves Chang knows much more about food than we did. But they're impatient and much less curious."

By eleven almost nobody was left from breakfast. The lunch crowd had not yet begun to assemble in the vestibule. Over near the seafood stand, Jerry Alvarez was putting out oysters on mounds of crushed ice, alongside bright red-orange lobsters, lined-up intensely yellow lemons, piled black mussels, a Dutch painter making his still life. He draped the ice with shining dark black-green seaweed. Everyone called him Jerry. His given name was Gerardo, but he said nobody could pronounce it. He placed some beautiful tender pink prawns in perfect rows on the ice.

Jerry, who was Bolivian and had a face and a luxuriant shock of black hair straight from the Andes, was wearing chef pants printed with big juicy red tomatoes and a white jacket. I asked him the best way to shuck an oyster, and he smiled his easy smile and led me down to the prep area in the basement. Placing a large mollusk flat on a board, Jerry held it with his left hand and with his right inserted the pointed knife in a tiny hole at the very corner, then prized open the shell. He cut away the muscle easily, removed the debris, and passed it to me to eat. With an anticipatory grin, he waited. I ate it. It was large and briny and very fresh, it smelled of the sea; a postcard of blue water splashed into my mind, but the thing itself went down with a slimy plop.

I'd have to try harder to like these things.

Jerry reckoned he had opened a million oysters, give or take, first at the Oyster Bar in Grand Central, then at Aquagrill in SoHo. Almost twenty years ago, he had heard about a new restaurant a few blocks down Spring Street from Aquagrill and he had wandered over to Balthazar.

I stabbed at the hard, coruscated shell of another oyster, this one smaller and more delicate, I stabbed my hand. "Not like that," Gerry said, explaining that you had to find the opening, the tiny hole where you inserted the knife. He did it for me and passed the oyster. "It's for you," he said with the kind of smile that told me how much he anticipated my enjoyment.

The cooks were watching, too. One of them smiled at me and I thought: he knows. He knows I can't stand these things, but I just smiled back sweetly and ate the oyster, and this one was smaller, better, sweeter, fruitier. Still, I was relieved when Jerry turned to making sauce for the lobster. It consisted of brandy, his own homemade mayonnaise, a little Tabasco, a little ketchup. I asked him what the measurements were, and Gerry smiled and said, "My measure is my hand." He said that it was how Escoffier had worked out most of his dishes.

At fifty-seven, Jerry had been in New York since he was twenty, when he arrived from Bolivia. Eventually, he told me, he would retire to Cochabamba, his hometown. I asked what he was thinking he'd do there. He said he'd like to see more of his own country and might also open a seafood restaurant. Bolivia is landlocked, Cochabamba about four thousand miles from the sea. "People are eating seafood, though," he said. "They are beginning to like new things." The seafood would come from Chile and Peru, Jerry said and smiled, thinking about his own restaurant. One day he would head home and create the seacoast of Bolivia.

All the time he was talking, I could not stop looking at Jerry's hands. The hands he had said hurt like hell at the end of a week at work, the oyster shells rough on them. I thought he must take good care of his hands because they were very soft, as if he had used endless creams and lotions to heal them after a week of shucking.

This was tough work. The shells were hard. My own finger was bleeding. I thought about a young Keith McNally shucking oysters at One Fifth soon after he had arrived in New York in 1975.

It took me about a year of e-mails with his office, but eventually I got on the phone with Lorne Michaels. Keith had said Lorne was his best friend. The producer of *Saturday Night Live*, which he more or less invented in 1975, Michaels was now also in charge of *The Tonight Show Starring Jimmy Fallon*. Not long before I talked to him, he had put on a show with Adele.

"We met when I was thirty," Michaels said. "I was Canadian, Keith had just come from London, and he was a familiar type. He was the maître d' at One Fifth, and we had our *Saturday Night Live* after-parties there. They didn't start until one in the morning at the earliest. He always had one foot in the theater, he was smart, knowledgeable, very well-read."

Down the phone came a warm voice, a blast of charm—it seems to me that a lot of successful guys who made themselves up have it, or maybe I was inclined to like Michaels because he was, like my mother, Canadian. Anyway, he was clearly pretty happy to talk about

Keith, and there was real warmth when he did. I also felt that Michaels was determined to protect Keith and wouldn't give away anything that his pal would mind, but then, they had been friends for forty years.

"I saw Keith last week in England," said Lorne Michaels. "He's a not-quite-retired English country gent." Michaels laughed in disbelief, and I asked if he thought Keith would be coming back to New York.

McNally had always loved walking, Michaels said, "I guess Keith is intending to walk the whole of England now." He paused for a moment, then added, "Though I think Keith is as restless at his core as I am."

CHAPTER 7

COFFEE WITH KEITH

K eith was eating hazelnut waffles at Balthazar around eleven in the morning, the waffles drenched with warm berries and syrup. I asked him why he thought Balthazar had been a success from the beginning. "It was the right place at the right time, I guess," he said.

"Like La Coupole in Paris in the 1920s, or Spago in LA for the '80s, or the '90s at the Ivy in London? Like that?" I said. "Or Odeon, of course, in New York in the 1980s?"

"I guess," he said. "I don't know. Have some waffles," he added, and offered me a forkful, then pushed the plate over to me and smiled.

Somebody once told me that a key to the great rock stars, or indeed the great movie stars, was that they did not—and this was almost unconscious—smile promiscuously. They held back and when they delivered, when they smiled, it was dazzling, it warmed you up and was a gift.

The waffles were delicious, nutty and fruity and full of butter.

Balthazar was a lot more informal in the early days, in the early 2000s, when I still ate breakfast every morning with Steven and Rona and the others. There were times then that Keith would wander into Balthazar; tallish, sandy haired, rumpled, seemingly diffident; he was said to be desperately shy, but shy didn't really seem to capture it. If Keith was interested in something or amused by it, he was pretty chatty, and he would occasionally sit down, stay a while, shoot the breeze about this or that, perhaps even pass on a bit of juicy gossip. Most of the time, though, he was a little evasive, a bit hard to catch, to pin down.

Enter Harry Lime.

Keith McNally named his company Third Man Management after his favorite movie. Mine, too, as it happens, though it made me feel a bit of a suck-up to tell him.

Harry Lime. The most famous, most dazzling character in *The Third Man*, Lime is also the most enigmatic. Played by a young Orson Welles, he is alluring and elusive; he appears and disappears, is thought dead and is resurrected. Harry, the handsome and corrupt American charmer whose self-obsession and greed destroy him.

McNally was an enigma, people said, a tough nut to crack if you wanted to find out what made him tick. I've always thought it was a little arrogant anyway, the idea you could, as a journalist, dive into somebody's gut and, after an hour or two, pull out any kind of truth. Only the greatest novelists have ever really clawed a whole human being out of words and onto the page.

Keith, however, charming, guarded, intelligent, shrewd, made the comparison with Harry Lime tempting. But the idea of Keith McNally as a version of Harry Lime never worked, of course, not even as a conceit. Better, perhaps, as Holly Martins, the teller of the tale, a character originally written by Graham Greene as Rollo Martins, an Englishman.

I dropped into Balthazar one day and saw Keith sitting at table 62, and when I went over to say hello, he mentioned that a great new print of *The Third Man* was on at the Film Forum. We were talking about the movie for a while when Keith asked, "What's the name of the guy who was buried in Harry Lime's grave?"

Keith had picked a minor character for me to identify, that was part of the game, of course. I was stumped. I rummaged around in my memory. I couldn't get it.

"It's Joseph Harbin," he said. (The plot turns in part on the discovery that Harbin, a hospital orderly, has been buried in Lime's grave in order to convince the other characters Harry Lime is dead.) Of course. *I knew that!*

After that, Keith asked what I'd been up to. I mentioned I'd been to Sag Harbor to visit some British friends we both knew.

"Nobody ever invites me," Keith said.

"I'm sure lots of people would love to invite you, love you to come," I said. "You wouldn't go, though." I added that because he now lived in London permanently, the first time since he was in his twenties, people didn't know where to find him, and also that, at Balthazar, he was missed. I asked what the hell he was doing in London anyway when he'd always said he didn't much care for Britain.

"People miss you, you get missed if you're only in and out, like Orson Welles," Keith said. So if it wasn't Harry or Holly, then maybe it was Orson Welles. Was Welles the secret alter ego? The brilliant but elusive filmmaker? Disappearing man? Was I getting warmer?

McNally had been a star for a long time, which carried with it all the usual baggage: from some, all you heard was how he allegedly punched a guy in a bar for poaching his staff; from others, that his generosity was profound, that Keith was a nice guy, just shy, just English or inscrutable. Asked about it, Keith would no doubt demur; he deflected any personal questions. An actor as a young man, it sometimes seemed he knew just how to play a situation.

Reserved, chilly, difficult, obsessive, and *hard to please*—Keith McNally had been called all these things. *Ferociously intelligent, immensely well-read. Shrewd. Sexy. Charming. Curious. Melancholy. Insecure. Fierce. Restless.* Fretful, mercurial, obsessive, he was known for making up his mind on the spot and changing it a million times. The decisions he made were often right, most people who worked with him said, but were not made without a certain agony.

He could be sweet, too. Sweet and also a pain in the ass and funny, with an English delight in winding you up.

In other words: Keith was an unreliable narrator to his own life.

"I like milking," he once told a reporter about the period when he had given up restaurants to run a farm on Martha's Vineyard.

The more I read articles about Keith McNally, including those interviews to which he had agreed, the less I knew. For months I pursued a big sit-down interview. He never said no. Or yes. I wanted to tear my hair out; I worried. I called people who knew him, but most of them were fastidious in protecting a friend.

One way or another, Keith resisted my efforts to sit down for a formal interview, perhaps because he was commuting between London and New York and barely had a minute. Perhaps. He was perfectly agreeable whenever we arranged to have coffee, or met by chance at Balthazar or one of his other restaurants, but that was it.

It took me a long time to understand that it both bored and embarrassed him, and that one of his pleasures—a distinctly British pleasure—was winding up journalists, especially those who asked silly questions: *Do you have an instinct for the next fashion in restaurants? How did you get into restaurants? Are you the Impresario of Downtown? Are you a genius?*

Reading some of the interviews, it came to me that Keith was more adroit than most at the British put-on, the play on words, the straight-faced half lie, the joke that's usually on you and can be very funny or obscure, ironic or impossible to decipher. It's a particular verbal style and you can hide behind it or it can reveal you. It is done better by Brits than anyone else. If you want to play in what's known in London as the chattering classes, it's a necessary art—or weapon.

Asked by *Bon Appétit*, Keith said the ideal music to segue from cocktail hour to dinner was "Elgar's Violin Concerto in B Minor, followed by Bach's St. Matthew Passion, followed by Herman's Hermits' 'I'm into Something Good.'"

True? Not true? Was this a fake-out? A send-up? A takeoff? A pasquinade, dare I say? Could be. On the other hand, I am also partial to Herman's Hermits. (Of the great classics, I prefer "Mrs. Brown, You've Got a Lovely Daughter.") Said the same journalist, "We always look forward to seeing your beautifully designed bathrooms. What inspired you to put as much thought into the loo as into the loup de mer?"

"That's an unkind remark," Keith said. "I put far more thought into my bathrooms than into my loup de mer."

Keith McNally was born in 1951 in the East End of London, when it was still a broken neighborhood, poor, working-class, heavily bombed during the war. "Our playground was a bomb site about ten blocks square. The East End had been wrecked, there was still a huge amount of debris," said Tony Gordon, who grew up near McNally and was pals with Peter, one of Keith's older brothers. "Peter and I instantly became friends at school. We were just kids then, and Keith was the younger brother, so he seemed like the baby. I lived in an old house—the bombs must have missed us. It still had an outdoor toilet, though. Where Keith and his family were, it had been badly bombed, they lived in a temporary prefab house made of cement and pressed asbestos, but it had plumbing and electricity. Their house was midway between school and ours, a few minutes, I was always around there.

"Keith wanted out as much as any of us, we all wanted better," added Gordon, who was working at the Balthazar Bakery offices when we talked.

Tony's dad did construction and was a postman; Keith's father, Jack, was a stevedore on the London docks and, later, a taxi driver. In the 2000s, Jack came to New York to live with Keith and his family on West Eleventh Street; most mornings he sat in the back at Balthazar, folding napkins, chatting to friends he'd made in the restaurant, including Steven and Rona. Jack was in his eighties then.

"I used to make Jack his Gin 75," said Jimmy Norris fondly, speaking of a cocktail of lemonade, gin, and a little Champagne. "He only drank one. I liked Jack. I'm Irish," Jimmy added. "My parents were immigrants. I felt like I knew him."

One of the very few interesting pieces about Keith was written by Allan Jenkins, an editor at the *Observer* in London. Jenkins got close enough to McNally to write about him thoughtfully and affectionately without being sycophantic. When I got hold of him, Jenkins said to me, "I like Keith very much. London, though, bit him evilly on the arse." He was referring to some of the reviews of Balthazar London, the restaurant Keith McNally opened in 2013.

When they met, Jenkins went to the East End with Keith, to his childhood home, and he wrote, "As we walk in the cold, winter rain he tells me about Joyce and Jack, his mum and dad. 'They should never have married,' he says. 'My mother was neurotic, cautious. She always felt slighted. We were never allowed to bring anyone into the house or sit on the green sofa or go into a certain room. My father was a docker, more easygoing, a keen amateur boxer and footballer.' "

To me, Jenkins said, "The need to escape for somebody like Keith was huge. It was huge for all of us. I was in foster care growing up, I was a Barnardo's boy from a little village." (Barnardo's is a charity founded in 1866 whose stated goal is the care for vulnerable children and young people.) "I couldn't wait to get to the big city," Jenkins added. "I get it. Keith comes from Docklands, now he can romanticize that world, but it was very hard."

More than forty thousand civilians were killed when the Germans bombed London, and a million houses destroyed. The Germans were particularly keen to destroy the docks and British shipping, as well as the East End, where the dockworkers had settled. In 1940 alone, thousands of tons of bombs fell on Bethnal Green, where Keith was born and grew up. "It was a pretty grim area," Allan Jenkins said.

In the early 1960s, I went to London with my parents. I was

about ten. We went to look at the East End where there were still bomb sites, still buildings in ruins. This wrecked world was shocking and incomprehensible to a middle-class child from New York. I had never suffered even the smallest discomfort much less the great horrors of war. I had never even been in an apartment without central heating or indoor plumbing.

"Keith was always smart, but it's a miracle that he and his brother Brian both got out," Allan Jenkins told me. It was Keith's mother's ambition—and Keith's own—that drove him; fear, too, Jenkins said.

In those days, when British kids turned eleven they took a test; those who did well went on to a grammar school, a free high school for bright boys (and later girls). If you failed, you went to a comprehensive school; some of them were very tough, more *Clockwork Orange* than *Downton Abbey*. Like his older brother Peter and Peter's friend Tony Gordon, Keith went to Coopers' Company, the local grammar school.

"After we left school, Peter McNally and I went around the world for a while," said Tony Gordon. "Keith moved into more arty circles, he acted. I'm not sure any of us even thought about university. It was not on our parents' financial slate."

At fifteen, Keith was working as a bellboy at the London Hilton when he was spotted by some producers and cast in a Dickens film.

He did some more acting after that, and then in 1968, he got a part in Alan Bennett's first play, *Forty Years On*. Also in the cast was Anthony Andrews, who would go on to star in *Brideshead Revisited* on television.

"We got on like a house on fire back then, and a few years ago he entertained us at Balthazar," Andrews told me. "I don't think Keith's changed a bit. We were all young and terribly enthusiastic, and we were in a hit West End play. We all contributed to the lyrics. John Gielgud played the headmaster, and Alan Bennett was in it, too, and we were all really happy to be there. Keith was a very gorgeous boy, very charming and talented."

• • •

In the 1960s, Gloucester Crescent in North London was a hotbed of intellectual activity. From open windows you could hear writers typing furiously. "'Competitive Typing,'" William Miller said to me, considering a title for his memoir. William, a television producer now, grew up in Gloucester Crescent. His father, Jonathan, had starred in the smash Broadway show *Beyond the Fringe*, with Peter Cook, Dudley Moore, and Alan Bennett, and Bennett lived across the road. In '68 or '69, he offered Keith a room in his house. The area was a crossroads of culture, intellect, theater, left-wing politics. In London, in those bohemian circles, there was plenty of jealousy, and it was incestuous in so many ways, but there was real appreciation for talent. "If you were invited in and you had intellectual curiosity and a little charm, you were on your way. The doors were open, the kids ran riot through the gardens, and everyone was always taking in waifs," William said, then added, "Keith was like a sponge.

"My parents became like his own," said William. "I adored him. He was the big brother I never had."

Sitting in his parents' garden in Gloucester Crescent now, William recalled, "Keith was incredibly sexy. I idolized Keith, and he was handsome. I used to follow him around. I was eight when Keith came to live in Gloucester Crescent. Alan used to let the actors he was working with come round to help with the plaster and painting of his house. Everyone was really cool, my dad was in his early thirties, incredibly famous and handsome and showing off, and people talked about who they wanted to fuck all the time. It was probably the first time Keith had heard grown-ups say something both so inappropriate and cool, and he must have been blown away."

The Miller house was full of books, the walls hung with art, some of it made by Jonathan himself. Both he and Rachel, his wife, were medical doctors, and Jonathan wrote and directed theater and opera, he painted, and made television shows about the brain. He hated the term "polymath," but it was the label that stuck to him. There wasn't much Jonathan Miller didn't know.

For years, whenever he was visiting New York, Jonathan, who often stayed with Keith, sometimes showed up for breakfast. Erudite, acid, and very funny, he held us—a table of intellectual thrill seekers—for hours, talking about *King Lear* or the Scottish Enlightenment or the phenomenon of the phantom limb in amputees.

At least once breakfast lasted until three in the afternoon. If we got lucky, Jonathan would perform a little bit of *Beyond the Fringe*. Our breakfasts, Jonathan used to say, reminded him of New York's great bohemian days in the early 1960s when he was on Broadway. Miller recalled seeing John Gielgud, who was in town, hitting on Dudley Moore at a bar—I think it was Gielgud. Miller saw Lenny Bruce perform—Miles Davis, too. It was thrilling. One day he brought Oliver Sacks, the neurologist and wonderful writer and Jonathan's best friend since childhood.

I got a glimpse of what I thought Keith McNally must have experienced when he was a teenager. In the years when I worked in London, I had been around this sort of seductive intellectual fast-talk, the wit and the jokes; it was pretty daunting at first until you learned to play, and you had to play if you were to stay in the game. Keith got lucky with the Millers, who adored him and are, to this day, among the most welcoming people I've ever met.

It wasn't hard to imagine the effect of all this on Keith McNally at seventeen. It was the 1960s. The British 1960s were not like ours, not exactly; like everything else in Britain, it banged up against issues of class.

Hard to imagine how stultifying life was even at the beginning of the 1960s, stultifying and clinging to a certain drab propriety. In London on that first trip with my parents, my mother pointed out a sign at the hotel informing us that dinner jackets were required. "To eat?"

my father said. But nothing captures the time quite as well as Philip Larkin's verse from "Annus Mirabilis": "Sexual intercourse began / In Nineteen Sixty-Three / (Which was rather late for me) / Between the end of the Chatterley ban / And the Beatles' first LP."

The American '60s were about styles of politics: Vietnam, civil rights, flower power, the age of the affluent hippie and well-fed protest was made real by the killing of four students at Kent State and the boys dying in Southeast Asia. What we shared were sex, drugs, and rock and roll.

The British '60s were about styles of style: Mary Quant made mini-skirts and hot pants; Vidal Sassoon made haircuts; Terence Conran told you that you could have furniture that was stylish, even fun, instead of your parents' dusty velour three-piece suite, antimacassars on the arms. You could go to France. You could get espresso coffee. In 1968, "Hey Jude" and "Jumpin' Jack Flash" were top of the charts.

When it came to class, it felt for one brief glorious moment as if real change was in the air, maybe a revolution. Class, the ever-present, immoveable fact of British life, seemed on its way out.

Britain would become an equal-opportunity backdrop for the young and talented; signs indeed appeared all over London announcing, CLAPTON IS GOD. A certain working-class aesthetic took hold; a working-class accent once would have held you back. (How many people I've met in England who have had elocution lessons!) But now accents like Keith Richards's became cool. The time was ripe for a young guy like Keith McNally.

The *Observer* editor Allan Jenkins said to me, "It was a special time, everything changing, and Keith floated on it all like a cork. He was taken by everything. You could buy rock records, you could read 'Howl,' there was the Pill, which meant there was sex, and an explosion of good times."

Almost as much as the music, the theater underwent enormous, incredible changes. From 1737 on—1737!— scripts had been licensed by the Lord Chamberlain's office, which amounted to government censorship. This lasted until 1968, when the censorship laws were lifted and the theater, the thing the Brits did better than anyone, got a new lease on life. Pinter, Wesker, Bennett, Stoppard were all young guys; so was Jonathan Miller. Peter Brook cast a young Glenda Jackson in a startling production of *Marat/Sade*. Keith was there in a hit play at the Apollo Theatre on Shaftesbury Avenue at the heart of it all. Four days after *Forty Years On* opened, the legendary anti-Vietnam protest and riot exploded at Grosvenor Square outside the American embassy.

"Keith is in some ways very theatrical. He's an invention of the theatrical, he loves the theater, and he's learnt from it," Allan Jenkins said.

Six years later, Keith went to New York. William Miller told me, "Keith had this little leather suitcase. And whenever he had extra cash, he put it in and it was exciting. He said, 'When this suitcase is full of money, I'm going to go to America and make films.' He intended going to LA, spent three months in NYC, and, as I recall, he never left . . ."

Keith McNally got to New York around 1975, just got on a plane and went—an illegal immigrant, he likes to add. Some of his enormous sympathy for the bussers at Balthazar probably came from the fact he had done their job when he got to New York; he knew the hard graft of a city kitchen. At One Fifth, where he was shucking those oysters, Keith became the manager. The place looked like camp Cole Porter, all retro décor, and bits from the interior of an old transatlantic liner.

Keith acquired a kind of following that included Lorne Michaels and the young cast of the brand-new *Saturday Night Live*, as well as Anna Wintour, the Artistic Director of Condé Nast and Editor in Chief of *Vogue*. "I met him when he was working at the bar at

One Fifth Avenue, the restaurant on Eighth Street," Wintour said. "He was in the process of planning the Odeon downtown with Brian McNally [his brother] and I told him it would never work because at that point Tribeca was such a wilderness, and no one thought that a restaurant below Fifty-Seventh Street would have any traction— but of course he was totally right, and I was totally wrong."

She went on: "Keith has always been a risk taker. London was a very small world, especially at that time. You were very much defined by where you went to school, who your parents were, what your accent was. I think New York opened up a world to him that maybe his own childhood didn't offer; he was always very clear that he wanted to do something different, be something different."

In 1980, I had never heard of Thomas Street. It was down south of Canal. I had never met anyone who had ever been there. That year, on the corner of Thomas and West Broadway, with his brother Brian and Lynn Wagenknecht, the woman he would marry, Keith McNally opened Odeon. It was his first restaurant, and it was in an area so bleak at night, if people went there, they went only to buy drugs.

Odeon lit up the night. The neon sign that read CAFETERIA blazed orange. The old Towers Cafeteria had been transformed into a gorgeous retro diner. Behind Formica panels, the young owners had discovered beautiful wood paneling. A Bakelite frieze of the New York skyline came from Woolworth's, and there was the huge mirrored 1930s Art Deco bar.

A wonderful place to eat and drink had literally appeared out of nowhere, an oasis in an urban desert.

Odeon was fabulous. There had been nothing like it since the grand bars in the midtown hotels of the 1920s and '30s; it was like a set out of vintage Woody Allen, like his *Radio Days*. You got a table at Odeon and you felt good and knew you had made it, more or less, though looking around the room, you inevitably realized everybody else was a lot more famous.

The nights were wired. Cocaine was the drug of choice in the 1980s, and there was plenty of it everywhere in the city. (I tried it once and was so paralyzed with fear that I might die—I had never been much good at drugs—I sat up all night and waited for the end.)

There were fights at Odeon, and famous people and the almost famous, but there was also a kind of warmth; you had come in from the cold of the dark, dank city streets, and people were, once you got inside, pretty nice. Nobody was snotty; nobody peered at you with the look that said, *How the hell did you get in here?*

It was almost startling, that you could go someplace incredibly trendy and popular and be treated in a human sort of way and eat really good food, even while you were watching a scene so cool, so filled with truly famous people—John Belushi, Andy Warhol, Scorsese, Basquiat—it was like being a tourist at a big party at the end of the known world.

The art scene was quickly becoming where the action was; the money, too. Henry Geldzahler—art critic, curator, guru, mentor—showed up at Odeon almost every night.

"Andy Warhol was frequently dining at Odeon during the early 1980s, almost always at a table for two, with a young guy," Michele Oka Doner said.

But let the late Seymour Britchky tell it. The most wickedly evocative—and provocative—and often unforgiving restaurant writer of his time, he understood downtown because he lived in Greenwich Village. His reviews were acute and very, very funny. In his 1985 review of Odeon, he wrote:

> Surely no observer can reasonably be faulted for asserting that trendy places are, ipso facto, dreadful . . . Apparently mindless of this reasoning, Odeon has contrived to become the ultimate destination south of Canal, while still producing yummy victuals . . . The crowd is very much Downtown Today. You see

the likes of this lady in pink slippers, black lace stockings, black leather miniskirt, a dinner jacket and dress shirt (sans bow tie)—all her hair is pulled to one side of her head, and her slash of lipstick looks like a wound . . . But the business side of whatever this world is is here, too, in suits and sunglasses, and the intellectual side, in steel-rimmed specs and bowl haircuts.

Britchky was uncompromising; he considered it his moral duty to check out restaurants and their food in obsessive detail—he went to each four or five times—and he loved the poached oysters at Balthazar, as well as the black chocolate mousse. "South of Canal, you cannot beat this place," he wrote, having also feasted on snails in cream sauce and praline ice cream.

Everybody went to Odeon. The owners had never expected this kind of success, and there was a kind of panic about it—and a joy.

Limos idled at the curb outside Odeon. Crack dealers and hookers looked on, curious or irritated. Odeon marked the territory. In fact, many decades earlier this had been a vibrant market area. Commodities in the area had changed: butter and eggs then; drugs now.

I've often heard people heave a sigh and regret the New York of the '70s and early '80s. What they remember is the music at CBGB and Max's Kansas City and Andy Warhol's Factory and Studio 54; they recall a time when artists squatted in cavernous lofts and the Lower East Side was cheap, if sometimes murderous.

The flavor of that lost urban world has become ever more potent in retrospect, as if in raising its ghosts, its fans might reclaim its spirit, its art and music. Perhaps it's also because people still went out at night; there were no cell phones or computers. In spite of the thousands of homicides and muggings, the craziness of crack—or because of it—and the malignant police corruption, there was a sense of intimacy in the city.

It might not make sense now. It certainly won't make sense to the Millennial who cherishes safety and coherence, but nobody was sensible in the 1970s. "Everyone was open-faced," said Michele Oka Doner. "The night was ours to claim. Sometimes we would go on to Area or Palladium; Tribeca was dark, abandoned. There was virtually no street life, especially after dark. I used to walk along the curb, away from hidden recessed doors, where muggers could lurk."

Michele could remember those days with a kind of nostalgia for the fun and at the same time, recall the muggings, the filth, the fear that hung over New York. She said that she'd rather live in the current Disneyfied city than be mugged by a man with a big gun, but she regretted the deliciously communal party that was New York in the 1970s. And we were young then.

Putting Odeon in a deserted area that turned into tony Tribeca gave Keith his reputation as a genius. Later, he lost Odeon to his wife in their divorce, left for Paris to make a couple of films, and came back. He opened Balthazar on a desolate street in SoHo. He seemed able to predict the next fashionable neighborhood, marking it as his own, before anyone else. It reminded me of the Delmonico dynasty in the nineteenth century.

Café Delmonico, which opened in 1823 downtown on William Street, was the first civilized place where a New Yorker could get decent coffee, a glass of wine, a French pastry. Over the decades, it grew into a restaurant, into *the* restaurant. Gradually, as the city moved, so did Delmonico's.

The big money went, so did celebrities. By the 1870s, '80s, '90s, it was one of the city's institutions where balls were held and politics discussed, and the likes of Charles Dickens was given dinners by the city's citizens eager to receive the great novelist. In the 1890s, the good, the great, the corrupt met regularly: Diamond Jim Brady, Mayor Jimmy Walker, Stanford White. (The best description I've read is in Caleb Carr's wonderful *The Alienist*, a thriller set in the nineteenth century.)

So savvy was this family, they knew exactly when to move the restaurant. They moved it slightly ahead of society, from the area around Wall Street to Madison Square to Times Square, getting in first, claiming title, changing the city. Delmonico's did two things for New York: it changed the geography of fashion, and it reinforced the city's love affair with French food.

As time went on and he opened more restaurants, people said that Keith McNally could sniff out the next big location, as if he were making a perfume and could find a rare bloom in a cracked sidewalk, as if opening good restaurants required a sort of taste for the dark side, the low life, a certain *nostalgie de la boue.*

People gave Keith credit for literally changing New York, for reclaiming whole neighborhoods and marking them as new and hot, places where real estate developers followed fast. He had done it with Odeon, and would do it with Balthazar, Pastis in the Meatpacking District, Schiller's Liquor Bar in the East Village, and then Cherche Midi on the Bowery.

"I think Keith is a genius at understanding neighborhoods. He picks his restaurant locations for his own particular reasons," said Richard Lewis, Balthazar's architect. "He finds places that other people don't want, that people don't see as worthy—you know, he looks for locations, for unusual things. If you were making a movie, you would look for great locations. I think he does that with restaurants . . . and he loves the old buildings, that, too."

Lorne Michaels told me he always thought Keith brilliant at creating great environments. "His attention to detail and his eye are fantastic—what he did with Balthazar and Pastis was amazing, especially Pastis because there was nothing in the Meatpacking District."

When Keith McNally opened Pastis, a terrifying real estate boom followed in which the meat warehouses, with blood still on their walls, were converted to multimillion-dollar condos. It was as if Keith had mapped his restaurants by an older New York map where you could just barely see the city's bones.

I remember when Meatpacking was a strange, broken, scary place where hookers worked the streets; you could smell the garbage from the river (the Hudson was a mess for a long time), and homeless guys warmed their hands over fires in trash cans. It looked like hell here on the fringes of the old industrial city, and it was exciting. I used to go to Florent, a restaurant where you could get terrific slabs of meat very late at night or early in the morning.

There was a thrill about the sense you were in a secret, abandoned city. People partied on the High Line, where they drank and got high, and some of them slept in the weeds that grew through the railroad tracks.

I used to ride my bike along the river. I loved the old industrial fringes of the city, the SRO hotels, the crumbling meatpacking warehouses, and I thought, from time to time, maybe I'd buy one or rent one. Then I'd move on. Only the smart, or the silly, or the brave bought property this far off the beaten track. No more. It's all taken now. Keith McNally took some of it.

Rarely did I have a conversation about Balthazar that didn't circle back to Keith. People who liked him, or did not, or were envious, his friends and the not so friendly, the customers, cooks, managers, everyone agreed that everything—the style, the look, the service—came from him. *Balthazar*, they all said, *is McNally. It's his DNA.*

And then, in 2010, he left again.

With his second wife, Alina Johnson, who had briefly worked at Balthazar, and their two small kids, Keith moved to London. The move sent a kind of shock wave through the restaurant business, but most of all through Balthazar.

Like so many Brits who came and stayed, were changed by the city and changed it—Keith Richards, Anna Wintour, Quentin Crisp,

David Bowie, John Lennon—McNally had seemed a quintessential New Yorker. He bought a house in Greenwich Village and sent his kids to the local schools.

Even so, he did leave. He bought a pretty house in London's Notting Hill and a country place in Gloucestershire.

"There's a divine discontent to Keith, if you like, or that's what I think," *Observer* editor Allan Jenkins said.

I couldn't say. Keith McNally somehow always remained just out of reach, no matter how charming he was over a waffle.

It wasn't until a canny friend of mine met him one evening that it all made a little more sense.

At Cherche Midi, where I was finishing dinner with a friend one night, Keith came by to say hello. In the next twenty minutes, he and my friend Frank, both autodidacts, both men of terrifying erudition and appealing passion, covered, though not necessarily in this order: Orson Welles's films—particularly how much better *Touch of Evil* is than *Citizen Kane*; the various cinematheques in Paris; New York architecture; the current state of British theater (pretty good). Also, I think, some aspect of design, possibly Constructivism, might have got a look-in, along with Beckett, Woody Allen, *Hamilton*, and the Young Vic production of Arthur Miller's *A View from the Bridge*. Later, I got a note from Keith saying he had enjoyed meeting Frank and inviting him to Balthazar in London.

On the way home, Frank, who is no pushover and not easily charmed, said, "You want to know what Keith is about? I think he's about whatever is good."

CHAPTER 8

THE SWEET MEN

I was watching Mark work on the cake that day just after noon. It was an opera cake, an elaborate confection that he loved. It was made of pounds of eggs, sugar, hazelnuts; of brittle made from the nuts; of chocolate ganache and cream. It took time. He whipped the egg whites and whipped in sugar and folded this into the flour. He baked the cake in sheets and cut them and built the cake with chocolate ganache and hazelnut buttercream, assembled it with an almost dainty touch.

Mark Tasker had been in since five. He was the man who had set me on course when I got lost in the catacombs. I watched him now as he cracked the eggs with one hand in that deft way real cooks have, one egg after another with a swift gesture, the shell splitting clean, the yolk and white sliding into the mixing bowl. It was quiet in the baking department, and all I heard was that crisp crack of the eggshell.

When Mark put his hands on the mound of dough, there was real intensity on his face. He examined the thick dough as he turned it gently; this was his baby. He loved doing this stuff, and not just the baking. He cared for the young women who worked with him and he kept a solicitous eye on them. One of the bakers was setting out little square rum-drenched petit fours, covering them with a large sheet of pale green fondant that she would cut afterward to fit the little cakes.

The baking room was big and light. It smelled even more potent than it had a few hours earlier when I had bumbled in. Pastry baking, the overwhelming, almost unbearably sweet and good aroma of sugar, butter, and chocolate, of nuts roasting, ginger and nutmeg. In a row of metal bins were three kinds of flour. The ovens were in a wall to the right of the entrance.

Improbably, a dozen chickens were roasting on spits in a huge glass-fronted wall oven on the opposite side of the room. Nobody seemed perturbed. Not an inch of space was wasted.

In his white chef gear with a flat cap to match, from his domain in the catacombs beneath Balthazar, Mark Tasker oversaw the cakes and pastries, tarts and cookies, for the Spring Street bakery and for Balthazar's catering department. A Scot in his fifties, Mark Tasker had been at Balthazar almost from the beginning. Like so many of the others, he arrived in a casual, roundabout way. "You could say I was an illegal," he said, laughing. His father was in the armed forces; the family moved around a good deal.

Mark was apprenticed as a teenager to a German baker in London, followed a peripatetic path that led him, eventually, to Philadelphia with a contract for work at a restaurant. The contract ended, but Mark had met a girl, and he said he snuck back into the United States via Canada. Eventually he got a green card and then his citizenship, settled in New York, married Renata (the woman for whom he snuck into the country), and they had two daughters, Lucy and Sophia.

Compared to the macho style of the prep guys and the line cooks, Mark's domain was more feminine, as if pastry in all its delicacy required a more serene ambiance. He mentored his young bakers, he encouraged them to invent and collaborate, and there were always a few young women in the kitchen, culinary school students or graduates.

Emiko Chisholm, working near Mark, had once carved a wonderful Halloween pumpkin into a Balthazar bread. On another occasion, she piped little roses into the pastry cream for a tart, even though the fruit would hide it. It was hidden art, art like charity, like a present. When I mentioned it to Mark, he just smiled as if to imply that that was the point, that the rose would be a secret gift. It was about doing what you loved even if nobody saw it, he said.

He was also without any pretension. Once I ordered a wedding cake for some friends getting married in my apartment. That afternoon, Mark and one of his guys carried it over, literally holding it between them as they came up Spring Street. It was three tiers of sunny yellow cake with creamy ivory frosting; around the bottom and on top, tucked into the layers, were fresh white flowers.

When I asked which of the cakes he had invented, he replied with British diffidence. "Nobody invents anything, really," he said. "But I love the opera cake we do. When people want something for a celebration I always suggest it, and we sell out of it by the slice in the bakery. I love that."

It was calm here, and most everyone, but especially Mark, seemed good-natured and quiet. He was a sweet man, and it was as if this sweetness went into the fabulous confections he made. In his domain at Balthazar, he ruled with a light touch. His staff always looked content and calm, too, as if they had imbibed Mark's patience. If he spotted a new dishwasher with ambition or interest, he tried him out. He often wished he could pay his workers more.

Emiko had begun placing purple and yellow edible pansies on a chocolate sea salt cake. Overhead the light was bright, and I could see how tired Mark was. There were times, especially before holidays, when he worked the best part of twenty-four hours a day. He got in at four or five; and at least once, I knew, he had worked until midnight because it was Christmas and he was making croquembouche, the pyramid of caramelized puff pastry, and bûches de Noël, those logs made of chocolate and chocolate mousse and cream and decorated with marzipan leaves and red berries, and gingerbread men with marzipan plaques in their hands that read, I ♥ NY.

At Thanksgiving there were pies, too, chocolate bourbon pie, pecan pie, pumpkin pie, and the best apple pie I have ever eaten. Mark Tasker was invested it his work in that particular way that bakers often were; with pastry, it was a fine, delicate craft, and Mark had once worked at Harrods in London decorating fancy cakes. He was a baker's baker, said Sim Cass, himself a kind of baking rock star who had helped start the Balthazar Bakery. "Mark is an artist," said Sim.

Around the corner from Mark Tasker, I found Andy Gomez pouring dense, dark, aromatic liquid chocolate from a cooking pot into a bowl. This was for chocolate sauce served with the profiteroles, arguably the best in town: three little light puff pastries stuffed with vanilla ice cream and arranged on a plate, carried to the restaurant by a runner who then poured thick hot Valrhona chocolate sauce over them with a flourish.

There was a time that a friend and I, eating supper at Balthazar, had ordered only the sauce, assuming if we put it on berries instead of pastry it was less fattening; except in the end we ate the chocolate sauce out of the little sauceboat with spoons.

Andy next tasted some rich banana ice cream, which is served with the banana ricotta tarts. "We took it off the menu like two times, and the customers were calling and calling and they say they want the banana ricotta tart," said Andy.

"These have been famous since we opened," added Andy, who made all the desserts for the restaurant. "I've been in Balthazar since it opened in 1997." Andy, at forty-five, was soft-spoken, meticulous, a kindly man who always wore a white cap in the kitchen. He kept a statue of the Virgin Mary above his desk in an alcove downstairs. He told me he loved food, his grandmother had cooked, and they ate rice and beans and sancocho, a hearty Dominican stew. He left home at seventeen and came to New York, where he lived on the Lower East Side, on Second Street between Avenues A and B.

Andy tried new things. He discovered steak with French fries. He worked making deliveries for a coffee shop until his uncle got a job for him at Aureole, Charlie Palmer's original and legendary restaurant on the Upper East Side. There, Andy first met Lee Hanson, who went on to Balthazar.

"I call him up and he says, 'OK, come on down.' I came here as assistant pastry chef," Andy said. "Oh my, it was crazy in the beginning. We were doing like eleven hundred people for brunch." It was so busy there were times he found himself running up and down stairs, working in the restaurant, preparing more sweets downstairs.

At his church in East Harlem, Andy worked to make sure new immigrants, most of them, like him, from the Dominican Republic, found housing and jobs, including some alongside him at Balthazar. I began to understand that at Balthazar, and across the city, the men—and they were mostly men—who worked in restaurant kitchens were tied together by nationality or blood or marriage. Some had come from the same town; others found their way to the same church. Uncles brought in their nephews, brothers worked together, fathers got jobs for their kids. Like every New York generation of newcomers, immigrants often began work where no English was needed—Latinos in restaurant kitchens; Jews, once upon a time, in sweatshops; and the Irish on the docks—and each had its own aspirations.

Down here in the Balthazar kitchens it was a largely Latino world, where Spanish was the common language. It was a culture in its own right, but not just a single culture. Each nationality had its own attitudes, its own history and cuisine, and if they all spoke Spanish, there were dialects and slang, and there were sports, too: the Mexicans were soccer players; the Dominicans rooted for baseball. Andy Gomez was a die-hard Yankees fan. "I'm with them in the good time and the bad time," he said.

It would be unrealistic to say of the guys who worked in New York kitchens that all—or even most—achieved Andy's level of success. The work was hard, the pay was often lousy, the conditions hot and hard, and unlike for the front-of-house staff, there was rarely any applause from happy customers or tips.

This was the real divide in most New York restaurants, friends who had worked in their kitchens told me. It was not between customer and waitstaff—especially not at Balthazar—but between back of house and front, downstairs and up.

But for men who did not speak English, it was a way in. For those who learned English there was a chance to rise in the kitchen hierarchy, and if you also had some skill, tenacity, a can-do way of looking at the world, and plenty of luck, you could make the system work.

Andy felt lucky. His daughter was in college and had decided on a teaching career; his two sons, also getting their degrees, were hoping for careers as New York City cops. It made him happy and excited that they had done so well, and that his daughter was also interested in food. "We do a lot of baking at home together. Also I got her reading a lot of books and getting a lot of ideas and working the recipes.

"Even when I'm not working," said Andy, "I'm thinking about ideas, because I love dessert. I feel happy when I look in the dining room and I see people happy, enjoying what they're eating. We used to go out the front door of the restaurant, and this one time I passed by a customer who was eating a Tarte Tatin, feeling the flavor, I could see that, and I was like, 'Whoa!' That made me feel proud. When I see people happy in what we do and where we come from, this is a dream come true. I didn't imagine it at all."

Over the years, whenever I went to Balthazar with my goddaughter, Justine, we almost always had the banana ricotta tart. It was very sweet and very rich, a dense almond cookie topped with a dome of ricotta dusted with sugar and caramelized with a blowtorch so that the crust was crunchy, and it was set on top of a puck-shaped helping of banana ice cream. It was finished with caramel sauce and a little vanilla crème anglaise.

We spent a lot of Justine's childhood at Balthazar. After school she would meet me for hot chocolate and sometimes shrimp cocktails. At her sixteenth birthday party, she came with her girlfriends, who, being New Yorkers, knew just what they wanted—apple martinis if at all possible—and could shoot the breeze with the self-conscious sophistication of women of thirty. Birthdays, graduations, we celebrated everything at Balthazar. Alice, Justine's late mother and my best friend, said to me fondly once, "I got the projectile vomit, and you got to take her to Balthazar for banana ricotta tarts and profiteroles."

Andy Gomez made some of the tarts for a baby shower when Justine was pregnant, and now that she has a little girl, she plans to raise Rosie on them. A piece somewhere—the London *Sunday Times*, I think—called Balthazar the most baby-friendly restaurant in America.

It all made me feel ridiculously sentimental. There was something wonderful about three generations—Rosie, Justine, and me—sitting together in a booth at Balthazar, eating banana ricotta tarts.

Lunchtime. At Balthazar's main door, people were pushing into the little vestibule between the outside door and the proper front door. Tourists in all varieties speaking French, Chinese, there were even a couple of Japanese. (There had been a falling off of the Japanese since their economy had gone bad.)

A well-known Brit, a movie director whose name I couldn't dredge up, ambled inside with the cool confidence of a regular. With so many Brits in New York, it was hard to tell who was an expat, who was visiting. Lousy tippers, the staff told me, except for the thesps; actors and film people were almost always great tippers.

At the front desk, Julia Mintz was already looking over the lunch reservations. She asked Asbury for a little help getting them to their tables, their coats to the cloakroom, the baby strollers to the disabled toilet on the ground floor at the end of the bar where they were stashed.

Asbury Wilkinson, one of the young hosts, was a handsome young man with a sweet face and dimples. He was working toward an acting career—he was hoping to audition for the Royal Academy of Dramatic Art in London at some point. No, Asbury had told me, his mother was not a particularly dedicated Springsteen fan, nor was his last name Park. It was simply that in his family the first male born to each generation was always named Asbury.

From the kitchen came the first orders: sautéed calf's liver with caramelized onions, crisp bacon, and mashed potatoes (I know a man who ate it the second he was released from a hospital stay); beef Stroganoff with buttered noodles that had the aroma of a rich beefiness; macaroni au gratin laced with huge amounts of cheese and bacon; a roast lamb sandwich with harissa; a cheeseburger piled high with frites.

To me, Balthazar often felt most like a Paris brasserie at lunch. On a wet day, when you could sit for hours with friends, consuming a few carafes of wine along with maybe a bowl of soup and plenty of the good bread. Thick pea soup in the winter, vichyssoise when it got warm.

Plenty of times, I'd sat here late in the afternoon, drinking coffee, ordering more wine, talking, gossiping, spotting friends across the way at another table. It always put me in a sort of daydream of a once-upon-a-time Paris when I lived there for a while and ate lunch every day with two girlfriends.

We always saw the same local workman in a blue jacket that matched his pack of Gauloise cigarettes, and he would polish off a robust soup or stew along with a glass of red, drink his café express, and light another smoke. He must have had a sweet tooth, too, because more than once I saw him cross the street to the patisserie and emerge holding a large chocolate éclair. Looking around a little surreptitiously, he would eat the pastry in two bites.

CHAPTER 9

RUTH REICHL, ERIC RIPERT, AND THE FRENCH THING

O n my wall at home is a photograph of Johnny Hodges at Brasserie Lipp in Paris. Taken by the great jazz photographer Herman Leonard, it shows Hodges, cool in cap and sports coat, sitting casually at the table, his gleaming sax resting on the white linen, a glass beside it. Standing next to him, a waiter in formal brasserie black and white pours the wine. Behind Hodges you can see Lipp's painted glass wall, the flower-shaped sconce, and a tilted mirror. On Hodges's face is a faint smile, perhaps wry or rueful. The waiter is white; Hodges, black.

The photograph was taken in 1958. This is the Paris of my fantasies, the Paris of the 1950s, when Americans dreamed (as they had in the '20s and '30s) of living in a city where there was a certain freedom; black jazz musicians went where they liked and played in tiny underground clubs, and Miles met Juliette Gréco, and artists and writers said important things, talked philosophy to one another at Lipp and La Coupole. I didn't make it for another couple of decades, but I was ever in training, the girl in black on the New York bus reading Camus in the original with the title in full view.

When I finally got to Paris, determined to write a novel on a napkin, I did see Simone de Beauvoir and Jean-Paul Sartre together at Les Deux Magots; Sartre was eating an enormous hot fudge sundae. It didn't matter to me if this was formally a café or a bistro or a brasserie. It was about the style and the flavor, and I had learned it from Ernest Hemingway.

Among Shane McBride's favorite writers was Ernest Hemingway, and among Hemingway's books, his favorite was *A Moveable Feast*. "I think it's a better book than *The Sun Also Rises*," he said, which made sense. Written in the 1920s, published posthumously in 1964, Hemingway's memoir made Paris an icon for generations of Americans. The references to Le Dôme and La Coupole—and to Brasserie Lipp—so potently evoke for the reader the world of the Paris brasserie. You can smell the beer, taste the herring.

"It was a quick walk to Lipp's . . . The beer was very cold and wonderful to drink. The *pommes à l'huile* were firm and marinated and the olive oil delicious," Hemingway wrote. "I ground black pepper over the potatoes and moistened the bread in the olive oil."

In our imaginations, it's always been like that, the fantasy of Frenchiness that puts you in a time and place when people broke bread together in big noisy brasseries any time of day or night, where there was great conversation, a sense of good fellowship. The yellow lights of the brasserie on the corner that illuminated wet black cobblestones on a drab Parisian night.

Balthazar had only been open five minutes, and already it felt, with its patina, as if it had been here forever; the self-possessed Gallic sense of itself, those high-backed red leather banquettes, the opalescent lights that made you look gorgeous, the steak frites and profiteroles and choucroute, the beer and red wine, the artists and writers, that elusive amalgam of the literary salon and the tavern, the intellectual and artistic ferment that had, down the decades from the mid-nineteenth century, blossomed in Paris. There were the celebrities. The social snobs. There was the eavesdropping, and everyone looking in the tilted mirrors.

It was Marcelin Cazes at Lipp who first had the idea of tilting the mirrors, letting customers observe themselves and one another, perhaps making sure they were having a better time than their neighbors. A secret hierarchy was also observed.

At Lipp, for a very long time, if you were not known, you did not get a table. At best, you were told you could wait twenty minutes; at worst, an hour, an indication you might as well leave. There was a visible pecking order. Keith understood that Americans, once willing to be intimidated by a snotty French maître d' in a dusty tux, had moved on, and anyway, Keith was not French; he was English, a working-class kid who hated snobbery.

"I know that Keith was affected by, inspired by, turned on by some of the great brasseries of Paris, like the Balzar or Boeuf sur le Toit, but also the grander places like La Coupole or Bofinger," Adam Gopnik said. I had never met Adam Gopnik when I invited him to Balthazar.

I liked what he had written about France and food and the Paris brasserie. It turned out that he was outgoing, chatty, sympathetic, a kind of natural denizen of the brasserie himself. We talked about mutual friends and about mutual interests, and this included Blossom Dearie and jazz and the winter—we were both crazy about winter—about which he had written a wonderful book. Balthazar made conversation easy the way a brasserie was meant to; it reminded me of France.

France has always been a magnet. The French, my generation felt, knew how to live, how to eat; they knew about wine and film and cigarettes and sex. The summer after my sophomore year in high school a group of us went to Tours to learn French. I shared a room with Steffi Finberg at a pension in the rue Léonard de Vinci that was owned by M. and Mme Jacob.

At suppertime the smell of kidneys drifted nauseatingly up from the kitchen. A large crucifix above the bed dominated the whole room, and it seemed a little scary and very exotic to us, and we wondered if the Jacobs knew we were Jewish. Kathy Boudin taught me to smoke in Tours. Sitting on a window ledge at her pension, I puffed away at a Gitane and tried not to choke to death.

We were sixteen, and nobody in France cared about your age, so we hung around vineyards where there were always free tastings of the local Vouvray. I learned to drink wine that summer. That was also the summer when, instead of going to class, we went to a local bistro, where we drank strong black coffee and ate jambon beurre, ham sandwiches on fresh crusty baguette. The owner got to know us and pretended to understand our horrible French. Being a regular was very seductive in Tours and, again, in Paris a dozen years later, where I lived for a while in an opulent, dusty old apartment building near the Champ de Mars.

We ate out four nights a week at least, with friends or on our own, and always at the same little bistro across the street from home. The same waiter—I think he disapproved of my decidedly unchic outfits—was always there. I almost always ate the same roast chicken followed by a lemon tart. At the next table was the couple—a tiny redhead in a beaded black hat; a large fat man in a three-piece suit, even in the summer—who had been feuding for years. Other regulars became friends or acquaintances, and after a while we were invited to celebrate birthdays and graduations. Everyone smoked and drank. An occasional writer sulked over his notebook and drank a lot of beer.

In that little place there was a sense that whole lives had been led. This was an entire hamlet, a community where you were known and felt good and safe. When the disapproving waiter suddenly disappeared and was replaced by a younger version who smiled more, it was never quite the same. We were told without much fuss that the old man had simply gone home one night and died.

It was then that I first read *A Moveable Feast*. When Paris was murderously attacked in November 2015, it was this memoir that seemed to offer hope. The book hit the French best-seller charts after the ISIS attacks that year. Along with candles and flowers, citizens of Paris placed copies of *A Moveable Feast* where the attacks had taken place.

As much as anything, Hemingway's book is about how American authors and artists found in Paris, in the city itself, an antidote to the nihilism that resulted from the horrors of World War I, and as often as not, they found it in the cafés and brasseries. The title in French is *Paris est une fête*, which translates as *Paris is a Party*.

Hard to believe, but the whole business of the restaurant only began in the late eighteenth century, and it began as soup. A "restaurant" was a concentrated bouillon for those too weak to take solid food; one "went to a restaurant to drink restorative bouillons as one went to a café to drink coffee," writes Rebecca Spang in *The Invention of the Restaurant*. As the word for coffee became the word for the place you drank it—the café—so with the restaurant.

People eventually started hanging out and chatting, and a social life emerged, and from this, by the 1820s, the restaurant as we know it—almost exactly as we know it—was a fact of Parisian life.

Unlike the table d'hôte, where you could not choose what to eat or with whom to eat it, the restaurant was all about choice, a glamorous public space where you could sit with whom you chose or all by yourself, choose what you wanted, be attended by your own servant (waiter), with the sweaty misery of kitchen work out of sight. It was also a stop on the way to a more democratic life—if you had the cash, you'd get the food.

A dinner out was attended by expectation, the thrill of possible celebrity, of seduction, a business deal, a celebration, an engagement or breakup, the pleasures of good food, the fizz of mild inebriation. Writes Rebecca Spang, "Like a theater, a restaurant was a stable frame around an ever-changing performance, a stage where fantasies might be brought to life." If, according to Spang, a restaurant was like a theater, there was always a certain frisson of uncertainty. Like a play, no two nights would ever be exactly the same; so there was this excitement, this possibility of delight, ecstasy, and often of laughter.

The brasserie as we know it came into being in the 1870s when Alsatians, fleeing the capture of their province by the Germans, made their way to Paris. With them they brought their skills as brewers ("brasserie" actually means "brewery"), a taste for big noisy collegial restaurants where you could get a brew, night or day, and the dishes they liked with beer, the herrings, the sauerkraut and sausages.

Some of the refugees went much farther. They crossed the Atlantic to America; most of them settled in New York around Washington Square. A French quarter took shape between Washington Square South and Grand Street, West Broadway and Greene; in other words: today's SoHo.

There were French butchers, cafés, shops, newspapers; you could buy peasant clogs; there was cheap food and cheap wine.

On Greene Street—my own block—was a dive called Taverne Alsacienne, a smoky basement joint that had its own clientele, men who played billiards and cards games like *écarté*, *piquet*, and *vingt-et-un*. Strangers were not welcome, according to Arthur Bartlett Maurice in his 1917 book, *The New York of the Novelists*. "A stranger in the Taverne Alsacienne in those days was very likely to be a spy or a detective, and the habitués were sensitive under inspection." It was part of New York's bohemia of the 1880s, though when the writer went looking for it fifteen years later, an older man told him, "You are too late."

For a century and a half, French food held New Yorkers in thrall. Not just the lowly brasseries but also the grand cafés with gilt ceilings and the gorgeous restaurants like Delmonico's. The restaurant *was* French. Rich Americans went to Paris, had their socks knocked off by this thrilling innovation called the restaurant—the restaurants of the Palais-Royal, and later the gilded fantasies like Maxim's, where every night was a party. Poor writers discovered the brasseries. High-tone ladies went to fabulous tearooms in the rue de Rivoli and ate meringues.

In the twentieth century, Americans ventured to smaller venues, the secret addresses for culinary delights in every quarter of Paris and out into the French provinces.

New York was in love; New York wanted French restaurants. Right through the 1980s, every critic and magazine felt compelled to publish separate roundups or rundowns of French restaurants. I looked at some of my old Seymour Britchky guides from the late 1970s and early '80s, and they are dominated by French restaurants: Lutèce, La Caravelle, La Côte Basque, Brussels, Le Veau d'Or— fifty-four French to half a dozen Japanese.

I, too, was raised on the idea that dining out *was* French, no matter if it was Charles French in Greenwich Village or Le Pavillon, grandest of all, where I went only once. Le Pavillon was very famous, the most celebrated restaurant of its time. It was also, reputedly, very, very snotty. On one of our nutty family expeditions, we went, my father, my mother, and I. It seems to me I had a rose-colored silk dress my mother had somehow acquired for me on a trip to France. I should remember what we ate; I think there was something that was flambéed at our table. But what comes back to me is how gorgeously my mother was treated, how they bowed and scraped, how they lit her cigarette and refilled her wineglass and admired her black chiffon dress. Me, I'm sure they thought I was a pretentious little pest. But my mother was on a pedestal the whole evening and we maintained a relatively calm demeanor, at least until we got outside on

Fifty-Seventh and Park and into a cab downtown, where we burst out laughing.

"What do you think that was about?" my mother said.

"I think I heard a waiter mutter about *Our Miss Brooks*," said my father, referring to a legendary television series and lighting his cigar. "They thought you were its star," he added.

"You mean Eve Arden, she's the one in *Our Miss Brooks*, isn't she?" said my mother. "Oh, well, and I was hoping for Bette Davis."

By the time food and restaurants had become a kind of national obsession and the television chef held sway, French food was pretty much dead, replaced by sushi and fusion, by tall food and raw food. The Italians also ruled, and there were restaurants serving dishes from provinces I had never heard of; out in California, where the food revolution had begun, at Spago, Wolfgang Puck was making pizza topped with lox.

"It took balls for Keith to put this kind of workingman's French food on the menu," writer, editor, and author Ruth Reichl told me on a wet day over lunch at Balthazar. "What Balthazar did was make that food hip. So people who wouldn't be caught dead eating frisée aux lardons with their grandparents were suddenly eating it with their friends.

"Would this have happened anyway? Definitely—Americans have a long and lasting love affair with France. We'll always have Paris, and it will always sell books and magazines." The only issue that *Gourmet* ever sold out when she was the editor, she told me, was her first Paris issue.

Although I didn't know Ruth well, we both grew up on Tenth Street in Greenwich Village. We had also both worked for *Metropolitan Home* in the 1980s, where Ruth introduced the new thrills of California food. Recently we had met at a friend's press launch, and I had asked her if she'd come have lunch at Balthazar.

In her review for the *New York Times* when Balthazar opened, her feelings had initially been a little less than ecstatic. But then she went back four or five months later:

> I didn't much like Balthazar when it opened . . . Oh, of course I liked the look of the place; its bold, sassy bistro airs were enchanting. So was the buzz: celebrities were everywhere and it was fun to walk around the enormous room trying to figure out why each of them had been seated in that particular place. One night it was a special thrill to leave the restaurant and find a panhandler staring resentfully at Jerry Seinfeld's disappearing back. But after I'd eaten my way through the bread basket (the bread is spectacular) and downed an oyster or two, I was always ready to leave; the food just wasn't very good.
>
> Then something happened. It got better. Lots better. I suddenly found I was gobbling up the short ribs (only on Saturdays) and longing for the good, garlicky brandade. Once, sitting in a traffic jam, I caught myself thinking longingly of the restaurant's steak frites. And after a lunch of pasta with broccoli rabe and roasted garlic, I couldn't wait to go back.

As the *New York Times* restaurant critic, Ruth described the food she ate, but she also always took you with her; she showed you the scene; she showed you herself. Ruth's second review of Balthazar a few months after it opened wasn't just about a restaurant or the food, but about her, a perfect selfie that told you—and included you in—what she liked and didn't, things that made her laugh, even a whisper of the schadenfreude we all sometimes feel about celebrities.

When I mentioned to Erin and Shane that Ruth was coming for lunch, there was a certain excitement. For a lot of people who had loved her writing about food, her cookbooks, her reviews, she was a name to reckon with. But, as I found out, there were readers to whom she meant something different, something more, to women especially.

Erin's wife, Maya, for instance, had had a connection with her own mother through Ruth's books. I think this was because in her writing, Ruth rarely seemed to hold back. She was revealing, sometimes startlingly so, about her own life, something I always admired, and envied.

So when she came down to Balthazar in the rain—she could not have been a better sport—to meet for lunch, what struck me most about Ruth was that she regretted nothing about her life, she said. Given it had not always been an easy road—I knew this from her books—she seemed a happy woman. Not happy in any giddy kind of way, not without an understanding of the brutality of life for farmworkers, or of politics and society, but happy in an alive kind of way.

Having walked from the subway, Ruth ran into Balthazar, her hair damp. She tumbled into a booth. Shane produced a three-tier platter of seafood. Ruth was ecstatic. This was charming in a woman who had eaten so many fabulous meals. Her enthusiasm was infectious.

"As you know, Balthazar's kind of food has always had a place in New York. All those places in the way West Forties that are still hanging on, the Chez thises and thats. Not to mention Tout Va Bien and Veau d'Or." (In my own memory, they were all called Pierre au Tunnel.) "But they were so geriatric—still are, in fact," said Ruth. "Then the great Italian craze came and wiped them off the map—at least as far as cool was concerned."

We both ate lobster. We drank Champagne.

She was on her way that evening to a new French brasserie in town, and I asked what she thought, if she had any notions about it in advance. "It won't be Balthazar," she said, retrieving a mussel from the platter of shellfish. "Nothing is."

• • •

Later in the week, I went to see Eric Ripert at Le Bernardin, his great French restaurant in midtown New York. The offices, below ground level, were different from Balthazar's. They were impeccable, sleek and beautiful; people sat at tidy desks, and there was a board-room, the walls lined with cookbooks.

If Ripert had any sense of himself as *le grand seigneur*, there was no sign of it. He offered a drink. I asked for a Diet Coke. He apologized because there was only Coke Zero. Ripert was handsome, charismatic, easygoing, and very tall; he spoke with an accent inde-cently well-suited to a famous Frenchman. And he had a sense of humor.

I spent only half an hour with him, but could detect not a speck of bullshit in this chef whom many consider the best in America, the owner of a restaurant that regularly gets three Michelin stars and the ripest praise from everybody else. We sat down with a couple of Cokes, and Ripert talked about Balthazar.

"I try to go to Balthazar as much as I can. Some people believe Balthazar is trendy, but for me it's eating at my favorite restaurant. They have great energy in the room and good service," said Ripert. "The food is very consistent. I've been going there for so many years, I know a lot of the staff, and I feel almost like I'm home. I always have a good bottle of Bordeaux, crab legs, shrimps, oysters, and clams, and then the steak tartare, spicy, or steak frites. And I call the bakery to ask them to reserve some cannelé for me." The cannelé, which resem-bles a little tower, is custard baked in a fluted copper mold so that its crust is caramelized and crisp, while its inside remains eggy, spicy, and sweet.

Ripert went on. "But it's always something in that menu that you crave. It's why you go back to Balthazar. Who doesn't want a good steak tartare? Who doesn't want a burger, who doesn't want a steak au poivre?"

Eric Ripert resembled a passionate convert reciting the catechism. I looked for something to disbelieve. Perhaps he and Keith McNally had been close pals for decades. But Ripert barely knew Keith. Finally, I figured that he just liked the damn place. And said so.

"I always take Balthazar as a reference for my staff. I'm like, 'We have to create menus where people, especially the regulars, should always have the desire to come back to try something that they're craving." Ripert finished his Coke. "Maybe it has fallen to us in New York to preserve some of the traditions of France."

If it was true, it was a satisfying little irony that it had been left to America, or at least a few Frenchmen and Francophiles in New York City, to hew to these wonderful traditions. *Indeed*, I thought. *Mais oui, Chef.* Right on.

A few dishes for brunch or early lunch.

SHANE'S GRILLED CHEESE A LA TRUFFE WITH HOMEMADE POTATO CHIPS IN DUCK FAT

Yield: 1 sandwich

I'm hanging around the bar at Balthazar one afternoon waiting to meet somebody when Chef Shane passes by, and I mention I'm dreaming about grilled cheese. Subtle hint, eh? Anyhow, he disappears into the bowels of Balthazar and returns with the most delicious grilled cheese sandwich I'd ever had. The secret? Clarified butter. "At home, I like to put some truffles in," says Shane, who later shares his secrets for the best sandwich I've ever eaten. "What kind of cheese?" I ask. Shane looks at me as if I'm nuts. "American cheese, of course; you can't make a real grilled cheese without it." So here's the deal.

INGREDIENTS

2 pieces good white bread, Pullman loaf-style

4 slices American cheese ("We use Land O'Lakes at Balthazar.")

3 thin slices tomato

3 strips cooked bacon

2 big tablespoons clarified butter

1 black truffle

Special Equipment:

Medium saucepan, ten-inch sauté pan

Spatula

Cooking spider or skimmer

Dish cloth/paper towels

The Potato Chips ingredients:

1 Idaho potato peeled on mandolin or food processor with very thin blade

1 quart duck fat (You can buy from dartagnan.com or, Shane says, "Make a duck and render the fat.")

Fine sea salt

Shane: "You can buy a nice frozen black truffle online; they're often cooked with some booze so they have more flavor. If you don't use it all, put it in the fridge and it will last a week.

"Put all ingredients down flat. Break up two pieces of cheese to cover slice of bread. Add so it covers the whole piece of bread. Add tomatoes, bacon, thinly sliced truffles to cover the surface, add two more pieces of cheese, and the other slice of bread. Press so it's nice and smooched. Wrap in plastic wrap, put in fridge.

"Soak potato slices in cold water. Remove, pat dry. Put duck fat into saucepan on medium flame (325°F). Call the cardiologist.

"Toss each potato slice in the hot fat, making sure they don't stick, then using the spider (or skimmer), move the slices around until completely

brown all the way through. Put on plate with paper towel on top. Sprinkle with fine sea salt. (We use it for the fries at Balthazar.) Set aside to cool.

"Remove sandwich from fridge, pour yourself a beer, put tablespoon clarified butter in sauté pan on medium flame. When butter is liquid, put the sandwich in, press down. When it begins to brown, flip it, and keep flipping until well browned, adding more butter if pan looks dry. Make cardiologist appointment. I keep flipping until the cheese starts to run out. Take out. Cut in half diagonally. Pile on the chips, and voilà!"

And to drink? "A beer," says Shane. I suggest a glass of nice cold Krug Champagne. "Krug would be great," he says. "It goes well with anything. Krug goes well with oxygen."

COUNTRY PÂTÉ

Yield: Enough for a party

INGREDIENTS

½ pound sliced smoked bacon (smoked bacon is best)

2 pounds pork shoulder

6 ounces pork liver

¼ cup chopped shallot

1½ tablespoons chopped garlic

½ cup chopped parsley

3 tablespoons chopped thyme

2 tablespoons salt

½ teaspoon quatre épices (This is a French spice mix made of ground white pepper, clove, nutmeg, and ginger. Some people add cinnamon to it, making it cinq épices.)

1 teaspoon black pepper

2 whole eggs, plus one egg yolk

2 tablespoons Cognac

½ cup heavy cream

Dijon/grainy mustard

Grilled country bread rubbed with garlic, for serving

Cornichons with garnish on the inside

INSTRUCTIONS:

You will need a food grinder to prepare this. The kind that goes with a KitchenAid works fine. It's best to freeze the grinder parts and to freeze the meat as well. There's less chance of the fats breaking down when everything is cold.

Preheat oven to 300°F. Freeze meat grinder parts. Cut pork shoulder and liver into cubes and place in ziplock bag in the freezer. Line pâté mold with cooking spray, then plastic wrap.

Mix liver with shallots, garlic, parsley, and thyme. Grind pork meat first, then add liver and herb mix as above.

Mix in salt, pepper, and spice mix. Mix eggs, heavy cream, and brandy together. Add meat mix to a stand mixer with paddle attachment. Add the egg mix and fold until sticky and fully mixed. Fold in extra garnish by hand.

In the terrine mold already lined with plastic, place slices of bacon over the plastic with at least 2 inches of the bacon hanging over the sides. Pack meat mix into terrine mold, pushing down well to avoid air pockets. Pack it so the meat is rounded on top rather than just a flat one. Fold the bacon ends over the meat mix.

Place into a deep roasting pan and fill the pan up with hot tap water until the waterline reaches halfway up the side of the terrine mold. Bake until interior reaches 160°F, about an hour and a half. Use a meat thermometer to test. When done, the top will look like cooked crispy bacon.

Place a weight* of about I pound on top. Cool. Then place in refrigerator until fully chilled. Remove from refrigerator for long enough so it's not cold but still firm and cool. Serve on a pretty country dish with a loaf of country bread. Or slice the bread and spread the pâté on it before serving. Garnish with cornichons.

*The weight could be a brick wrapped in foil, a box of salt, cans of soup.

TO DRINK:

Rosé with this country dish. A solid, quality rosé meant to pair with the meal. Château Simone's 2014 Côtes de Provence Rosé Palette, arguably the best of the best in Provence. It's from a teeny tiny little appellation near Bandol, and Château Simone owns almost all of it!

OYSTERS

How to Shuck an Oyster

Jerry, Balthazar's master oyster-shucker, puts the oyster on a flat surface, surrounds it with his left hand (he's right-handed), and sticks the tip of a small but deadly oyster knife into the tiny hole at the tip until he pries it open. He cuts the oyster muscle from the shell, and if there are bits of shell he removes them with the oyster knife and disposes of them.

Shane likes only lemon with oysters and sometimes a dash of Crystal hot sauce.

TO DRINK WITH THE OYSTERS:

Rebecca Banks has definite ideas. "My hands-down pairing choice for oysters will always be Muscadet from the Loire Valley. It's classic—briny, low alcohol, and lots of lemon-lime acidity.

"Alternatively, Picpoul de Pinet is a little unknown appellation in the Languedoc (South of France) and a classic pairing with local oysters. I think of it as the Muscadet from the south; it has a bit more body but is still crisp and refreshing.

"And finally, I'm a huge fan of a very light rosé with oysters. A briny, high-acid Sancerre rosé or Chinon rosé from the Loire Valley would be heaven!"

PART
THREE
BEFORE TWO

CHAPTER 10

THE GREAT PORT
OF BALTHAZAR

S hane was standing in his office, his jacket on, when I went down to see him. He was talking to Kelvin Arias, who shared the cramped space where they usually sat back-to-back on rickety office chairs, staring into their computers. "Come back down after one," Shane said to me. "We'll cook the gumbo. It's much quieter down here after that." He was just on his way out, heading over to Cherche Midi on the Bowery, another of the McNally restaurants.

Halfway out of the door, Shane reminded Kelvin, who was the chief steward, that he needed jalapeño peppers for the gumbo. He asked for Crystal hot sauce, and Kelvin said that was fine; it was just one of the million things that went into getting food on the table at Balthazar.

Whenever he was putting something new on the menu, like the gumbo, Shane asked Kelvin to get the ingredients; for the most part, Kelvin had internalized all the sources for just about everything in the way of food, and only had to make a phone call. He had been at Balthazar for almost twenty years.

"The first thing I do when I get in every morning is check with

Kelvin," Shane had told me. "He's the steward for Balthazar. He orders all the produce, protein, dry goods, pretty much everything except the wine."

Kelvin was usually in by five in the morning. Most of the deliveries arrived before two in the afternoon—this meant he could pick up his three kids from school in the Bronx, where his family lived—when the freight elevator stopped and made it difficult to get heavy crates down into Balthazar's basement.

With his swept-back gray and white hair and slightly suave face, Kelvin resembled a character from a Buñuel film. He picked up a sheaf of receipts from the morning's deliveries.

Every morning, Kelvin put things downstairs to rights. "We organize all the mess that is left over from the night and we clean it. The guys at night, they often put food in the wrong place; we put them in the right spot, and then we wait for the deliveries, meat, fish, produce, bakery. They start coming, sometimes by six, we put it all away as fast as we can, because we don't like it too long outside. After we do this, we go through the walk-ins again, icing all the oysters."

Like everyone at Balthazar, Kelvin had the health department on his mind. For as long as anyone could remember, the inspectors had come once a year, and they came more or less on a schedule. You knew if they were coming. You could get ready. Now they came more often and without any warning. This caused a low buzz of apprehension around Balthazar, though Kelvin kept his cool most of the time.

In the prep room, he looked over a delivery of fish before he put it in a walk-in. He took each fish from the box, felt its flesh to see that it was firm, sniffed it to make sure it was fresh. The fish was fine, Kelvin said, and smiled. If Balthazar was a great port, Kelvin was its head harbormaster.

I went and stood at the back entrance to Balthazar on Crosby Street, where I thought about Kayo Dugan. In *On the Waterfront*, Dugan,

played by Pat Henning, tells his pal Terry Malloy (Marlon Brando)—
they both work the docks—how he dreams of the sweet day when a
ship will bring a cargo of "crisp" Irish whiskey instead of the bananas
they're always unloading. Whiskey, fruit, all of it hauled up out of the
hold in cargo nets, onto the Brooklyn docks in Red Hook (though the
film was shot in Jersey).

Red Hook is less than five miles from Spring Street. I guessed
that most goods came in by road or air or in containers now, but the
image of the old ships, the men fighting for work, those huge nets
bearing food and booze, stayed in my mind.

Kayo would have felt lousy had he known that his beloved Irish
whiskey was not so popular these days, and that to attract a younger,
hipper drinker Bushmills had come up with a honey-flavored whiskey named Black Bush. ("How that name slipped through the focus
groups, I'll never know," said Rebecca Banks, Balthazar's director of
wine and spirits.)

All week crates of spirits came in at the Crosby Street entrance:
Grey Goose vodka from France, newly fashionable rye whiskey from
Brooklyn, Kentucky bourbon, Cognac, Grand Marnier, liqueurs in
green and blue. There was wine, of course—Sancerre, Chablis, Bordeaux, Burgundy, Champagne. Balthazar served only French wine.

Every month, twenty thousand pounds of beef came in on Pat
LaFrieda's white trucks, each of which had a drawing of a little black
cow grazing in bright green cartoon grass.

The beef, for the most part, had arrived at LaFrieda's in New
Jersey from Arkansas City, Kansas. One hundred ten pounds of
mussels had been sent from Prince Edward Island. Twenty cases of
sweet butter, and cheese, Tomme de Savoie, Sainte-Maure, Fourme
d'Ambert, as well as the fifty pounds of Gruyère and twenty of Par-
migiano Reggiano that were used every day.

From all over the country produce came into Hunts Point Market in the Bronx every day and then to Balthazar. Cartons of green

things—lamb's lettuce, peas, arugula, asparagus, celery. Boxes of big russets, the potatoes from GPOD in Idaho. Fruit, too: pears, plums, lemons, apples, strawberries, blackberries, blueberries. Edible yellow and purple pansies arrived for Mark's chocolate sea salt cakes, and the sea salt.

Supplies, too: paper towels; menus; china; cutlery; napkins, white with a blue stripe. Peanut oil for the French fries, mustard, ketchup, cocktail olives, and bright red maraschino cherries.

On Crosby Street, it was cold and damp; a tiny flutter of measly snowflakes was falling onto the pavement from a sky the color of oily oysters, and an icy fog had wrapped itself around the city, hiding the tops of the buildings. Easy to imagine Balthazar's back entrance as the gangplank to a port where supplies were sucked in every day, to imagine myself on a wharf. I imagined I could smell the sea.

A mile from Spring Street was Corlears Hook, where the Dutch, the first Europeans—unless you're rooting for the Vikings as first, or for Giovanni da Verrazzano, who got as far as the tip of Manhattan around 1524 but was blown off course—arrived in Manhattan in 1624. They came to stay.

They found an island ripe for plundering: dense with fowl and game, it was lush with plums; freshwater ponds stuffed with fish, mullet and bream, estuaries were encrusted with mussels, oysters, and scallops. You could pick up oysters the size of plates, or use them as stepping-stones to cross a stream.

The English went to New England to flee religious persecution (and immediately turned to persecuting others), but the Dutch came to New York to make money. We were never religious; money, land, and booze were our gods. If there was profit to be made, those early Dutch didn't care who you were; some of them made friends with the Native Americans and learned their languages.

Commerce and real estate were always the driving force in Manhattan. (The word "hooker" is said to have come from Corlears Hook because prostitutes went where the business was.) New Amsterdam, as it was known, was, in fact, merely the function of a corporation. The Dutch East Indies Company ran the show.

Still, except for the worried overseers at the top, those big grim Dutchmen in big hats with ruffs around their necks, New Yorkers were always convivial; and there were almost as many taverns on this island as settlers. We began as we've gone on: no religion, little ideology, a lot of hustling, and a certain tolerance that came with the Dutch; in its day, Amsterdam was the most tolerant, liberal city on earth. "Such an unruly population required servicing," writes Russell Shorto. His marvelous book *The Island at the Center of the World* is a brilliant evocation of those first settlers, and the city itself: "The island spawned taverns and breweries with remarkable speed . . . one quarter of its buildings."

By the 1660s, the English had taken over and imposed their autocratic will and their laws on Manhattan; much of the Dutch history was lost.

I knew something about the Dutch because all New York school kids learned about Peter Stuyvesant, and Stuyvesant's church, St. Mark's Church-in-the-Bowery, was a few blocks from where I grew up. But Shorto's book was a revelation. Among the first settlers were Dutch and English, Jews, Catholics, and Protestants, Walloons, Bohemians, married women, whores, Mohawks, Montauks, free blacks, African slaves, fur traders, and a large number of tavern keepers. "With its geography, its deep harbor and its rivers," Shorto writes, "Manhattan was exquisitely placed as a depot, a wharf for the whole country and the rest of the world. This never changed."

Dwight James was late that morning. Most days he arrived at Balthazar by nine, but today Dwight, the produce man, was late, though Kelvin was not especially worried. Balthazar's chief steward had a cool head, and he was a New Yorker. "Traffic," he said. "They'll get there." Without his even temperament, Kelvin would have gone nuts in this city where streets were permanently jammed with traffic and construction work.

Every morning Dwight left home in the Bronx before dawn to get to his produce people near Hunts Point Market. As soon as his truck was loaded, he made for downtown to Balthazar (and other restaurants), as he had been doing for years. Dwight was a familiar face in the Balthazar catacombs, drinking a cup of coffee after he unloaded his hand truck and shooting the breeze with Kelvin.

Kelvin had started out as a dishwasher, but that didn't last long because Vinnie saw something in him. Vinnie DeFrancesco, then the chief steward, was always on the hunt for smart new kids, for a little talent or ambition, something out of the ordinary.

"Vinnie saw that I could learn a little more," said Kelvin, who at seventeen came to New York from the Dominican Republic. "And he takes me as his assistant, and I do that alongside him for nine years."

Money was always on Kelvin's mind when he did the ordering. Storing the food was one thing, costing it was something else, and with soaring food prices, everybody at Balthazar was obsessed about budgets. Shane tried explaining how it worked, although the figures were, he said, rough and always changing. About 12 to 15 percent of Balthazar's budget went to food. He broke it down for me. "You have $70,000 to spend for the week most of the time. At Christmastime, it's $90,000 to $120,000. November to January is great. And then January to February is like, 'We're in the shitter,'" he said. "Spring is good, it's graduation time, then June and July are pretty dead, people are out of town, but we're always kind of busy here."

"Kind of busy" meant four hundred covers (at dinner) instead of seven hundred, and if brunch wasn't a thousand people, it was eight-fifty. There was always the perception of being busy,

Shane said, but if you lost two hundred people per meal, it hurt your wallet.

Everybody at Balthazar was always tormented by food prices, exchanging alarming news about how they had gone sky-high and were spiraling out of control.

At first I figured this was restaurant gibberish, a little bit of hogwash, to justify rising prices on the menu, or because the rent on Balthazar, which had tripled, had to be taken into account, and you could shift the money this way. I asked around. It was true: food prices were going up. If you were using local produce and the best meat, you could be undone by the weather. With produce, the weather killed you; the price on grain for the cattle killed you. If there was a bad winter, lobsters went up to eleven dollars a pound, whereas the summer of 2016, they were three bucks and every chef in town put lobster on the menu.

A salmonella outbreak among chickens around the country had sent the previous chief steward, Vinnie, into a state of despair. Food stats were a knotty business and all-important. It took a steady guy to untangle them. Vinnie kept his head about the chickens and found substitute producers, but it made him gloomy. Gave him the blues.

When I ate breakfast at Balthazar every morning, Vinnie DeFrancesco used to come upstairs and stop to pass the time of day for a few minutes. He was still Balthazar's chief steward then. I met him for coffee recently. He was now the director of purchasing for all seven of McNally's restaurants; he had moved from Balthazar's basement to the McNally offices over on Prince and Broadway.

At 4:45 every morning, Vinnie walked the few blocks from his apartment to the office. He did his paperwork. He talked to Kelvin. He looked at his computer. "I used to verbally give orders. I knew everyone. Now you do it on a computer. I can't stand it," he said. "I used to be able to talk to everybody, all the suppliers every day, and that's my strength." The business of purchasing has always been as much about relationships, about the dealing, the bargains; in local dialect, about the hondling. In this, Vinnie was a master.

Vinnie had a classic New York face, an Italian face; he was seventy-four and fit for his years. He had been an avid bike rider, and when Keith McNally was planning a trip through Provence, it was Vinnie who helped him buy and customize the perfect bicycle. If he didn't spend his days worrying about beef prices, he could have been a New York prosecutor played by De Niro. His was a true, deep face, etched with history, tough and generous.

"Well, the funny thing about Vinnie is whenever I talk to him I'm like, 'How's it going?' He'll say, 'Well, you know, I got a new bird,'" Erin said. "He has this house on Long Island, and he loves birds. They have birds. He has a lovely wife, too."

Vinnie DeFrancesco was born and grew up in Williamsburg, but this was not the Brooklyn of hipsters and fancy food; this was an immigrant neighborhood dominated by Italians back to the 1860s. By the 1950s and '60s, the neighborhood had seen overcrowding, poverty, crime, drugs; it was a tough place. When Vinnie's parents divorced, he was still a kid at a Catholic school. "I had problems at home and drifted to the streets, got involved with the wrong people, you know, did drugs," Vinnie said.

At sixteen, he was thrown out of high school. He spent years in and out of prison and on the streets, and then, Vinnie said, "I took a look around and I realized that this was going to be it for the rest of my life or I was going to die young. And I essentially came from a really good family. I had a lot of roots as a really young kid, what was instilled in me in my formative years. The Jesuits have a point, you know?"

He reached out to his father, who got him to the Fortune Society, which helped people coming out of prison. "I was sort of lost at the time," he said. "But I walk in, and I felt that I was with people that knew me and understood me and everything, you know? There were people that had been in prison. I just felt comfortable, and it was a place to hang out, talk to people, and blah, blah, blah," said Vinnie, who became a counselor there for sixteen years; he became the director of counseling, but he wanted something else.

Vinnie had married, and his wife knew somebody, and Vinnie was in at the opening of Mulholland Drive Café on the Upper East Side. He went in cold as the steward, had never worked in a restaurant before. By sheer force of will, brains, and personality, he made a success of it; he got to know the food purveyors all over town and eventually found his way downtown when Balthazar was in the works.

"So I went down there," Vinnie said, "and I briefly met Keith and Riad"—one of the original chefs. "The first time—oh, man, what a nasty place that leather factory was. We had just a general conversation about the industry, who I knew, who I dealt with, and that was it. I got hired."

Vinnie was still using 65 percent of the suppliers he used in the early days. "They're all tried-and-true and good suppliers, you know?" he said. First thing in the morning, he speaks to them. "I'll take emergency calls. I can troubleshoot things if I'm there that early. I start doing pricing. I'll have all my prices in, all my produce, you know, all my fish prices, and what the computer does is it highlights and picks out the lowest price—which you don't always order from, not necessarily just because it's the low price. It all depends on the quality and what you like better, but it gives you a good guideline on, you know, price control."

In the beginning at Balthazar, there was no budget, Vinnie said. "You just made it up as you went along. Everything has changed drastically now. There's a lot more at stake because the cost of food is so high. It's mind-blowing, and anybody opening a restaurant, you have to question why you're doing it. Your Balthazar customer knows quality of food. You have to keep it consistent," he said, noting there were a lot of people he had to keep sweet to make it all work. "You have to have a personality to work at Balthazar," he said.

I liked listening to Vinnie on the egg market or the impossibility of getting halibut for New Year's Eve, and his urgent call to Shane and the decision to replace it with turbot, or the terrifying rise in cod prices. You could imagine guys all over the country, buyers, suppliers, farmers, chefs, linked together by this need for food, for ingredients, for the right price.

Over at the office, I saw Vinnie watch the price fluctuations, heard him talking to mates around the city, assessing the news on pigs or butter or weather conditions in the Nebraska wheatlands as carefully as the guys on the floor of the commodities exchange or the stock market. Born into tough urban Brooklyn, he was, nonetheless, as bedeviled by prices as any farmer or Chicago mercantile hustler might once have been trading frozen pork bellies.

As a child, my mother thought pineapples grew in cans, but that was in Winnipeg, where she was born and raised, and where it was forty below in the winter. I didn't have much idea, either, about where food came from; as far as I knew it came from Bert's grocery on University Place, which was run by an avuncular guy named Bert, and from a fishmonger next door or the butcher shop around the corner on Eighth Street. The first supermarket I remember was Gristedes on University Place, though my aunt Shirley, my mother's sister, had a D'Agostino's near her in Stuyvesant Town; we were jealous of this because Dag's, as it was known, was said to be the best in the city.

For fancier stuff, there was Jefferson Market over on Sixth. You got fresh fruit and orange juice at the original Balducci's, which was then at the junction of Sixth and Greenwich; I liked to pop in and watch the oranges dance on top of the juicing machine. Cake came from Babka or Greenberg's, bagels and corn rye from Ben's on East Houston, smoked fish and the like from Russ & Daughters. I can't remember my mother ever buying pasta, or making it. For Italian, we ate out.

There were one or two school trips to the countryside—my school was, after all, called City and Country—where we milked a cow. Our summers were spent on Fire Island, where nothing at all except beach plums grew. Everything, every bunch of celery, each apple, a salami, was carried by ferry across the Great South Bay to Fire Island, though I suppose a bit of the fish was occasionally caught and eaten by locals. When the boats docked, local kids made some money by meeting the new arrivals and dragging their groceries home in Radio Flyer red wagons.

With Balthazar, I was spending so much time looking at food, listening to talk about food prices, thinking about it, I got the idea that I'd like to see where some of it came from before it arrived on Crosby Street.

Bread, beef, potatoes, wine, oysters; these were iconic brasserie staples, and they were consumed in enormous quantities at Balthazar. I wondered what happened to the wheat milled in Pennsylvania and the flour that came into the Balthazar Bakery in New Jersey. The beef processed in southern Kansas. The Widow's Hole oysters delivered weekly by Mike Osinski. The Château du Taillan that I often drank at the bar.

Farm to table was a way of life now, of course; the closer the farm, the cooler; there were people in Brooklyn who smoked their own pastrami and grew their own salad, and others who brewed bourbon there. But most food still came into New York from farms around the country, and I wanted an idea of the six degrees of separation between the Black Angus cattle in the Flint Hills of Kansas and the steak on my plate.

To get to the end of the line with any food massively consumed in this country was an enormous task. Originally I had the faintly crazy idea of harvesting wheat or going to Idaho to dig up a potato, marking it with my name, and trying to find it when it arrived in New York, this one particular potato, and was then turned into frites at Balthazar. I didn't quite manage it, though I did drop by the Irish Hunger Memorial on the west side of Manhattan, where they grow spuds on the roof.

It's an odd sort of museum, the sloping roof covered with dirt and planted with potatoes. Excepting those few Brooklynites smoking the meat and somebody in Long Island City who grew arugula—I think it was arugula—urban life has so completely taken us over that agriculture, the rural life, seems of another age, certainly another place. Odd, to only understand potatoes at a supermarket or a fancy farmer's market or a museum.

The museum does sit near the Hudson River. From it you can see the way the ships came in the nineteenth century, carrying millions of Irish to America and away from their own country, where the potato had fed them and then, with the famine, killed them.

LE BAR À HUÎTRES

PLATEAUX DE FRUITS DE MER

LE GRAND

OYSTERS
CLAMS
SCALLOPS
MUSSELS
SHRIMP
PERIWINKLES
CRAB

LE BALTHAZAR

OYSTERS
CLAMS
SCALLOPS
MUSSELS
SHRIMP
CRAY FISH
PERIWINKLES
CRAB CLAWS
LOBSTER

LES HUÎTRES

EAST COAST

BLUEPOINT
SALTAIRE
BELON
MALPEQUE
WELLFLEET

WEST COAST
KUMOMOTO
FANNYBAY
SKERLPOINT
COOTKASOUND
HAMASAKA

SHRIMP COCKTAIL

CHAPTER 11

UN-AMERICAN BREAD

Not long ago it was revealed by Sam Sifton in the *New York Times* that a great many people around the country were so crazy about good sourdough bread, about baking it themselves, that they cherished their starter as they would a child or a dog. Sifton, surely the wittiest of the *Times* food writers, noted that "a sourdough starter comes into your life the way a turtle might: as a pet." People give their starters names. A long way from the day when Julia Child said, "How can a nation be great if their bread tastes like Kleenex?"

Bread. Good bread. Bread with a crunchy, thick, dark crust still warm from the oven, smothered with wonderful butter. There have been times when, on my way home from Balthazar's Bakery on Spring Street next to the restaurant, I've gobbled up half the loaf I bought before I got to my door, a four-minute walk.

The signature Balthazar bread, this pain de seigle, a dark French sourdough rye, had a thick, crispy crust that was lightly caramelized, but not at all sweet. Inside, it was soft but not mushy, and deep. When I did get home, a friend who was staying with me looked at the naked loaf and asked, feigning innocence, if it was a ritual to denude the bread of its crust. "You kind of flay the bread, right?"

Flayed. Denuded. I went back to the bakery to get a loaf that was intact.

It was around lunchtime, and inside the bakery was packed. More people were outside on Spring Street, talking on their phones, impatient to get lunch.

Balthazar Bakery, a jewel box of a shop, was adjacent to the restaurant on Spring Street; it had a pretty painted ceiling, mirrors, a chandelier, had its pastries displayed on glass shelves behind the front counter: tiny lemon meringue and raspberry chocolate, the coconut cakes and glistening pear tarts, croissants and orange brioche; there are Madeleines in chocolate, pistachio, and lemon, Proust's little tea cakes.

Shelves on both walls held the bread: baguettes, white sourdough, square loaves of white bread, raisin pecan bread, multigrain bread, chocolate bread, and ciabatta. Then there is the pain de seigle, the French sourdough rye that has been served at the restaurant since its doors opened.

With five customers inside, it was like the Tokyo subway at rush hour—at lunchtime the bakery sells sandwiches, soup, and salad. Behind the counters, the young staff took it in stride. Even as a woman in a fur coat, discovering there was no pain au chocolat left, stomped out as if she had been denied some essential right, Maryanne, the young manager, smiled and wished her a good day. Other customers waited patiently eyeing the pastries—and oh, those pastries.

I bought an extra loaf of bread that day, and it was this bread, this boule of French rye, that Jean-Georges Vongerichten and other famous chefs had clamored for when Balthazar opened. When Keith McNally lived in Paris, it was on the rue du Cherche-Midi. On the other side of the street was Poilâne, the bakery that made dark country loaves fashionable.

For a long time, dark bread had been for peasants, but Poilâne brought them back into fashion, and the heavy, zaftig French boules became desirable in a world that had wanted thin white baguettes with a delicate, brittle crust. In Paris not long ago I paid Poilâne a visit, and Balthazar Bakery is clearly its first cousin, not just the bread but also the shop itself.

Even as late as 1997, it was not easy to find good bread in New York. Here and there a restaurant served a decent Italian or French bread, and it was OK, but there was nothing like the loaves you got in France—that you went to France *for*.

You wanted ethnic bread, that was another case. There was plenty of it—this was New York—and on Atlantic Avenue you got pita; on Bleecker Street, Italian semolina loaves; and there was Indian naan to be had in Jackson Heights. Polish rye from Greenpoint wasn't bad. Jews had it pretty good, too, the ones who knew their way to, say, Ben's on East Houston Street for bagels—the old, hard, boiled kind that nearly broke your teeth—and corn rye, a loaf that was both dense and light. It wasn't actually made with corn, but its outside, coated with cornmeal, crunchy and a little crisp, this I liked ripping off.

These were exceptions in the United States, though. Most bread came in a package. So alien were these "foreign" breads that even a packaged rye—commercial stuff—was seen as exotic. "You don't have to be Jewish to love Levy's" was a legendary 1960s ad, indicating that even ordinary Americans could enjoy this foreign stuff.

So it wasn't surprising that when Balthazar's great bread appeared on the table, people went nuts. It was served at the beginning of meals, and some people consumed baskets of it. There was good butter, too, at a time when bowls of olive oil had begun appearing at restaurants, and no olive oil was ever as good as sweet, fresh pale yellow butter, not with bread, anyway. So many people ate so much bread they were no longer hungry and, to the chagrin of the Balthazar staff, ordered less for dinner. As a result now, until a customer orders, the bread is served only on request.

• • •

Just before Balthazar opened, Paula Oland was hired as the chief baker; it was a casual affair for her, something to keep you going, extra money to get by. "It was just a little consulting gig, or that's what I thought it would be," she told me.

As a partner, Paula had Simon Cass. Keith McNally knew that Sim could bake; they had worked together for years, and Sim had been the DJ at Nell's, the club Keith ran for a while. Sim was profoundly loyal to Keith, and when he called, Sim left California and came back to New York.

"We worked together and collaborated on developing the initial breads at Balthazar," Paula said. "We had never known each other before. And that was a nice collaboration. We saw eye to eye. And Keith was OK with everything, you know—except he didn't like our croissants, really. I didn't tell him that I hadn't ever made croissants before."

So Mark Tasker was recruited. "I could do croissants," said Mark. "The baking took place in a cupboard in the basement under the restaurant. It was very hot and so small, and it was hard to stand up straight." As a result, Mark took himself and the dough into the refrigerated walk-in, where he formed the croissants next to the oysters. "The baking was pandemonium," Mark said. "It was crazy busy, it was brilliant. We had such a great time, it was really hard work, and we all enjoyed what we were doing, and we all really wanted this place to succeed." I always got the feeling Mark wanted everybody to succeed.

Before long, the bakers in the Balthazar basement ran out of space. "I think the bakery is now the garbage room," Paula said. "The oven was a pretty good oven, but it didn't have enough ventilation, and we had a fire. It all broke down." Last year, sometime around 2016, I heard that the bakers were negotiating for a brand-new oven that cost a million bucks.

In December of 2000, the bread baking moved to Englewood, New Jersey, just across the George Washington Bridge. Paula, Sim, and Mark went with it, but Sim left soon after, and Mark returned to Spring Street; sending fragile fancy cakes across the George Washington Bridge and down New York's potholed streets had been a disaster. The cakes wobbled. They broke. He set up in the basement of the restaurant again.

Soon there were four locations for baking bread and cakes and making ice cream and desserts: Mark Tasker's under the restaurant, which turned out cake and cookies for the Spring Street bakery and also for catering; the room next door to Mark's, where Andy Gomez made desserts for the restaurant; the Spring Street Bakery itself. Then there was the commercial New Jersey bakery, which was also known as the Balthazar Bakery, and which eventually spawned its own retail shop. (Same name, too!)

Around sixteen miles from Englewood to Spring Street, it took the Balthazar trucks, the pretty yellow trucks with the familiar logo, about half an hour without traffic to deliver bread; with traffic, it was always a crapshoot.

"We've gotten so big now we get the flour in trucks that look like they've got udders and they hook us up and pump it into the building, about fifty-five thousand pounds every ten days or so," Paula Oland said when I went to see her in New Jersey. She said it with a certain regret, the fact that she was making so much bread, there was little time for her to experiment with new flavors or for ordering flour in boutique quantities. "For a bit, we were getting some from Anson Mills in South Carolina, but it was coming in little boxes by UPS; I'd love to experiment with sprouting rye, which is a northern type of grain."

It was impossible to say exactly where the wheat she used came from originally, she told me. "So now I depend on Martins Creek in

Pennsylvania to get us something that tastes good, and we get two different white wheat flours of different strains. Probably it comes from somewhere in the Middle West or the Great Plains," she added.

I had seen wheat growing in Nebraska, where, under a hot blue sky, it—and nothing else at all—grew to the horizon. From the road you could sometimes see a red barn, a grain silo. Then they would disappear and there was nothing but the wheat again and the sky. It went on forever; it had a hallucinogenic quality and made me think in a random way about those amber waves of grain, about Big Agriculture and genetically modified organisms, about why so many young women attribute evil to gluten. I thought variously about the time I had done a little inept threshing during a wheat harvest in the Rift Valley in Ethiopia; and how for Stalin wheat was a weapon he used to starve the Ukraine. Fifty-eight million tons of it are produced every year in America.

Paula Oland was the kind of baker who would have loved to get to grips with the wheat itself, how it was milled for her flour, its exact composition, its provenance and poetry. In her office at the New Jersey bakery, I felt that in some profound way she was as concerned with the elements she used for her bread as a painter with her palette of paints, not just the colors but how they were made, where the pigment came from, how it was ground.

An artist, Paula left Canada, where she was born and grew up, and headed to Los Angeles. To support herself at art school, she turned to cooking and baking. "Cooking was a way to make money and turned out to perhaps be my first passion," she said. Making her way to New York, Paula started a small firm called Ecce Panis. It was the best bread anyone had tasted.

Small, trim, pretty, with a modest, almost diffident manner, Paula seemed to have a phenomenal competence, a can-do attitude as well as an instinctive passion for her art. It somehow went beyond the ingredients or a recipe. This was a woman who was born to bake bread, something as mysterious as an eye for true color.

"It's fun to bake, you know?" said Paula. "It's fun to catch the little bread on the cusp, catch the wave, sort of, and cut it and have it come out beautiful, that and the mixing."

Outside, the word BALTHAZAR was written across the hundred-year-old redbrick building. Inside, the first impression was of almost startling light and whiteness. With 14,000 square feet of space, the industrial ceilings had enormous skylights that opened to let in sun and air. The workers were dressed in white with white hairnets or caps, and everything seemed to have a fine coat of flour that also floated on the air and was visible in the slanted beams of sunlight.

At a long stainless table, two rows of workers in white were shaping the dough. Here the men and women chatted, and sometimes laughter broke out among them. A young woman, making apple galettes, was smiling—something about the fruit tarts pleased her, or maybe she was thinking about a song she liked or her boyfriend. In another section, men in white were placing the shapes on huge wooden paddles. These were tough guys with big arms, men who worked too hard; their faces were lined with the effort. With dough on them, the setters were heavy as hell.

Loading them into the ovens was backbreaking work. It took two guys, one in front and one in the back, to lift the setters that held the unbaked dough on them. They slid one load of dough into the oven, and then, bracing themselves, pulled it back out. Over and over they did it and you could see that some of them, even the younger guys, were bent from the work. But the pay was decent and there was a community at the bakery where many of the workers had been for years.

Like the kitchens at Balthazar, cousins and uncles and brothers brought in family members from time to time. Most were Latino. The women forming the bread sometimes talked softly among themselves and the Spanish chat drifted on the floury air.

"Yes, many employees are Hispanic—and there is a broad range of origins throughout Central and South America, all the way to Chile and Argentina," said Paula with real fondness for the employees. She was also interested in the cultural differences. "Also a smattering from all over the world. I love that part, although it can be challenging to blend cultural differences. It's a mixed bag." She thought for a moment. "Most employees arrive here liking fairly bland bread, but the longer they're here, the more they switch to other varieties. They sweep the racks clean of pastry at the end of the day."

It was hot. The ovens made the area almost unbearable in the summer, though makeshift tubes blew cool air down into the baking area. It got easier later, around one in the morning, when the bake of the day finished.

"There's a break and then we start again," said Paula. "We do some larger breads that need to be sliced overnight, and then we start—the mix starts around three-thirty in the morning. We work around the clock." Balthazar's bread was always delivered fresh. "We mean for everything to be baked at night and eaten the next morning. Breakfast pastries are not intended to sit on the shelf. Deliveries to Balthazar, to the bakery and the restaurant, go overnight to arrive early in the morning around five a.m., and there's another delivery of bread later in the afternoon for the restaurant service."

Outside in the parking bay was a fleet of yellow trucks and vans with the Balthazar logo. When the bakery moved to Jersey, it had about thirty accounts. Now there were five hundred accounts, 190 employees, profits of around $17 million, and a retail shop attached to the bakery. Every week, the restaurant alone ordered 111 of the large dark boules, 330 of the white levain, 248 plain croissants, 168 sticky buns, 147 orange topknot brioche. And more. Along with the bread, the morning pastries—brioches, sticky buns, some of the rustic tarts like those apple galettes—were now made in New Jersey. Mark no longer had to make croissants in the fridge.

On high metal racks near the ovens, bread had been set to cool: the big ryes, white loaves, onion breads, knobby dense cranberry pecan bread, were on those racks. The aroma was heady.

I had always figured that the big *B* etched into the signature dark Balthazar loaves was a riff on Poilâne's *P*, which that Paris bakery was famous for. Not so, said Paula. "It's funny, it happened when we started, and an Ecuadorian baker we had just did it one night. And then one morning I came in, and there were these *B*'s with all these—it looked like Our Lady of Guadalupe, all these rays coming out from her, and they were really beautiful. I was like, 'Oh, that's great.' So we just did these *B*'s, and he had surely never seen Poilâne." Paula let slip a smile. "And then Poilâne switched to this beautiful *P*, which they might have copied but, to be honest, was better than ours."

Bread, real bread, Paula explained, was generally made only with flour, water, and fire. First the flour was weighed, and the bread was shaped and mixed by a team of women. The starter—there was no yeast in these breads—took time, too. "The bread just has got a lot of moisture to it, which is not the same as a leavened gumminess. Let's try some," she said, and we went over to the side of the bakery, where she placed a couple of just baked loaves on a ledge.

"Would you like it with some butter?" she said.

Having already stuffed a piece of it into my mouth, I said, "Is the bread better with butter?"

"Everything is better with butter. I hope you don't mind salt in your butter," said Paula. I didn't mind. She gave me a huge chunk of it, still warm, smeared with salty butter. "This is a nice piece," Paula said. Nice. It was, without any doubt at all, the best thing I had ever eaten.

"What about some apricot jam? Jam is good, right?" she asked.

The jam was good. I stuck my spoon back in the jar. There were chunks of apricot in it, and it was sweet but with a tart spring in its step.

After some more eating, Paula said, "You see, these breads are naturally leavened and without yeast; it means it's not too sour. We don't like the bread to be too sour. We don't want it to change the character of the food it's served with. It's always supposed to be a supporting player."

It was mesmerizing, thrilling. Wheat, flour, the bread, these seemed like living things when Paula talked. She made me want to bake, to get my hands in the enormous mounds of dough, to cut it, to shape it, most of all to tear into that warm crust and eat it. She was devoted to her work, almost pious about the bread, but she was also funny. Her descriptions of bread run to "gummy," "sticky," and "chewy."

"Is gummy different from chewy?" I asked. I loved her use of words that really spoke to the sensation of eating bread.

"Yeah, gummy's kind of a wet thing. I like wet, but this is just a bit too sticky," she said, inspecting a fresh piece of bread. "Gummy is kind of sticky, but I like a bit of stickiness."

Munching, Paula explained that anything in the interior is called crumb; the rest is crust. With the dark bread, she said, "The crumb gets a pleasing kind of gumminess to it. The bran are little sharp bits of the outside of the wheat that will kind of clip away at the gluten strands, which are these nice sort of gelatinous protein formations.

"Look, breads are just an evolution from one thing to another, and I like really large breads. I like the way the crumb is and the crust—you get a substantial crust, and yet you still get a rather wet crumb because there's just so much mass to them," she said, and reached for a freshly baked baguette.

"Baguettes are baked twice a day, and we have kind of a rivalry between the day crew and the night crew sometimes, and then we'll show off the daytime baguettes to the night crew to see if they can get a similar result," she said. Paula's bread had no preservatives; she didn't believe in them. Besides, nothing was shipped farther than a few hours away.

We went on eating, and B Young—everybody just calls him B— joined us. Paula's colleague and husband, he fell in love with her bread before he met her. "When I interviewed for the job, I was relocating, and I just kind of assumed that there was a crusty European guy who had invented the rye bread, which I had tasted in the restaurant. I thought, *This is the bread I want to make every day,*" he said.

Real bread making is more art than science, and clearly Paula was an artist with perfect pitch for crust and crumb, for a certain elusive alchemy. "Isn't that called magic?" I said.

Paula laughed. "Don't look behind the curtain," she added with the slightly rueful air that told me she somehow always wished she could do more, or better. Her self-deprecation, her modesty, was the real thing, the quiet virtue of authentic talent. Like Mark Tasker and Shane McBride, Paula was self-confident but without any need for squawk or swagger.

"So, I'm a fairly intuitive baker, I guess, for better or for worse," Paula said. Again, my mouth full now of a delicious moist ciabatta (don't cut it, tear it), I said I thought this was true art. Perhaps a little uncomfortable with the compliment, Paula said, "At this stage, I'd suppose a better understanding of technology and science might serve me well, might make production easier." She sliced into a loaf of the pain au levain, the white bread that was also served daily at Balthazar.

"There's less bran in the white bread," Paula said. "There's some ash content, but you're just lacking the bran, and because of that, you can get a more open, less gummy interior if you choose. You're just tasting the inside of the wheat; you're not getting that texture from the bran, which has just been sifted out basically."

Did Paula create new breads, did she invent them, dream them up? I asked, but she demurred; she shrugged. For ten minutes B Young had been listening to us talking, watching Paula fondly, and then, clearly unable to keep his mouth shut, he said, "Can I just answer directly a question that Paula evaded? Every really good idea in the bread department has come from her. The bread is popular and successful. It comes from a real place from a real person," he said. B looked at her. Paula blushed. He said, "Someone should speak the truth about this. It's a really collaborative process, but Paula is a really insightful baker, and these ideas are all her ideas."

Paula, deflecting the compliment, just said to me, "What breads would you like to take home with you?"

CHAPTER 12

EVERYTHING BUT THE MOO

Postcards from Kansas

O n the plane out to Wichita, I got to chatting with a guy while we were both in the aisle waiting for the restroom. He asked why I was headed to Kansas. I told him I was going to look at some cows. "Oh, I raise some," he said. Turned out he was from Vermont and cattle were his hobby, but he was actually going to Wichita to look at aircraft stuff, which was the other big business in the state. He said, "So do you raise dairy or beef cattle?" I tried not to laugh out loud because it was a perfectly reasonable question, and he seemed a nice guy. How could he know he was talking to somebody who barely knew the difference between a cow and a heifer? I didn't know much about Kansas, either, except for *The Wizard of Oz*.

Wichita. "Wichita Lineman." Kansas. The Atchison, Topeka and Santa Fe. This is mythic stuff, there's even a Western called *Wichita* with Joel McCrea and Lloyd Bridges. Wyatt Earp met Doc Holliday in Dodge City not far to the west. Everything about the West, about the myths, always seemed to have started in Kansas, Missouri, and Nebraska.

Oil made Wichita a boomtown in the early twentieth century, and on its heels came an aircraft industry. Clyde Cessna made private aircraft the means of transportation for the western man once he got off his horse. Early on, it was also a progressive state. Formed as an anti-slavery state in opposition to Missouri, Kansas was one of the first with women's suffrage, first to institute workers' compensation. Not so much anymore. Wichita is home to, among others, the Koch brothers.

But I had come for the cows. Pat LaFrieda, the butcher who provided Balthazar—and all of McNally's restaurants—with its meat, introduced me to Creekstone Farms, where their beef was processed. And Creekstone invited me for a look at their facilities in Arkansas City, Kansas. To get to this town on the border with Oklahoma, you flew into Wichita and drove south awhile.

I had been planning this trip for months. There was this, and it hung over me: I was going to Kansas to see a cow killed. For all the talk about cuts of beef and good grazing, and the incredible niceness of everyone I talked to on the phone at Creekstone, no matter how many people said this was not the meat industry as Upton Sinclair had described it in *The Jungle*, this was, nonetheless, about death. That was the deal, and I was nervous.

Friends looked at me as if I'd lost my marbles for spending vacation time doing this. I usually said I was doing it because, as a journalist, it seemed right; if I ate steak, if I was now writing about Balthazar's great steak frites, I should witness the whole process. I sounded very pompous.

With me on the plane was Artie, my fellow. I wasn't crazy about going alone, and he had agreed to come so long as he didn't have to witness the actual slaughter. "I've heard if they miss with the stun gun the first time, the eyes bleed," he said. He claimed he knew quite a bit about rural things and animals.

• • •

The next morning we were on our way to the Flint Hills, Kansas's great virgin grazing lands.

In the front of the van were Nate Stambaugh and Brandon Ford, who was driving, an elbow out the window, the other hand easily on the wheel. He drove this country for thousands of miles every week. The cattle procurement man, Brandon was Creekstone's contact with the ranchers. Nate, the director of food services for Creekstone, dealt with restaurants and retail shops. He was a culinary enthusiast, and the tattoos on his arms left you in no doubt about this. Among them were a fried egg, chicken and waffles, crabs, oysters, a whole pig, cornstalks, and a burger with bacon, tomato, and lettuce.

With us in the back of the van was Erin O'Shea. One of very few female pit masters, Erin was the owner of Percy Street Barbecue in Philadelphia; brisket being her signature dish, she was a good customer of Creekstone, and they had invited her for a visit.

Good chefs, bad restaurants, great food, hard work, favorite meals, Nate and Erin were busy trading stories about the food business: how Erin and some friends spent a month's wages when they were younger on a meal at Per Se; how much they'd like to meet Francis Mallmann, the great Argentine chef; about "Lambstock," where Nate had just been and where he had tasted every variety, baby lamb to raunchy mutton; about brisket, beer, and bourbon; about successes and failures.

What ran through it was a pleasure in food and in feeding people. Listening to Nate and Erin O'Shea in the car, to Shane McBride at Balthazar, and to Dave Chang, and then to more people I met on the road, it seemed to me that these chefs and restaurant owners and suppliers each cared enormously about what they did.

They knew their business from the ground up. Food—the sourcing, cooking, serving, selling, the thinking about it and talking about it, and especially the gathering together to eat it—made them happy. They had no pretensions as far as I could tell, even if they did yak for hours about the quality of some cut of smoked pork they had made in a backyard someplace. Best of all, they were the antithesis of the stuck-up, smug foodies of a couple of decades ago, the chefs and proprietors of restaurants where the stars (both senses) were all that mattered and the food required an explication de texte before you understood what was on the menu.

After my one meal at the French Laundry in Napa, after the young acolytes who served had deposited with hushed reverences seventeen tiny courses and I had eaten them, I'd had it. I had not been allowed sparkling water or salt with my dinner. After I left, I wished only that I had asked for ketchup.

Kansas was flat and hot. We drove for hours until we got to the Flint Hills, where everything was green.

Alan Geiger, the owner of the ranch where we stopped first, was lean and self-contained, a Gary Cooper of farming who seemed to belong to the landscape. He was waiting for us in his yard where we all shook hands. Large shining machines, the kind required to service a cattle-ranching business, were in the yard: harvesting machines, too, sprouting blades and grinders, mean as machines in *Mad Max*. Gazing out beyond the yard to a grassy field where a herd of his cattle grazed, he said, "We just like easygoing cattle."

A Victorian-style farmhouse was a dozen yards away. From it emerged a little kid—Geiger's grandson—in a big cowboy hat with a couple of toy six-shooters. Alan Geiger hugged him and kept talking.

Operations like his own, Geiger said, did pretty much everything from calf to cow, which was how he put it. They planted their own feed; they bred their own cattle and fed their herds with the food they grew.

"These guys like Mr. Geiger here, he will grow his cattle on his own grass," said Nate Stambaugh. "After that he'll put them in pens on his land and feed them—they call this finishing them—with the alfalfa and corn they also grow." The sense of a one-stop breeding and feeding operation seemed to Nate the best of all worlds, as far as I could make out. It meant the cows were kept in their own native environment, at least until they were sent for slaughter.

We left the Geiger place, but we were still in the Flint Hills, one of the last unbroken grasslands in the country. On the plane out I had been reading *The Worst Hard Time*, Timothy Egan's book about the Dust Bowl. Worst hit was the part of the Great Plains where southwestern Kansas meets the Oklahoma Panhandle.

Earlier, what had been Native American grazing land had first been overrun by ranchers. The ranchers grazed their herds and then the price of beef fell, and they sold the land off to farmers. And the farmers, spurred on by high wheat prices, tore up all the grasslands, which were natural to the area, in a frenzy. For twenty years, from the beginning of the twentieth century, they planted wheat.

With the 1930s came the Depression, as well as a drought that lasted six years. There was nothing for the crops to hang on to, and the whole of the land turned to dust and blew away. It came back in apocalyptic storms, in black clouds that contained the dust. It killed the land and everything around it. There were very few original grasslands left in the country, and of what remained, some of it was here in northwestern Kansas.

The Flint Hills, a lovely, green sixty-mile strip of unbroken grasslands, never tilled or turned over, was one of the oldest natural grazing areas in the world. According to Nate, "It has just always been great grassland, native grass that they utilize every year to grow cattle on."

Nate ran through the specs on cattle here, how they were raised and fed and what you called them. The singular of cattle is cow, but cattle and cows are almost always used interchangeably. A heifer is a female that has not had any calves; once she has, she becomes a cow. A steer is a bull that has been castrated.

Given that cows and bulls had certain hormones that changed with age, Creekstone processed only steers and heifers. Then Nate passed me an Altoids tin. I opened it, ready to dig in for a mint.

"It's not to eat," said Nate. "It wouldn't hurt you, though. It's silage, the good stuff, a mix of corn and hay and wheat the cows are fed on, silage raised on the same farm where they are fed." I shut the tin.

We drove to another farm. Nate had stopped talking. Erin O'Shea was quiet. We turned off the main road out of the pretty countryside and found ourselves looking at a desolate vista. On an abandoned airfield, bulldozers were pushing silage into little mountains beside a gravel road.

On either side of the long dusty road were large pens holding the cattle, and there were a lot of them, hundreds of heads of cattle in scores of pens, as far as the horizon. A sea of cattle. Nate looked at his watch.

Most of the animals were standing at the edge of their pens, feeding from concrete troughs where their carefully controlled diet was delivered regularly. This was where they bulked up. Black Angus, their sleek hides shining in the sun, gained three hundred pounds in three months.

"They'll put twice the amount of cattle on grass for a shorter period of time," Nate said. "Then, for three months, take them off the grass on sileage, and in three months make a five-hundred-fifty-pound steer weigh eight hundred fifty pounds. Most of our cattle are eighteen to twenty-four months, although a few bump up at thirty." (Apparently the aging was sometimes inaccurate and the only sure way to tell was by the animal's teeth.)

Three hundred pounds in three months sounded a lot like force-feeding to me, but Nate explained that this was how you get the marbling that everybody craved in their beef. Without it, "You're not going to get the prime side of the beef that everybody's looking for. Marbling is everything. Marbling is what makes a piece of beef 'prime,' and of all the beef sold in America, only about 4 percent or less is prime. Marbling is the deep white veins of fat you see in your steak before you grill it; marbling is what gives American steak its outrageously delicious flavor."

Marbling, then—those three hundred extra pounds—produced the beef that Americans craved, the great piece of delicious beef, grilled to a char, red or blue inside, dripping with juices, the smell wafting up into the summer air, the charred smoky beefy smell, the deep taste, the crispy bits of fat. When I left for Kansas, I had no moral issue with eating beef. I had always loved steak, but the feeding up of the cattle out here made me fretful. Was it finally just a question of go vegetarian or shut up?

I asked Nate about quality. About allegations that the pink glop I'd seen on television went into fast-food burgers. What about the environment and hormones? Did "natural" meat imply there were no antibiotics, no hormones? Finally, what about this business of stuffing the cattle on a regime, day after day, until they were fat enough to satisfy our desire for marbled meat?

Nate told me that the USDA definition of "natural" meant minimally processed, meant that the meat did not have anything unnatural added to it after the animal was dead. The industry, he said, had got really tricky in wording and labeling. NEVER EVER was the label to go for. It meant there was an affidavit somewhere from the farmer that there had been an auditing process to make sure that the animals had never received an antibiotic. If they had, they were kicked out of the system. What then? "They go to a different program," said Nate. Everyone had what was called a G schedule, and there was a USDA website where it was possible to look up any beef packer. This would tell you the specifics about their cattle.

Before the trip to Kansas, I had tried reading up a little, but I found that the big business of beef, and indeed all meat, was a complex tangle of agencies and laws. With the US Department of Agriculture's complex system of grading beef, I was lost. Other agencies were just as impenetrable. Add to it the breeding of cattle, the feeding methods used by ranchers and processors, the work done by packers and butchers, and I fell into an almost impossibly arcane and often intentionally deceitful world. This depressed me, but it also made me feel curiously detached—so many rules, so much paper, so many mandates—from the hard reality.

We stood in the road and watched the immense animals, heads down, just eating and eating, on schedule, fattening up. I was trying not to be sentimental about the cattle. I probably would have been all right, but just as we were about to get back in the van, the cattle stopped eating. Those out in the pens stopped moseying around. All of them, hundreds of animals, turned their heads in one direction. It was as startling as if a bomb had gone off.

The cattle had seen something or they had smelled it, and it had scared the shit out of them; and they turned all at once as a herd and bolted. They made a beeline in one direction, away from whatever had scared them. A terrible collective whimpering rose up.

"That was the rendering truck," somebody said.

A rendering truck meant death for the cattle. Sick or injured cows were picked up by the truck and killed, and the meat was rendered for tallow or other kinds of fat; sometimes it went into dog food.

The cattle had smelled it. The fear had caused them to stand dead still at first, and then run like hell.

A trio of cowboys was beginning the roundup. "Come on, ladies, we've done this before," one said. "Come on." The cattle were back in their pens, the rendering truck gone. Two of the cowboys wore big hats, the other one a baseball cap and sneakers. There was no posturing; this was not a role in a movie. Nobody was playing at cowboy. It was just a job. The three men sat easily in their saddles and made affectionate noises at the cattle. They coaxed them into a tidy herd and onto the long dusty road and out the gates of the ranch. Waiting trucks would take them overnight to the Creekstone Farms processing plant in Arkansas City.

In the van on our way back to Arkansas City, we joked around about my cow—Daisy Mae, I called her, the pretty cow with tag number 805 on her ear—the one I had imagined I'd see through all the way from the rich grazing lands of the Flint Hills to Creekstone's plant, to Pat LaFrieda's in New Jersey to be butchered to Balthazar's specific needs—petite tenders, ground beef, steak au poivre—and then to Balthazar itself. One cow made sixty-seven boxes of meat, Nate said.

We were joking because we were nervous—at least I was, and so was Artie. Erin O'Shea didn't want to think about it.

Creekstone Farms, widely considered one of the very best beef processing plants in the country, was designed by Temple Grandin. Grandin, the renowned professor of animal science who has been autistic all her life, is a legend in the livestock business; she has long been one of the great innovators in the treatment of cattle in modern times. Grandin's autism enabled her to "see" as cattle see; as a result of this, and years of study, she designed facilities that were kinder to cattle. At Creekstone, everyone was very proud of what Grandin had done and often talked about her visits to the plant. "She was here only the other week," said Brandon. "What she's done is make a better way for cattle to be treated, so they feel less fear."

So there it was: "They feel less fear." All the time I was in Kansas I was wondering what it meant to talk about how a cow felt. If the Grandin system led to less fear, if cattle actually felt less fear, what else did they feel? Did they feel pain when they were stunned just before their throats were slit?

The next morning at six a.m., Nate Stambaugh picked us up at the Best Western, which was pretty much all there was in Arkansas City apart from Creekstone.

"We want to be known in the industry as the guy that's small enough to do it right, but big enough to provide availability to restaurants like Balthazar that are doing higher volume," Nate said on our way to the plant.

Creekstone was a boutique operation; it processed about five thousand cattle a week, while the big players handled more than twenty thousand.

Just off the road was a cluster of featureless buildings that in the dawn light resembled a secret military base or a nuclear storage facility. Nate was straightforward about it. "It's a slaughterhouse," he said.

The lobby had the immaculate feel of a corporate retreat. A man in a blue hard hat—Don Morrow, fourth-generation meatpacker and committed Christian—greeted us. He helped us understand the safety rules and made sure we were kitted out with white coats, blue Wellington boots, hard hats, and hairnets. During this process, Don said, "these cows have a lot of great days and one bad second."

We were shown the processing plant from a second-floor window first. Below us scores of workers in white overalls were working on the carcasses of cattle that hung by chains from a huge track in the ceiling, as in a vast dry cleaning shop. The thing I found hardest to watch was the moment when the entire glossy black hide was whisked off the cow all at once to reveal livid white flesh. Peeled. Skinned. Flayed.

In the center of the room on a raised platform were the rock stars of the operation, wiry, tough men with huge saws in hand. "They're an elite on the processing floor," Don said as one man split a carcass with exquisite precision. "These guys are the best, the highest-paid. It takes ten years to learn. If they're an inch off, they cut through the tenderloin, rib eye, and strip, it could waste hundreds of dollars. These men are really fit. They have arms like my legs."

Downstairs on the floor, we were taken through the whole process backward, beginning with the cardboard boxes ready for shipping. I wondered if this was intended to acclimatize us to the place before we saw the killing.

Workers in the most dangerous areas, where razor-sharp knives were constantly in use, wore chain mail aprons, gloves, and shirts that gave them the look of medieval warriors.

Steam baths, a thorough chilling, a check on lymph nodes, livers, and kidneys, all this was done to avoid the risk of infection, Don told us. We passed close to a bunch of severed heads. On the floor was a large canvas container of tongues, the big tongues that had perhaps belonged to cows we had seen grazing yesterday. Artie looked queasy.

At Creekstone, a point of pride was that every bit of an animal was used, and conservationists agreed this was a sane approach to food. "Yup," somebody said quietly. "We use everything except the moo."

At the back of the Creekstone plant was the pen for the cattle designed by Temple Grandin to minimize their distress. A continuous winding passageway led the cows gently in single file to the point of slaughter. In this way, we were told, not for the first time, they felt less fear, less stress.

I looked around for Daisy Mae, but it was impossible to find her in the crowd of docile black cattle, quietly waiting to mount what at Creekstone they call the "Stairway to Heaven."

The cattle walked up a sort of escalator from the pen to a platform where a man with a stun gun was waiting. The cattle were docile and followed, one after another, mounting the escalator. As each animal reached the platform, the man placed his stun gun precisely on its forehead and triggered the bolt. Instantly, the animal dropped to the floor, tumbled down a chute, and was immediately hoisted by one of its back legs to that overhead track. It was brain-dead now; in some cases, the cow's legs kept twitching. We were not shown the place where, in the sequence of all this, the animal's throat was slit.

Erin O'Shea, the pit master from Philadelphia who was famous for her tender, juicy beef brisket, turned her face to the wall.

In the brutally cold room where his prime beef was aging, Pat LaFrieda fiddled with the temperature controls, the air circulation, and the dehumidifiers. "The meat is decomposing," he said when I visited him at his plant in New Jersey after I came back from Kansas. "But it's controlled, not rotting."

We walked the aisles of fine slabs of beef, sides of beef set out like fine fur coats hanging in storage. Pat added, "There are sixty-five hundred pieces in here. That's a million and a half dollars." Pat, a tall, handsome man who looked as if he had been raised on good beef himself, appraised his inventory lovingly. "It's a growing trend. We age it up to a hundred twenty days, but that's as far as we go."

The beef comes into LaFrieda's place from Creekstone Farms neatly packed in boxes. Before the Meatpacking District was gentrified, it was where meat arrived, was butchered and packed. Trucks rolled in from the Midwest and were backed up to the warehouse loading platforms—warehouses that were now condos and designer shops and restaurants—then slid onto immense, vicious metal hooks. Men in bloodstained white coats worked all night and into the morning, and the mornings, when it was hot, used to smell of blood.

"It's better than the old days, when from the kill to the delivery was ten days. We can do it in three now. It's much fresher. Nothing is frozen here. Restaurants want their product tomorrow morning," said Pat.

Beef arrived at the LaFrieda plant in primal cuts, the cut-down pieces of carcass I had seen butchered in the Kansas Creekstone plant. These were then turned into a variety of cuts as ordered by the restaurants.

The orders continued coming in through the evening. At three the phones were turned off, but the computers kept spitting out orders printed on labels with the LaFrieda logo. Pulling a label out, Pat showed it to me. "'Fifty pieces Creekstone beef cheeks, cleaned, send all,'" he read. "You see, this restaurant wants us to remove the sinew on the cheek and send it as well as the cheeks."

The labels were sent into the clean, white, air-conditioned rooms where butchers in white coats, shower caps, and hairnets turned the primal cuts from Creekstone into rib eyes steaks, New York strips, tomahawk steaks. Meat was also ground to order in small batches for burgers—this was done to specific recipes for Minetta Tavern and Cherche Midi or Danny Meyer's Shake Shack chain. Recipes were secret, closely held by Pat LaFrieda. He could not, for instance, share with me the recipe for Shake Shack. Burgers that could be the stuff of industrial espionage.

Pat himself generally worked from around six in the evening through the night, helped with the cutting at the family plant, and he was always conscious of the USDA guy on the premises, who was apparently as secretive as the CIA.

The meat business was more carefully regulated than a nuclear facility, said Pat. This was good, he added thoughtfully, checking an immensely complex chart of regulations. Sitting at his desk in a green plaid shirt, Pat was pensive. "You don't hear about a lot of food-borne illnesses from meat from a USDA plant," he said.

In the morning, the fleet of white LaFrieda trucks waiting in the factory bay outside rolled off to deliver meat up and down the East Coast, from Baltimore to Boston. An hour later, one of the trucks pulled up at Balthazar's back door on Crosby Street.

Like a number—a dwindling number in the age of corporate food—of fourth- and fifth-generation food purveyors in New York, Pat LaFrieda did not set out to be a butcher. His father forbade it because the business was tough and sometimes dirty. Pat was desperate to do it, but he went to college and, with an MBA, ended up on Wall Street. He hated it.

Pat's great-grandfather had arrived from Naples and had opened a butcher shop in Brooklyn in 1922. The shop moved to Manhattan. Within a few decades, the LaFriedas discovered there was better money in selling to restaurants than to individuals, and so they moved out to New Jersey, got a fleet of trucks, and, eventually, a reputation as the best around, much of this thanks to Mark Pastore.

Pastore was Pat LaFrieda's first cousin. For a decade, he played salesman, PR guy, relationship maker for the LaFrieda label. He was, as he told me himself, a very gregarious guy. He liked hanging out and making friends and doing deals. "I could go in a room of fifty and make them all my friends," Mark said. "They say I'm the man behind the curtain."

When he was around nineteen, Mark started "on the scales" (basically the checkout desk), with Crown Meat, where he learned the business until his cousin Pat invited him to join the family business.

It turned out that Mark's greatest talent was in the critical New York art of schmoozing. He ate out seven days a week, ate everywhere, knew everyone, especially the chefs. "I break bread with them," he said. "New York is a city of who you know. But you got to have the product." Mark also took an interest in the farms and the farmers. "I go and meet them and look at animals, and then I look at the meat when it comes in, and if there's ten pieces of meat in a case, I pick the top three and say, 'These are for Keith McNally.' If you say this is the best strip steak anywhere, it better be the best."

When Frank Bruni, then the *New York Times* food critic, gave Minetta Tavern three stars, noting it was the best steakhouse in the city, this was for Mark Pastore like the Second Coming. It was probably with Minetta that McNally helped make LaFrieda the celebrity butcher, the most famous of the meat guys.

There followed a stampede, chefs heading to New Jersey, beseeching Pat, standing around in the aging room, gorgeous beef brushing their heads, pleading for a special recipe. Something new. Something different. Please, Pat!

"Restaurant people say, 'Give us a different cut, Pat,'" Pat said. "But it's very difficult to do anymore. I took the rib eye cap off a rib eye, which turns it into a rib eye roll. You clean both sides, and you roll it and tie it—this is the juiciest part of the rib eye, the spinalis muscle, it's got more intramuscular fat than the rib eye. But I can't really invent parts of the animal that don't exist."

Celebrity Meat, meat that was branded (both senses), beef with a calling card, a provenance, became a must-have for New York's top restaurants. Before I saw the LaFrieda name on the menu at Minetta Tavern, I had never really considered the particular origins of my slab of steak or my humble burger. Humble no more, the high-tone burger soon required the kind of attention to age and provenance you might look for in a bottle of fine French wine.

When I got back from Kansas, one night I found myself at Balthazar, staring at the menu. It made me think about the cattle in their pens out on the prairie, eating around the clock with docile obedience—except the idea of obedience was a human characteristic, and these were just cows, after all.

"Here the cows feel less fear," I'd been told in the well-designed processing plant in Arkansas City, Kansas. *Less* fear?

I didn't order the steak, not that night.

CHAPTER 13

GOD'S POTATOES

A shortage of the brown-skinned GPOD Idaho russets always gave Vinnie DeFrancesco a really vexatious case of agita. If he couldn't get enough of this particular spud, it could lead to a shortage of the frites, the French fries for which Balthazar was rightly famous. These were always the best frites in town, maybe the country. Skinny fried potatoes, fleshy, fluffy, tasty, and dense inside; the outside, crispy and golden and brown. "We like to say GPOD stands for God's Potatoes on Demand," Kevin Searle, the company manager, told me. Idaho sounded a godly place.

So much were these fries rightly adored that no other potato was ever good enough for Balthazar. When Keith McNally opened Balthazar in London, he tried eight kinds of British or Euro potato, didn't like any of them, and considered shipping the GPODs across the pond. People thought he was nuts, but then, they had probably not tasted Balthazar's French fries.

Balthazar sold a staggering amount, frites served in piles on the steak frites, with burgers, on their own. "Without these potatoes, there are no frites, and without frites, there would be no steak frites," Vinnie told me. "Potatoes, we always get them from the same source, they are GPOD ninety-count, grown in Idaho. The prices can vary from eighteen to thirty-five dollars per case, and when the crop is about to finish, they start becoming very expensive. We use about twelve to fifteen cases per day, depending on the day of the week."

At one point, Vinnie, being a persuasive guy, convinced a distributor on Long Island to build a shed and stockpile the potatoes, which are harvested only once a year in Shelley, Idaho.

I'd planned to visit Shelley during the harvest, maybe dig up a couple of my own spuds. This was the best time to go, I was told, because during harvest Shelley goes into party mode. At Spud Day, there are sack races and cook-offs, and people play around with the potatoes and feast on them and dress up as spuds.

The potato's origin in the high Andes—far, far from Idaho—was the gift of the New World to the Old and, because you could feed workers cheap on them, very popular with the bosses. Potatoes fed South American silver miners in the sixteenth century, and eventually fueled the industrial revolution. They were also the poisoned present of imperial England to Ireland; when the potato famine came, it drove the Irish—literally half of the country's population—to the United States, Canada, and Australia.

Still, Marie Antoinette wore a headdress of potato flowers to a fancy dress ball (let them eat spuds), and a staple of Jackie Kennedy's diet was a baked potato with crème fraîche and caviar.

French fries, as a dish, did not have a particularly glamorous origin, though; France and Belgium both claimed it. The likelihood was that it got its name from American GIs who ate them after the war in Belgium. Everybody was speaking French, of course, so the GIs referred to the food as French, and so the name.

Near the Snake River, Shelley, Idaho, where the GPODs came from, was a remote but ravishing stretch of countryside within sight of the Blackfoot Mountains. I had driven the length of the Snake River on a summer vacation once, but somehow I had missed out on Shelley.

When I phoned Kevin Searle, the manager at GPOD, who comes from a long line of potato men, he was very nice. I told him how sad I was that I couldn't make it to Shelley Spud Day. I had family obligations. He said that, instead, he would send some potatoes to me personally, potatoes that had just been dug and sorted, as near as possible to the earth they had come out of.

My potatoes would be coming out of land worked by Kevin's cousin, Bryan Searle, which gave me a connection and made me happy.

"Bryan's father and my father are brothers," Kevin told me on the phone. "My grandfather Leo Searle settled in the Shelley area to begin farming. My father and his brothers followed him, as have some of Leo's grandsons, of which I am one. Growing up on a potato farm was a special way to be raised," said Kevin. "We learned about the earth and how to till and take care of it. We were taught to work hard, respect the soil that grew the crops, and take pride in being a part of the farming community that puts food on the table of our fellow Americans. I loved farming with my cousins and the dream of being the next generation to carry on the family tradition."

Did I hear Kevin sigh down the phone?

He went on: "For me, this was not to be, as I was captured away in a different mode of helping with the farmers' potato crop. I am the fourth generation to be involved in the potato business in my family. And I now serve as the general manager at GPOD of Idaho, a fresh-pack potato facility serving the area growers for forty-seven years." Kevin said he took great pride in helping facilitate the potato movement of local growers to their East Coast clientele who loved GPOD of Idaho potatoes.

Caught up in the almost lyrical recitation of family potato farming, I waited for my Idahos with some excitement. If I couldn't dig them, maybe I could at least carry them over to Balthazar, get them fried up, and eat them, thus feeling they were somehow *my* potatoes.

• • •

It took some time, a few weeks, but finally a large box arrived with a couple of dozen potatoes, the fine big russets, beautifully packed in a classic potato sack. They had been quite scrupulously cleaned and packed, but I liked to think I could smell the rich Idaho dirt. The burlap smelled nice, too. During the Depression poor people made dresses out of these sacks; on Amazon now there are fashion items or fancy towels made from them.

For a day or so I posed my potatoes on the sack and took their picture. Truth was, though you could make an art object out of anything, on its own the potato had limited visual charm. I called Shane. He said to come over, so I walked my potatoes to the restaurant. This probably looked a little odd; there were not usually people carrying potato sacks filled with potatoes around SoHo.

When I got over to Balthazar, I gave Shane my spuds and he handed them over to Diógene Peralta, who, with Ramón Alvino and Daniel Estrella, was a master potato peeler. "These guys do nothing but peel potatoes all day long," Shane said.

A few deft moves and my potatoes were done, after which they were chipped—cut by a little machine into the right-size strips—and placed in a large container of water to soak overnight. This took a lot of the starch out and made a crispier fry. I was impatient.

The next day the chipped potatoes were taken to the prep kitchen, where at the far end of the large room, they went into the fryer with peanut oil. José Antonio Moya, who was the fry guy that day (there were usually two or three), shook them in the basket, turned them out, started again.

"This was a first job for an aspiring cook. All you do are the fries, all day," said Frank Ortega, one of Balthazar's sous chefs.

Then upstairs to the kitchen, where, just before they were served, they were fried a second time, again in peanut oil. Twice fried, they were crisp outside and soft inside, and just about perfect, and by the time these babies arrived at the bar where I was sitting, they had been transformed. The lumpy, dull-looking, but pure and nourishing American spud, the culinary workhorse that went into the manly staple known as "meat and potatoes," had become glamorous chips; dunked in mayo, skinny, crispy, salty, golden, warm, they had become French.

The critical thing here was digging out those dark burned extra-crispy bits at the bottom. This could be a furtive activity. When I scrabbled, unembarrassed, for the last tiny fragment of potato, it made me feel like an old hippie getting the last hit off a joint.

CHAPTER 14

OYSTERS

The Living Truth

Kumamoto, Fanny Bay, Skookum, Nootka, Royal Miyagi, Wellfleet, Beau Soleil, Island Creek, East End, Glidden Point, Hood Canal, Chatham. So many varieties of oyster were sold at Balthazar in any month and according to the season that it was sometimes tough for the waiters to learn the names, the region, the taste and size, though this was a requirement of the job. Oysters were a big deal at Balthazar from the beginning, but then, they had always been an essential part of the grand Parisian café-brasserie, like La Coupole or Bofinger, where there were always bushels of oysters on stalls outside the restaurants. On mounds of crushed ice, they always looked better than other oysters, and so did the yellow lemons. These had always seemed to me a more perfect yellow, a Parisian yellow. I thought that, given all this, I'd better get a handle on the oyster thing.

Shane suggested I visit Widow's Hole Oysters on Long Island because they sold a succulent product and Mike Osinski, its owner, had a good story to tell. He liked hanging around with chefs, too. And I had always liked the North Fork.

About a hundred miles out from New York City, at the far end of what's known as the North Fork, is Greenport. It was still a pretty town, still more blue collar, certainly less moneyed than the Hamptons to the south, and I was happy to drive out to check on some oysters.

On the way out I saw how much had changed in the area since I'd last been; there were bigger, newer houses everywhere, though the area still had a rural air with its vineyards and farms, and guys like Osinski with his oyster beds. Mike, of course, was a pretty recent interloper, having set up oystering after he left Wall Street.

It took Mike Osinski a while to get his oysters into Balthazar. It felt a little like getting your kid into a decent New York school, and he had been pretty pissed off about it, he told me.

"So I walk in, I say, 'I got a new oyster farm, I'm selling to Le Bernardin, and the Four Seasons, and Union Square,'" Osinski said. "'Would you like to buy some?' And this crotchety old guy, he says, 'How much?' I said, 'Sixty-five cents an oyster.' He says, 'You'll never get sixty-five cents from me. Get the hell out of here!'"

I figured the crotchety old guy was Vinnie DeFrancesco. I could imagine Vinnie thinking, *I'm not paying this uppity newcomer that much for an oyster.* I imagined the little confrontation: Vinnie was no patsy, his life dedicated to getting the best and the best prices for Balthazar; Mike Osinski, a man with an obsession for his oysters was no pussy when it came to confrontations. All the time I was with him, he kept saying, "Why eat food that's dead when you can eat wonderful fresh living food?"

On the lawn of his house one afternoon, looking at the water where yellow buoys marked his oyster beds, Mike crossed his foot over his leg, took a steaming bowl of oyster chowder from Isabel, his partner and wife, and picked up the story. "So about five years ago, we're driving down making a delivery in the city and we're going past

Minetta Tavern and I said, 'Stop!' Isabel's driving, right? I told her I'd heard it was a good restaurant. I got in. Riad and Lee—Balthazar's original chefs—were there and I give them my 'I got an oyster farm, blah, blah, you want to try some samples?' They say, 'Yeah, sure.' You know, they're good guys. They come out to the truck, and I'm shucking oysters on the back of the van, and they taste some and they say, 'These are great,' and they ordered for three or four of their restaurants. And that's how I got into Balthazar." Mike Osinski sold about a million oysters a year now.

When I visited Mike, he was getting eighty cents or even more per oyster and prices were going up. Soon, it would be a buck minimum. At their place in Greenport on Long Island, he and Isabel put in crazy hours tending their oysters. "I like three years on an oyster," Mike said. "You can sell them at two. Most people sell them as fast as they can, usually at eighteen, sixteen months. The less time in the water, the bigger the profit for the grower because there's less time before you sell. But you've got a better animal at three years. Plumper meat, thicker shell, more desirable." Mike knew this because he ate his oysters all the time. He ate them with pasta, with polenta, in his wife's chowder, for breakfast and dinner. He loved oysters a lot, so he ate them whenever he could and he talked about them with evangelical fervor.

It was 1999 when Osinksi bought the place. He was only forty-five, but he had retired after making a bundle. He bought the big house on the water to get away from the city. Without local permission, he built a dock; this got him into trouble with the local authorities, which pissed him off.

Eating his oyster chowder, Osinski said, "So I go to a local lawyer. I said to him, 'I'm a New Yorker. I'm not going to get homered out here by the home team.' So he rolls out this map of Greenport Harbor, it's a hundred-year-old map. I said, 'Hey, what's the big box there in the water next to my house?' He said, 'Look carefully, see the tax IDs are the same. You own that. Write to Albany and get a copy of the deed.'

"And I did. And I have a copy there. 'We, the people of the state of New York by the grace of God, free and independent,' it says, all handwritten, beautifully cursive, and it gave us five acres out here. Actually it had given this to the previous owner. And nobody knew him. Everybody forgot about it until I stumbled upon this." In a *what the hell* sort of moment, Osinski said to himself, "'This used to be the oyster capital of New York. I'm going to grow oysters.'"

What Mike had discovered was that his house on the Peconic Bay came with the title to five acres of underwater "land," starting from the edge of his property. It was all his and it was like discovering that just by chance, having no idea at all, there was oil on your land when you thought all you'd bought was a weekend house.

Once, Long Island had been nothing but oysters; from Montauk to Orient to Riverhead, for thirty miles, the Peconic Bay was one solid floor of oysters. Greenport alone had supplied fourteen train-loads of oysters a day to Manhattan. There were canneries, ship-yards, oystermen, and oyster shuckers here all through the early twentieth century.

The native Lenape Indians had eaten oysters. European settlers found there were oysters for the taking, and they took them and ate them in enormous quantities. In New York, oysters were sold at markets, in restaurants, off stalls. The nobs ate them, and they were also the preferred working-class snack. It was bar food, but then, so was caviar at the turn of the twentieth century before we fished out all the local sturgeon.

Then, in the 1920s, there was a huge cholera outbreak. "The waters had been so polluted people died in droves from eating shellfish," said Mike Osinski. "After that you could not sell oysters without a lot of restrictions. Matter of fact, even today, the only food you cannot sell from a truck or food stand in the city of New York is an oyster."

By around 1960, overfishing and pollution had killed New York's oyster trade. All around the city and Long Island, all the rivers, streams, ponds, coves, bays, all of them were done. Slowly, over the last few decades, there's been a comeback, in part because of people like Osinski who are willing to put in the time and the methodical attention to reviving the oyster trade. Mike had the money, and he had a house on Long Island right on the water. Besides, he was sick of people calling him evil.

He told *New York* magazine that he had been called the devil by strangers because, in the early 2000s, he had compiled software that eventually turned mortgages into bonds. It nagged at him, he said, that in some way he had played a role in the housing and mortgage crisis and the economic crash. We were talking *The Big Short*, he said. Oysters were, in part, his redemption. Growing up in Alabama and Cape Canaveral, Mike Osinski had earned his keep digging ditches and hauling shrimp, and he got into computers at Emory University. Turned out he was a natural at writing software, and by 1985, he was at Salomon Brothers.

New York was a dream. "I had the desire, I bought into the stupid song, 'If you can make it here,' that reverberates to everywhere in the country. And people come to New York to have that feeling of being, you know, in the nexus of all this ambition and lust and power."

And then he was out. He had signed a contract that forbade him to work on Wall Street for the following five years. He had socked away plenty of dough, and so to Greenport.

Once, Mike gave me a rundown on how oysters make babies. In the best of all natural worlds, they spawned around the Fourth of July, and they spawned best where the water had a lower salinity. "In nature, the oyster would spawn and attach onto its parents. They'd form a reef. They're the northern reef-building animal. So, they would take the cultch—they call that cultch, *c-u-l-t-c-h*—and then they'd go back in August, scoop it up, hydraulic dredges, and it would be covered with spat, little tiny millimeter baby oysters, and broadcast it across the bays by the billions. And they grow the stuff on the bottom. Bottom culture. So many die with bottom culture you have to have your own hatchery. What we do is called off-bottom culture." Mike looked up.

I was hanging on to this explanation like an oyster baby to its parents' shells.

A nursery system moved the babies into the creek on Mike's property. At an inch they went into cages out in the bay. The buoys in the water had tags, each one indicating a cohort of a certain age—apparently multiple oysters are a cohort—and Mike knew how old they were. "You have predation there, you have starfish, oyster drills, scungilli, they attack the oysters. But they didn't care, they had so many billions. But eventually, they were overwhelmed with starfish and oyster drills, and now you see off-bottom cultures coming back. But you have a huge amount that die—if you're going to do bottom culture, you've got to have your own hatchery. You can't afford to buy and then throw it out on the bottom, right?"

Osinski walked out to his dock. He spread his arms wide and sighed and smiled, pleased with himself and his operation. Out on the dock, he looked a little like the Jesus of oysters who was working the water to bring truth to the world. I followed him. He turned to me.

"Now you're at an oyster processing plant," he said. "Beautiful meat's here." Still in his evangelical mode, Mike leaned forward. "But there are more growers all the time. More and more people are eating oysters. So there's a big rising demand every year, and really, it's the best piece of meat you can put in your mouth. As far as nutrition, the omega-3s are off the chart." He told me the Chinese were the world's largest producers of oysters; 99 percent goes into oyster sauce. To be honest, I had never actually considered that oyster sauce has oysters in it; I thought it was just something that came from the Chinese restaurant with the rest of the food.

All the time that Mike Osinski was talking about oysters, oyster babies, oyster spawn, oyster sauce, oysters with grits, I was wondering if he was going to offer me a sample. He did not. I was glad.

I have always felt bad about my antipathy to oysters. I thought it marked me as a culinary lout. People like me who didn't have the taste for them were philistines; that, or they were kosher, which was never my problem—I had always been crazy for lobster and shrimp.

But I had never liked them and I wasn't sure why. It made me feel I had missed out on something, and that I would never quite make it in the food world. Everybody loved oysters.

I was on the rack, one of my own making. It seemed silly, this not liking oysters. When I met people who would not eat caviar or Roquefort or anchovies, I thought them childish.

Clams were good, but clams had no poetry, no sex appeal; clams were the plain-Jane sister to those sensuous oysters. Nobody sat around reminiscing about clams they had eaten. Even as a player in a great spaghetti alle vongole, the clam could not compete.

For chrissake, I thought, *oysters in Oyster Bay do it, and Cole Porter said so, and I love Cole Porter.* In a more practical, less tuneful way, they were tremendously eco-friendly. Oysters cleaned the water, acted as a natural filter. Also, they provided wonderful protein without many calories, and they could be eaten raw, cooked, boiled, fried, baked, stewed, broiled.

Again, as I had with Jerry, Balthazar's oyster czar, I tried and failed. One more time I committed myself to them. The problem was with me, not the oysters. One Thursday afternoon, as soon as Mike Osinski had dropped off his Widow's Hole oysters at Balthazar, Shane suggested we try some.

In his office at Balthazar, he opened a bottle of Muscadet and set about shucking the oysters. "I love the whole process, opening them and eating them with a nice white," said Shane. He placed a round platter with half a dozen oysters on the desk in his tiny office downstairs. Frank Ortega, the sous chef, stopped in. Both of them looked expectant. They ate.

"They're briny and plump and delicious, and they have a deep shell," Shane said. I gave my attention to the deep creamy shell, with its curves and ridges made by the sea, the interior almost opalescent in a certain light, the luscious-looking creature firm, plump, and moist.

I ate one. Shane said, "Well?"

"Lovely," I lied. "Delicious. Yum."

"Have another one."

Shane and Frank each took an oyster, swallowed, closed his eyes, and said in that celebratory way . . . "YUM!" I saw it now as I always saw it: the look of rapture, the expression of bliss that always appeared when somebody had eaten an oyster. It always seemed to me that this went beyond the simple satisfaction with a delicious morsel of food. The expression carried with it an almost metaphysical sense—or did I mean existential?—that in eating and enjoying the oysters, something perfect had been experienced. As if they had dined with poets and philosophers—a plate of oysters with John Donne or Jean-Paul Sartre. Or was it the myth of the oyster as an aphrodisiac? Did eating a few turn certain friends into lovers of great prowess? Was I an atheist in the world's most exquisite cathedral?

"Are they alive?" I asked Shane.

"Sure," he said, echoing Mike Osinski.

"Why would you not eat them?" Mike had looked at me and asked. "I don't know why people put dead meat in their mouths. Every meat you eat is dead except for oysters."

It was one of those things you learned late in life and that made you feel like an idiot for not having got it earlier. The truth was that I had not known that oysters were alive when you ate them. Literally, actually alive, breathing and sentient.

Thomas Huxley wrote, "I suppose that when the sapid and slippery morsel—which is gone like a flash of gustatory summer lightning—glides along the palate, few people imagine that they are swallowing a piece of machinery (and going machinery too) greatly more complicated than a watch." Oysters have a brain and a nervous system. (So much is the oyster a living creature that there have even been attempts to anaesthetize it before eating.)

In any case, sapid and slippery, that was exactly it. My fellow, Artie, who had driven around with me in Kansas, was from England, and he only liked his fish fried and wasn't all that interested in oysters one way or the other. I asked if he had known oysters were alive when you ate them.

"Alive?" he said. "You're kidding."

I said, "Truly."

"How do you mean, alive? You mean they're reading Jane Austen and listening to Miles Davis?"

When I expressed my reticence about oysters, Ruth Reichl said, "But they clean up the water and they're delicious and good for your health and they taste wonderful." Also, Ruth added, "They do read Jane Austen."

CHAPTER 15

A GLASS OF
GOOD RED

Rebecca Banks grew up in rural Pennsylvania, where people didn't drink wine. "Not people I knew," she said. "My family did not drink wine, they really didn't drink at all. We lived across from a cornfield."

We were sitting at the bar, sampling a bottle of red wine Rebecca had brought up from the Balthazar cellars—cellars being the various cupboards and little rooms down in the catacombs where the wine was kept. The director of wine for Balthazar and the rest of Keith McNally's restaurants, to a pretty large extent Rebecca was also responsible for the booze. She kept up with trends and styles; she always knew which gins—there were gins made in Brooklyn now and hipsters loved the idea—had come onto the market; she was clued in to the fact that the younger "soms" (as she called sommeliers) were fond of Madeira.

"Personally, I'm excited about fortified wines like Madeira and Sherry over Vintage Port and Sauternes for after dinner," said Rebecca.

Small, dark, pretty, with a head full of wild curls, she lived in

Brooklyn with her husband—he was in the movie business—and two kids. By age and style, she was a perfect denizen of the new Brooklyn; her heart, though, was always in France. If she could happily riff on Sherry or bourbon or tequila, when she talked about French wine, she really lit up.

At Balthazar, there was only French wine. If a customer asked for, say, a nice Chianti, instead the waiter might offer Chinon Rouge. Instead of a Napa Cabernet, a bottle of Bandol.

The waiters learned it all so they, in lieu of a California or Australian Chardonnay, could offer you a French white from southern Burgundy—Chassagne-Montrachet, Meursault, or Nuits-Saint-Georges. Or tell you that French Chardonnays were a little subtler, but still exhibited buttery and nutty flavors and aromas from spending time in oak barrels. For a California Merlot, a right-bank Bordeaux, Saint-Emilion and Pomerol; or a Vin de Pays de l'Hérault in place of a super Tuscan.

The bottle we were sampling while sitting around at the bar was Château du Taillan. "I like this," said Rebecca. "It's accessible and approachable, it's easy to drink alone or with food. Secondly, I appreciate that an otherwise stoic and sometimes stodgy wine like Bordeaux can be fruit-forward and fun and a value, like the Taillan." She added that it was clearly a well-made wine that wasn't trying to be anything other than a Cru Bourgeois. "It is honest and delicious—and generally a crowd-pleaser."

Rebecca was right. This was good stuff. This was an immediately delicious wine that climbed into my mouth and said, *Hello, have some fun, eat a steak frites.* Never was a good, happy Cru Bourgeois going to trick you with hints of something you could never understand. No faint undertones of walnuts here; I could never smell those walnuts the experts were always talking about anyway.

"Actually, that isn't generally an aroma or flavor descriptor that would be used," said Rebecca, amused by my lack of wine smarts.

"Common Bordeaux descriptors might be 'barnyard'—in other words, manure—pencil lead, forest floor, tobacco, pipe tobacco, cigar smoke, maybe cedar shavings," she said. By this time, I would have been happy with the walnuts.

Un bon verre de vin rouge. A glass of good red. Wine was as critical to the life of a brasserie, as potent a symbol of its essence, as anything else. I liked the Taillan by the glass and also the Franc Lartigue Saint-Emilion 2009, which was beautifully open and fragrant. So when I decided I'd go look at one of the vineyards, I was torn, but I was taken with the idea of a château entirely owned and run by women. So to Château du Taillan I went. It was just after Easter when I got there. I had been visiting friends in the deep southwest of France, and from there I went to Bordeaux.

Every year on the first day of October, Armelle Cruse walked her hectares at the Château du Taillan. With the sun rising over the Gironde, Armelle picked a grape, worked the skin off in her mouth because this was what she wanted to taste, this was where the key to the winemaking was. All the time she was walking and tasting, she was pondering if the time for the harvest was right or if she should give it a day more.

All this was going through her head, she told me when I got to Taillan in April. She said she constantly worried about issues of acidity, flavor, bottling, and, most of all, the sales. Tourism, too. Armelle, who owned the Taillan vineyard along with her sisters, was always consumed by the burgeoning relationship she saw all around her between tourism and wine. All the big vineyards understood it, and Armelle was convinced that with a small operation like hers, only these two things in tandem would keep her going.

"To make money, you need the tourists," she said. She did not seem angry or pissed off or even disdainful. It was the way of the world. She was right. I had worked on and off for travel magazines, and there was a voracious audience for experience. People, especially people with dough, didn't want to just travel, just visit a place, they wanted to do it, make it, eat it, get married in it. Sometimes it was a theme park version of experience they sought—I once heard of a group who went to Mali to hear the music and lived in an air-conditioned tent. But there it was, and Armelle knew it. Tourists who came to her château and saw wine being made bought the wine, spread the word.

Small, slim, elegant, and utterly French in her high-heeled oxfords, Armelle Cruse seemed to glide across the bright green lawn. (I just sank into it.) Blond and fine-boned, she was a mother of two. She got a bottle of the château's white wine and we sat on the lawn at a little white wrought-iron table.

On that lovely day at the end of a harsh winter, the tranquil scene around us belonged to a distant, quieter time. Across the green lawns of the park that surrounded it was the eighteenth-century château: an immaculately poised piece of architecture, an almost Platonic French château, the soft golden stone seemed to glow as evening came on.

The sun was going down. In the lush countryside here just outside the city of Bordeaux, the dusky light sucked the green from the fields and lawns and turned them purple. Everyone who worked at Taillan had gone for the day, it seemed, and it was quiet and, except for Armelle and me, nobody was around. The magic hour, photographers call it. It was a dream of French wine country.

We sipped the wine.

"You must use tradition to be modern," Armelle said, her dog, Helios, at her feet.

With a small vineyard, you needed promotion, you needed visitors to the wine shop on the premises, you needed, Armelle said again, tourists. And this was why she smiled when, on the balmy spring night, as if in answer to her comment, a tourist—plump and bald, wearing shiny tennis shoes—appeared. He greeted us shyly and said he was visiting in the area and wanted some wine to take to his friends' for dinner.

"You are in luck," said Armelle, who rose from her chair. "We are usually closed now, but here I am. How can I help you?" A sale was a sale, after all, and this was not an easy business.

I followed Armelle into the shop and watched her sell the guy four bottles of wine, two of the red Cru Bourgeois, the really good 2010 stuff, and a couple of the Dame Blanche. Unusually for white wine, it was made from 100 percent sauvignon grapes. Most white Bordeaux was a blend of sauvignon blanc, sémillon, and a little Muscadelle, and the variety added balance to the blend. If a winemaker thought his terroir more suited to a specific grape variety (and had enough of it to justify bottling), he might choose to use only one grape. It was what Armelle had done for her Dame Blanche. It was light and went down easy, which was most of what I cared about in wine.

Happy, the guy in his shiny sneakers left, clutching his bottles, and we returned to the little table and drank until it was time to go in for dinner.

Henri Cruse, who was from Germany, bought the Château du Taillan in 1896. He made wine and raised horses. Armelle and her sisters are the fifth generation at Taillan; when she was only twenty-one, her father died unexpectedly and she took over the winemaking. The only one of the sisters with an interest in wine and a degree in oenology, she was ready.

Gradually she sold the horses, but she maintained the house and the vineyards, the cellars where the wine was made and stored, and she added the shop.

We went into dinner with Armelle's mother, Madame Guille-mette Cruse. Her house was next door to Armelle's. (In fact, the whole property was owned by all five daughters, but only two of them worked on it; the others were shareholders. Armelle and her family lived in the house, but it was also used for weddings and family reunions and Christmas.)

Madame Cruse was about eighty and sprightly; a slim woman in trim pants and a sweater, she exuded extreme elegance. She was friendly and spoke English for my sake, but there was an ineluctable sense of Frenchness about her. At the table, she explained that the utensil beside my plate was a fish fork. (I knew what a fish fork was for, but I thanked her for telling me with what I imagined was extremely French politesse.)

Afterward, we sipped coffee in a sitting room filled with chintz-covered armchairs and the knickknacks collected over a lifetime. At Madame Cruse's feet was her dog; his name was Asterix.

I had been invited to spend the night and given a large, pretty room that looked over the front of the house. Not the room, though, or the view, but the riding boots were what I would remember.

On top of a large armoire were three or four pairs of beautiful riding boots, properly polished, with old-fashioned wooden boot trees in them. Armelle had told me that she and her sisters all rode.

I had trouble sleeping that night. I lay in bed in the large old room, the shutters still open, the window looking out on the long drive and rows of trees and the lawns, and I was supposed to be thinking about wine and how it was made and then sent to New York and Balthazar, but the thing that stayed in my mind were the riding boots. This had been a place where everyone rode the horses that Armelle's father loved; there were pictures of horses on the walls. So I tried to sleep and thought about boots and horses, and also the green bathroom.

In the bathroom that adjoined my room the fixtures were pale green porcelain, and all I could think of at first, a thing that floated into my head, was from a book I read a hundred years ago, *Lost Horizon*. In James Hilton's 1933 novel, a traveler to Shangri-La—the lost world, a hidden and ancient paradise—discovers that the modern bath is "of a delicate green porcelain, a product of, according to the inscription, Akron, Ohio."

I felt nearly as far away here, no radio with me, no TV in the room, the vineyards out back, the wine made pretty much as it had been for centuries. I fell asleep and woke up, unsure if this was a dream.

The next morning I went downstairs; Armelle had been up and out soon after five. I had breakfast with her mother. The domestic French breakfast often seemed to consist of pots of yogurt and hard toasts out of a package, nothing at all like the glammed-up baskets of gilded pastry and fresh bread at Balthazar.

After that I met Armelle at the wine cellars. Long flights of stone steps went down into the cellar, where the wine was resting in bottles and tanks. Great stone arches held up the ceiling. There was barely any daylight, and Armelle seemed to speak more quietly, as if out of respect for the resting wine.

The smell was cold, the smell of ancient stone and dirt. Wine had been made here for centuries, even back to the time when Eleanor of Aquitaine ruled the region; my favorite of all female monarchs, she outlived her husbands, including Henry II, who had her locked up in a tower for years.

In these cellars, first dug in the sixteenth century, I felt the history of the region creeping up with that smell. "Cloisters, ancient libraries . . . I was confusing learning with the smell of cold stone," says one of the characters in Alan Bennett's play *The History Boys*. Even more apt, perhaps, is another line in the play: "History is just one fucking thing after another." One fucking movie after another, Eleanor of Aquitaine actually always appears to me as Katharine Hepburn in *A Lion in Winter*.

"Shall we go up?" said Armelle. We climbed the steps from the cold cellar. She told me that the 2015 Cru Bourgeois was looking good, and later she wrote to me, "It's a very nice year. Easygoing, no problem of vinification, maturity is nice. Lots of sweetness and tannin in the wines, and I am very happy at each weekly tasting."

After the grapes were harvested, the wine was made and placed into French oak barrels for twelve months. Of the oak barrels Armelle ages the wine in, 10 percent are new oak barrels and 30 percent are one-year-old barrels. (The rest could be older barrels or stainless steel tanks.)

Moving wine from a cellar in France to a restaurant in New York took some doing. In the fifteenth months after the harvest, usually in the spring, the wine was bottled and stored at the winery, until Frederick Wildman and Sons, Ltd., the distributor, placed an order. The wine was shipped by truck from the winery to the temperature-controlled warehouse in Bordeaux that belonged to the Compagnie Médocaine des Grands Crus, a Bordeaux *négociant* and merchant. From there it went by truck to the port at Le Havre, where it was loaded into temperature-controlled containers for the Atlantic crossing.

Unloaded at the docks in New Jersey, the containers remained sealed until they reached Western Carriers, where Frederick Wildman stored its wine, along with hundreds of other distributors. Roughly seven million cases of wine were stored in over two million square feet of space at this dedicated wine-and-spirit warehouse in northern New Jersey. A massive operation, it was secretive and carefully controlled. Not exactly the rope net Kayo Dugan used to pull up his whiskey in *On the Waterfront*.

When Balthazar put in an order, usually ten cases at a time, the wine was trucked to Crosby Street from New Jersey the next day. Leo Ramirez, the steward for wine and spirits, received it, put it in the right place; cellar master Mark Mason looked after it; Carolyn Morosanu, the corporate beverage buyer, entered the details into the computer; and Rebecca considered if she should order more.

Sold both by the glass and the bottle at Balthazar, Château du

Taillan brought in over ten grand a month. As with most restaurants, Balthazar's real profits are in the wine and spirits. "Most restaurant wine-list markups range from two hundred to four hundred percent of wholesale cost.

"We don't really mark up expensive wines much," Rebecca told me. "If you have a three-hundred-dollar bottle and only sell three bottles and you raise it by fifty bucks, you make only a hundred fifty. It's nothing in the grand scheme of things. But by the glass, when you're selling, I don't know, sixty glasses of Sancerre in an afternoon, or three hundred glasses in a weekend, it does make a difference whether you raise it a dollar or not. So that's how we figure it," she said. She had first put Château du Taillan on the Balthazar list in September of 2014. In the first six months, 184 bottles were sold; so were 3,706 individual glasses.

We were finishing our bottle at the bar when I asked Rebecca how she got into her trade, and she told me—like so many others at Balthazar—she fell into it.

She had studied fashion and design, and worked for a while as a stylist, but when she got an internship with Balthazar's first wine director, the late Chris Goodhart, one of the legendary originals at the restaurant, she fell in love with the work and stayed.

"For a while I kept thinking there was something wrong with me because you never hear about people staying in a restaurant this long. It's been twelve, thirteen years. But it's a show. Every single day," she said.

I asked if she had discovered some kind of talent, some kind of connection with the wine.

"Well, definitely having gone to culinary school, I went to the French Culinary School in New York, and taking the wine classes, it was like . . . I got it. And it seemed to tie in very seamlessly to art and fashion and music. I grew up playing the piano, classical, for the most part, in a jazz band at school. And I enjoyed traveling. I traveled through college and after college. And then working here was just so exciting, because I was around food, I was around wine, I was learning, I was talking to reps and winemakers." And her family? Rebecca said, "Maybe I should tell you that my mother does drink wine now—White Zinfandel and Moscato." She grinned at the idea of her mother sipping these unsophisticated wines, then added, "I try to keep my comments to myself."

"Another one?" Jimmy Norris was on duty. He had been the bartender at Balthazar for years, had lived through the *Sex and the City* days, and had a kindly, humorous face that said he had seen it all. It was only around two in the afternoon and the weather outside was gray, bleak, the city still swathed in a dank fog. I ordered another glass of Château du Taillan. He pulled the cork and poured it into my glass. *Un verre de bon rouge.* Good red wine. I sipped it and the taste was easygoing and sunny, and it made me think about Armelle's little vineyard in Bordeaux, drenched in the evening sun.

CHEF SHANE'S "FIRST TURN OFF THE SMOKE ALARM" STEAK FRITES

Yield: Plenty

INGREDIENTS

Grilling steak (beef tenders, hanger steak, thin New York strip)

Fine kosher salt

Black pepper, freshly ground if possible

6 Idaho potatoes, brown russets if possible (6 brown-skinned Idaho russets are best, but any kind will do if it's a white-fleshed baking potato)

2 quarts peanut oil

Good sea salt to season the fries (it sticks to them better than kosher salt)

Shane's method for the home cook:

"First, turn off the smoke alarm. Then, you pick your cut of meat, but a traditional steak frites is an inexpensive cut of beef. Here at Balthazar we use the 'petite tender,' but you could use hanger steak, or skirt steak or a strip steak—make sure it's no more than an inch thick.

"Season it like crazy, both sides, salt and pepper (kosher salt is best, and cracked black pepper from a pepper mill if possible). Get your—I hope it's cast-iron—skillet smoking hot. A trick is you put your oven to 500°F, put the skillet in for 10 to 15 minutes, pull it out, put it on a high burner,

throw in a couple of drops of canola oil, then drop the steak in. Literally sear that side for probably 3 minutes, flip it over, and put the skillet in the oven for another 2 or 3 minutes still. It's done. You'll have a well-seared, medium-rare charred steak. You could do it in your backyard on a grill if you have one. Obviously, we grill it here at Balthazar, but we use a—you know, we have a 36-inch-wide commercial grill that has 90,000 BTUs, which you're not going to use at home unless you plan to burn your house down.

"When I make a steak at home like that, I open the windows, I turn on the fan, I close the bedroom doors, with the small anticipation that my entire house won't smell like meat for three days. That's the steak. The steak's the easy part.

"The French fries at Balthazar are a two-day process, almost. Your best bet, for real, is go buy some frozen French fries, throw them in your oven and bake them until they're nice and crunchy, toss them with salt, and put them with the steak, but if you're determined to do it yourself: Clean and peel the Idaho potatoes, put them in cold water for a while, then chip them, make strips out of them—in other words, cut the French fries. Put them in cold water again, change the water twice. (It's the chipping that's hard, and if you're dead-set on doing French fries, go buy a little machine for it, and God bless you.)

"Take them out, put them on a kitchen towel, put about 2 quarts of peanut oil in a fryer or deep pot (like a stockpot), turn up to medium heat for the first blanch. They come out, they look limp and flaccid, kind of off-white—this is how they should look. Let them rest a little if possible, then fry again at higher heat in the same oil. You'll know they're done because they'll look brown and crispy and delicious. We use fine sea salt to garnish.

"Put the French fries all over the meat and the plate. My kids and my girlfriend, their favorite are the fries at the very bottom that are soaked in all the meat juices and the melted Maître d' butter. (Mix your butter with shallot, garlic, parsley, tarragon, and chives, or anything you like.)"

TO DRINK:

"Rhône Valley wines are terrific with steak and fries, particularly southern Rhône: Vacqueras La Roubine '12. Vacqueras is a stone's throw from Châteauneuf-du-Pape, a touch more rustic, and half the price! Another option would be: Bandol Le Galantin '09 (from Provence)."

POTATO ONION LOAF

Yield: 2 loaves

I chose this out of all of Balthazar's breads because it's utterly delicious, especially when served warm with lots and lots of salty butter.

INGREDIENTS

Special tools:

Gram scale

Dough scraper

Tea towel or cotton/linen cloth

Covered Dutch oven or cloche

Cooling rack

Potato starter ingredients:

90 grams peeled, chopped potato

112 milliliters water

54 grams all-purpose flour

24 grams whole-wheat flour

1 gram instant yeast

Cooked potatoes and onions ingredients:

1 large potato

1 pinch salt

1 medium onion

1 tablespoon butter (approx.)

Dough ingredients:

700 grams all-purpose or bread flour

2 grams instant yeast

275 grams potato starter

340 milliliters water

150 grams roasted potatoes

22 grams sea salt

85 grams cooked onion

This is a complex recipe, but if you can do it, you'll be baking wonderful bread. It comes straight from Paula Oland, Balthazar's head baker and a woman who knows her stuff.

Paula says: "This bread is based on the potato bread we have been making since we opened in 1997. It is redolent of potato aroma, which, along with butter-sweated onion, makes for a very moist, long-lasting loaf. Ours is made with a sourdough starter and no additional yeast, but the following recipe uses a potato starter made with a minimal amount of commercial yeast. I would encourage anyone who maintains a sourdough starter at home to use it in place of the starter in this recipe, if they choose to.

"Bread bakers typically use weight rather than volume measures, so that's what I have done.

"It calls for instant yeast—this is not the same as either active dry or fast-acting. Its main advantage is that it can be added directly to flour. If using granulated or fresh yeast, it needs to be mixed with a bit of the water (heated to lukewarm temperature) prior to adding it to the rest of the ingredients. Instant yeast is about twice as strong as active dry, which is about twice as strong again as fresh. The amount of yeast in this recipe isn't terribly exact, and it is small.

"After trying this (or any bread recipe), I encourage experimentation with different wheat flours from local sources, keeping in mind that those with more bran will behave differently, absorbing and releasing water at different rates. Whole-grain flour will produce a closer crumb than that which has undergone more sifting."

Day 1

TO MAKE THE STARTER:

In a small pot, cook potato in water, covered, until very soft. Do not drain. Cool in water until lukewarm and weigh—you need to have about 275 grams of finished weight. If you don't, add water to make up for that which evaporated. Mash, then add the flours and yeast. Beat to combine. Cover and keep in a warm place to rise overnight.

TO COOK THE POTATO AND ONION:

Scrub and then roast a potato until slightly underdone. Dice, season with a pinch of salt, and set aside.

Peel, quarter, and slice an onion. Sauté in butter with a pinch of salt on very low heat for about 20 to 30 minutes, or until slices become very soft and golden.

Day 2

TO MAKE THE DOUGH:

In a bowl, combine flour and instant yeast. Add all of the starter, about 275 grams.

Add water and two-thirds of the cooked potato, and mix to combine. Let the mixture rest for about 20 minutes.

Add salt and knead on slow speed or by hand for 10 to 12 minutes, until dough is soft, almost smooth (except for potato lumps), and has elasticity.

Resist the urge to add *any* additional flour. Add onion and remaining cooked potato, and continue mixing to just roughly combine.

Set in a draft-free place—an oven with a pilot light would do—for about two hours, or until risen and web-like underneath. Fold the dough a few times to de-gas it and let it rise again, covered with plastic or a lid (I prefer to refrigerate it, where it will continue to rise slowly overnight).

Note: If left at room temperature for this second "proofing," it will go much faster than the first. Do not let it over-proof or collapse, as it will develop off flavors and a whole range of problems.

Day 2 or 3

SHAPING AND BAKING:

Get ready: clean cloths (on a pan for easy transportation); flour for dusting; rice flour or fat—a neutral oil, soft butter, or other fat of your choosing; a Dutch oven or two.

Knock the dough back once again to deflate. Divide the dough into two pieces and form them each into soft, round balls. Invert one piece to expose the rough part and flatten. Roll toward yourself, giving it some gentle tension, yet not tearing the surface. Flatten the final 1 inch or so to about ¼-inch thick—a rolling pin might help.

Dust the final edge of dough with flour (preferably rice flour) or even oil, to prevent the dough from sticking to itself, before rolling it onto that

seam. Leave the seam on the bottom as you place it on a heavily floured (preferably with wheat flour) cloth. Make a tall pleat in the cloth before repeating with the other round of dough, which will go on the other side of the pleat.

If you do not have enough room in your oven for two loaves in two Dutch ovens *at the same time*, keep one loaf in the refrigerator for half an hour to slow it down. Cover with plastic or another towel and allow to rise for at least a couple of hours. (If not starting with refrigerated dough, much less time is needed.)

Preheat oven to 500°F with covered Dutch oven or cloche placed inside from the start of preheating. Preheat both for about 35 to 40 minutes. The interior of the pan needs to be hot.

The fully proofed dough should hold indentations of your fingers for a bit when ready, but still have good spring toward the center.

When ready to bake, get organized, as the Dutch oven will be really hot to handle—thick or double oven mitts are not a bad idea. Remove the pan from the oven and remove its cover.

Invert a ready loaf onto your hands and carefully lay it into the pan. With your oven mitt (!), replace the lid and gently set the pan into the 500°F oven for 10 minutes. Turn the oven down to 450°F and continue to bake for 30 to 40 minutes, until loaf is quite dark. Remove to a cooling rack—it should sound a bit hollow when you thump it on the bottom. Reheat and repeat for the other loaf, making adjustments to baking as you see fit.

*Note about hand-kneading: soft dough or those with high hydration or added potato and other ingredients are quite sticky. If kneading by hand, they will be messy for a while, but eventually, as the gluten strands form, the dough will begin to clean itself up off your work surface. You might begin just by beating it in a bowl, then as the gluten strands begin to form, turn it out onto the counter (you can even lightly oil the counter) to continue kneading. I recommend using a couple of plastic dough scrapers—one in each hand—to slap the dough mess back and forth onto itself. Watch a clock if you must! Depending on how you knead, the dough will take the same amount of time as if you were using a mixer on low speed—12 minutes or more. The dough will change and eventually come together.

TO DRINK:

Fresh coffee. A cold beer. A glass of red wine. A coffee milkshake. What's *not* good with great bread?

COQ AU VIN

Yield: Serves 4 (2 if very hungry)

*I love the deep, intense coq au vin at Balthazar with its rich
flavors of wine and bacon. If you habitually prefer eating out
like I do, and your home cooking is minimal and marginal—
like mine—you are going to screw this up unless* you pay
attention. *I didn't kill anyone, but my chicken was tasteless,
so Chef Shane came over to my place and talked me through
it, one tiny detail at a time. "It's a recipe," he said. "A French
recipe, which means you can't just say, 'What's the difference
if I leave out the thyme?'" I didn't, I said.*

"What did you do?"

*"I sort of didn't cover the chicken in the marinade
completely."*

"What else?"

"I think I didn't cook it long enough."

*Shane downs several glasses of wine and resumes
his equitable stance. "So . . . we begin," he says.*

INGREDIENTS

1 3-to-4-pound chicken, cut into eight pieces (your butcher will do this for you)

½ pound bacon, cut into ½-inch cubes

2 carrots, peeled and cut in half lengthwise

1 onion, cut into medium ¼-inch dice

2 bottles of good red wine (Shane likes a nice Côtes du Rhône)

1 quart chicken stock

½ tablespoon tomato paste

1 bay leaf

¼ teaspoon fresh or dried thyme leaves

4 cloves of garlic, minced

½ pound button mushrooms, cleaned, dried, and cut in half

½ pound white pearl onions, peeled

½ pound butter

5 tablespoons canola oil

Salt and pepper

TWO OR THREE DAYS BEFORE YOU COOK:

Put the chicken, 1 bottle of wine, onion, carrots, bay leaf, and thyme into a large plastic bowl or plastic bag, cover, and put in the fridge for two or three days—the longer it marinates, the richer the sauce.

ON THE DAY YOU WANT TO COOK:

Put everything in one area for ease: all ingredients; a large saucepan; a large pot, like a Dutch oven; a strainer, sauté pan, plate. Open second bottle of wine and keep close.

Cut up slab bacon into little cubes like lardons.

"OK," Shane says. "We've marinated the chicken. Remove it, pat dry, put on a plate. Strain out the veggies—carrot, onion—from the marinade, set aside, skim off any crap from the marinade, put in saucepan, and simmer for 20 minutes on a medium flame. Render lardons [or bacon pieces] in the Dutch oven, remove when cooked, leave fat in the pot.

"Preheat oven to 350 degrees.

"Brown chicken in the bacon fat, set aside. Sauté veggies and garlic in same fat until the carrots have a little color. Add tomato paste, mix it around with the veggies, and when the paste turns the pan bottom black, add Cognac, and flame.

"Add chicken stock to marinade and add to tomato paste mixture. Bring to boil and skim.

"Add chicken and bacon pieces. Cover, put it in the oven for three hours or until tender. Drink the extra bottle of wine.

"While drinking delicious wine, sauté the button mushrooms in 2 tablespoons of canola oil in the saucepan over medium heat until soft. Add 2 more tablespoons, sauté pearl onions, and set both mushrooms and onions aside.

"Remove the pot of chicken from the oven. Remove the chicken from the pot with a slotted spoon, set aside.

"Strain out the cooking liquid, throw out the solids. Put the liquid back into the pot, bring to a simmer, skim impurities off as they surface.

"When chicken is tender, remove everything from the Dutch oven—chicken, veggies, bacon, with a slotted spoon. Set aside. Strain out the cooking liquid and throw out the solids. Place the liquid back into the pot. Bring to a simmer and skim impurities off as they surface.

"Cut up the carrots into ¼-inch pieces.

"Turn up the heat and cook down the liquid (reduce it) to about half. Reducing liquid is just allowing it to evaporate. Reduce by ½ to ⅔ until nice, glossy, and thick. If you like your sauce really thick and sticky, reduce it a bit more.

"Put in chicken, carrots, bacon, mushrooms, onions; check seasoning;

add salt and pepper, another splash of red wine, and serve. Or, if it's the night before, let it cool down, put in fridge. The next night you can put the whole pot in the oven at 300 degrees for about half an hour. Serve with egg noodles, rice, or just slabs of French bread."

TO DRINK:

Chicken is great with a medium-bodied red: red Burgundy, of course, or for a change something a little earthier, like a Cabernet Franc from the Loire Valley. Try Chinon "Gabare" Grosbois '14.

PART
FOUR

AFTERNOON

CHAPTER 16

COOKING

In the prep room, a young man who was carrying a big pot of French onion soup from the stove to a table began to sing. He was singing in Spanish and his good light tenor rose across the room. Nobody stopped work, but it was quieter now downstairs, at a little after two. Upstairs, lunch was under way and the restaurant was jammed; down here, there was hardly a sound except the sweet romantic voice of the young man with the onion soup.

"Come on, let's do this, we'll cook gumbo," Shane said.

By now I knew my way to Shane's office, and he was waiting for me, a blue and white apron tied around his waist. Shane had seemed a little withdrawn, almost dour, when we'd first met, but I had mistaken shyness for reticence. Now he was smiling and talking about the gumbo he was going to cook. He handed me an apron, which I put on. I knew I looked like, if not a fool, a complete imposter. I was no kind of cook. I followed Shane into the kitchen. "It takes time. You'll get bored probably," he said.

A few of the prep guys were starting on dinner, one of them—a red, white, and blue scarf tied around his head—seasoning duck breasts that he had arranged on a large flat tray. A rubbery dark pink octopus had been set to soak in a large bowl of water.

I had asked Shane if I could watch him cook something, and he had suggested the gumbo. A favorite of his, he was planning to put it on the menu as a special.

One of the sous chefs had put out the ingredients on a table. Two pounds of smoked bacon, a pound and a half each of tasso ham and andouille sausage. Shane started slicing and dicing, turning it into a small mountain of pork cubes with the deft flick of his knife.

"Your knife?" I asked.

"Yes," says Shane. "Though I'm less obsessive. There was a time when I slept with my knives. This one is Japanese, four hundred bucks."

Gumbo, the way he made it, consisted of the meat he was cutting and the Trinity, the holiest of New Orleans ingredients, a mixture of celery, onion, and green pepper. On the table was a pile of the vegetables, already finely diced. Also: butter, flour, okra, garlic, and hot sauce ("I like Crystal," Shane said), and the filé powder, critical to Creole cooking, a spicy herb made from the dried and ground leaves of the North American sassafras tree. A big pot with four quarts of chicken stock was on the stove, but, of course, to make the gumbo Shane needed a roux.

"A lot of people make roux with just butter and AP flour," said Shane. "I like to use the pig fat, too. The roux is key. It's equal parts by weight of flour and fat. It's a thickening agent."

"Any kind of flour?"

He laughed. "You don't know what AP flour is? All-purpose. Out of a bag. Like from the grocery store? When the roux's hot, it's like napalm and it will literally burn a hole in your arm. At CIA . . ." He started his story.

Shane's alma mater was the Culinary Institute of America. "They always tell the story about the boy who ate the roux. And they're like, 'Oh, you know, we had a student, and he didn't know what roux was. And it was roux day, we were making roux for the first time, and it smelled so appetizing that he decided to take a big spoonful of it and eat it right out of the pot.'"

Shane was loving it, he spun it out, he imitated the boy who ate the roux. "His tongue fell off. It was incinerated to a crisp." I was laughing, and Shane was laughing, laughing and enjoying the effect; so completely at home, in the kitchen, his former shyness melted away.

"You believed it," he said to me about the apocryphal story. "Didn't you?" This made him laugh even more. I was beginning to see that Shane liked joking around and fooling with you. He feigned a throwaway manner when he cooked, as if it was easy, as if anyone could do it. Something in Shane, who was intensely private, made him feel that to make an overt fuss was not proper.

The things that made him a great chef were personal; he kept much of his feelings about his art to himself. If the food he made was great, if people liked it, if his bosses were pleased, that seemed enough.

Against one wall of the kitchen were two huge stoves, one French style with a flat top, the other with six burners; both had ovens; both were made by Jade, which made large heavy-duty commercial stoves. Shane heaved a thirty-five-quart pot onto the flat top. He put all the diced meat in and turned up the heat.

"I left part of my liver in New Orleans," he said. As with so many chefs, it was a city he loved and from which he had acquired a passion for its raunchy, quintessential dish, the rich gumbo that was adored by everyone and was also a symbol of the city's messed-up, mixed-up history. Shane, a man for whom the pig was a gift from the gods, who competed in Memphis every year at the big barbecue cook-off, inevitably made his gumbo rich with pork.

Rendering the fat was the next task, and to keep the pork from burning or sticking to the sides, Shane picked up a paddle you could steer a canoe with and began pushing the meat around.

"Come here and smell this," he told me. "This smells really good, this is going to be rib-sticking wonderful when it's done." Shane inhaled the sizzling pork, a look of bliss on his face.

It smelled wonderful. The aroma was like bacon frying but better; this was the essence of pig. Inside the pot, the rendered fat was the color of liquid gold. Putting the canoe paddle aside, Shane added two pounds of plain unsalted butter and stirred it until it began to melt. "The butter gives it a better flavor," he said, stirring some more and straining the mixture, putting the cooked crispy pork into a large pan on the table. It would go in later. The rendered fat went back on the burner. He began adding the flour—AP, as I now knew.

"OK, look in the pot now," he said. "With a normal roux, you just mix up the butter and flour, cook it a couple of minutes, and you're done. For a gumbo, you keep cooking it until the color changes, and you get to something like chestnut, then mahogany, and that gives a depth of flavor. You stir every couple minutes for around twenty-five minutes. You can smell it, it smells nutty, it has a texture like wet concrete, beyond peanut butter. OK?"

I said OK, and he put in the Trinity, the onion, celery, and green pepper dice, then added garlic and jalapeño peppers. "I let that residual heat kind of aromatize the garlic."

"How much longer?"

"I told you. It takes time. This is why we don't make little pots of gumbo. This will make enough for about forty people. Chicken stock next," he said. "I add hot chicken stock because if you add cold stock it takes longer. So I'm just stirring until it thickens up and goes from broth to thick-as-milkshake thick. You have to keep stirring or the gluten in the flour will burn, so you stir until all the flour breaks up and none of it sticks to the bottom. About thirty minutes, until it's coming to a boil, and when it does we'll add half the meat and the chicken and let that cook for about thirty minutes more. When the chicken is cooked, we'll add the okra that I cut into small slices, season it with Crystal hot sauce, salt and pepper, cook another twenty minutes, throw in some shrimp if we feel like it, cook another minute or two, and it's done, except for . . ."

"What now?"

"Eat it. Over rice. With cold beer to drink."

Shane fixed two bowls of the gumbo. Standing at the table, we ate it. It was spicy and deep, thick but not sticky, redolent of the crispy pork and the liquid fat, the hot sauce, the garlic, all somehow magically layered together in a way that I could also taste each of them distinctly. The guys in the kitchen gathered around for a taste. Shane sampled the gumbo again and smiled briefly. "Not bad," he said.

Frank Ortega had arrived at two o'clock. He was the sous chef for the evening shift, which usually began around two. He had already checked on the tarte du jour—it was poached pear in red wine tonight—and the raw bar.

Sometimes when Frank Ortega was downstairs, checking ingredients for Shane or doing certain familiar chores, he said his mind wandered a little to the beautiful furniture he was making. It was slow going. Frank was trying to reclaim the lessons his father, a construction worker, had taught him about craftsmanship when he was a kid in Mexico, before he left for America. A friend who had already settled on Staten Island bought him a ticket. Frank had never been on a plane. It was his first time out of Mexico.

When he arrived, he stayed with his friend on Staten Island. He was seventeen. He didn't speak English.

It was 1990. Without English, the only work Frank could find was washing dishes for a catering company. He got lucky. The Italian chef at the catering company took an interest in him. It was the first time Frank had cooked anything at all; in Mexico, his mother did the cooking. Now he paid attention; he watched how his boss made meat sauce and meatballs; he got a chance—washing salads, then cutting vegetables. "Once he gave me the opportunity, I took advantage of it," says Frank of his first boss.

"By then I was very good with cutting—because they would do small garnishes. You know, they would make a swan out of an apple for display, or flowers. I saw my original chef making tomato sauce, that's sort of what I still do now. And I've tasted all different sauces, and that's the basic, and I still use the same recipe."

Everyone in the kitchen spoke Spanish, no time for practicing English. Instead, Frank went to the library at night. He was on his way. He paid close attention to what went on in the kitchen, too.

Frank moved up. He studied. He learned. Whenever somebody asked if he had worked the line, he said, "Give me a chance," and before long he was working in an Italian restaurant, where he made all the pasta, the raviolis. He learned how to cook fish; he worked brunches and poached eggs and made hollandaise and home fries.

His boss often described all the big-deal restaurants in the city—Manhattan was always The City if you were in an outer borough. (I was reminded of a very young Tony Bennett, growing up in Queens, looking across at the Manhattan skyline.)

So Frank got the ferry. He went into Manhattan and had dinner in a nice restaurant, he told me. Smiling nostalgically, Frank said, "And that was fun."

He wanted more. He read up. He read about the famous restaurants in the city. His English was fluent now and he sent out résumés. He got a job at Fresco on Madison Avenue. Frank had made it into The City.

The chef was a screamer; Frank was intimidated at first. He stuck it out, but he wanted a job as a sous chef. He had worked the line; there was nothing he couldn't do in a restaurant kitchen.

When Geoffrey Zakarian took over Patroon on Forty-Sixth Street, Frank got his chance.

"I used to open the restaurant at six in the morning, and I had to be there until eight, nine—five, six days. But it was good, because I did the ordering, I did some of the line, I would expedite one day, I'd oversee everything that was going on," Frank said. "Patroon got three stars from the *New York Times*. So that was good. I learned."

Zakarian left Patroon to open his own place, promising Frank a job in due course, but Frank couldn't sit around not working, so he went to Balthazar for what he thought would be a short spell. It was early days and the place was jammed.

"We were always packed with people, so there were orders and orders and orders, and it would just stay full throughout the whole night." Frank paused to look around the kitchen where we were talking. "People here know what they're doing, several guys have been here at least seventeen years. Sure, there was some screaming. Sometimes I did the screaming," said Frank with a mild smile. "It's all mellowed out now. Shane is very, very mellow."

Frank's own ambition was to rise to chef de cuisine, to run his own kitchen. There was a certain confidence about him; he knew he was going to make it.

I asked if he thought many of the other cooks were as ambitious. He was thoughtful. "I think sometimes people are happy just making their wages and they are comfortable within their community and their family," he said thoughtfully. "I try to encourage people to learn and to do other things, but a lot of the time, people don't want to learn other things or don't want to see other things.

"We have a couple of older guys, one of them that preps and he's been here from day one. His sons worked here, and they finished school. One of them is going to the Police Academy already. You know? So it changes."

Frank looked around, a little preoccupied, I knew he had to get back to work. I put away my notebook. I knew that Frank and his wife had a house in Bayonne, New Jersey, and I asked if he had any children. "A daughter," he said, and told me that, having graduated from Columbia University, where she also got her MA, she was waiting to start her PhD in Art History, possibly in Chicago.

Then Frank told me his daughter was born when he had just arrived, when he was seventeen, and that her mother had died in childbirth. For two or three years after that, while he learned English and learned to cook, Frank had taken care of the baby on his own.

He smiled. "Things change," he said again.

Around three in the afternoon, the evening cooks began arriving and started their own prep for dinner. By now, Frank was slicing creamy onions paper-thin. A cook in a hairnet removed a tray from the oven, and the chickens on it were bronze and shining from the butter under the skin and the olive oil the outside of the birds had been painted with. These birds were three-quarters roasted and would go up to the main kitchen to be finished to order.

If you ordered the roast chicken, before it was carved, it was brought to the table to show off its plump, bronze loveliness. As you reached for it, it was whisked away back to the kitchen for carving and plating and the addition of creamy, rich mashed potatoes. My friend Jan didn't believe this, she believed that there was what she called "the show chicken." "I swear it's always the same chicken," Jan would say. "I swear to you I can tell, this is their show bird, the presentation fowl, and the ones you eat stay in the oven until they're carved. Trust me."

I still haven't told her that I know different now.

In the kitchen, thick cuts of beef dusted with cracked black pepper were removed from another oven. Still raw inside, they would be grilled upstairs. Around the prep area, the cooks were picking up speed.

It was these elaborate preparations that let Balthazar serve hundreds of meals at a speed that made customers happy and also meant a more profitable night. If there was something to celebrate behind the scenes at Balthazar, the guys who really deserved the kudos, it was here; the prep kitchens downstairs were where the hard work got done.

The salad man, Fausto Perez, put an enormous bunch of yellowy green frisée lettuce in an industrial-size red plastic salad spinner, dried it, removed it, cut it, bundled it into a stainless container, then swaddled it in plastic wrap. On the counter were big leaves of dark kale, a bunch of pale dill, piles of bright green asparagus; all were quickly washed and chopped. Mushrooms were sautéed. Bright red and yellow peppers cut in pieces, baby carrots orange and glowing with oil went into a stainless steel bowl. Gerry was looking into a pot of soup he had made, stirring and looking at it, but thinking about some new oysters he had sampled and wondering if he should order them for Balthazar.

As the food was prepared, it was packed in plastic crates to be carried up to the kitchen. It was hard, repetitive work, but for the most part the men got on with it looking reasonably content. Unless I was kidding myself; there was no way for me to really tell what they were thinking. I didn't speak the language.

At other restaurants there was a lot more resentment, even disdain for the management, a feeling from the workers that "they're owed," as one ex–general manager said to me. "That they're owed plenty, and so there's a lot of 'stick it to the man' kind of thing."

I asked Jerry about it; he was always open to questions. He told me that when there was a problem, little groups formed and you'd hear the guys mumbling, hear the discontent. Guys with their heads down in clusters around the kitchens would grumble plenty. It was a way of blowing off steam, said Jerry. "They stand around for a while," he said. "And then they go back to work."

"Cogs in a machine, no ambition," a long-gone Balthazar manager had told me with careless condescension. But this was not a machine; the men were not cogs; these were professionals who knew precisely what they were doing and why. I must have shown up in the prep kitchens a hundred times, just stumbling down the metal stairs at odd times of the day; nobody knew I was coming. Clearly I was an outsider, but I had the chef's permission to hang around. It didn't take long to realize that people doing hard and concentrated work didn't much care about your presence unless you were a real pain in the ass.

Most of the time the guys in the kitchens went on working efficiently, one or two smiling, a few chatting to one another. The men I got to know a little would look up and smile or nod. Once or twice we shared the misery of the state of the Yankees.

Peter Nelson, the photographer I worked with, was also an experienced documentary cameraman who had been in some very tough places. He loved cooking, he baked a mean blueberry pie, and he was a volunteer fireman in the Catskills. A big guy with a mustache and no pretensions, Peter fit in with the guys downstairs. After a month, he said to me, "You know what I think about the guys here? I think they really do give a shit."

Against the opposite wall, another cook was making bar snacks, slicing Balthazar's dark rye bread very thin. He coated the slices with olive oil and Parmesan and grilled them. More cooks arrived.

The kitchen filled up. I tried not to barge around, or slip, or crash into a guy carrying a huge blackened pot of French onion soup.

Shane watched me, laughing.

I got the feeling Shane understood that I wasn't crazy about cooking, that I was preternaturally lazy when it came to the prep, the slicing and dicing, then watching things on the stove and waiting. Either I sliced my finger, or I burned myself. I don't much like cooking, to tell the truth. I figure you have it or you don't.

My pal Steven, who was half Italian, would simply peer into the fridge, pull out a handful of magic—some dill, some cilantro, a few old tomatoes, a clove of garlic, a piece of mozzarella—put the pasta in a pot and whip up something fabulous. He did it with wonderful ease and real style. Or my best friend, Alice, who lavishly enjoyed sitting down at night with her tattered volume of Julia Child's *Mastering the Art of French Cooking*, making dishes from it with exquisite patience. This was the kind of detailed work she adored, and as a result she made some paradisiacal chicken in cream sauce, a salmon mousse light as air, duck for my birthdays, and cherry clafouti.

I always loved having people over, and with so many good places to buy stuff near me I never had to cook much. I always felt a little guilty until Nigella Lawson, the British cookery writer, saved my bacon. "If you don't like cooking, why bother?" she said. "Why cook when you can shop?"

Shane and Frank and the others in the Balthazar kitchens cooked for a living. Few if any, except Shane, had gone to cooking school. They had learned on the job. Frank Ortega had spent years washing dishes and learning how to make a rose out of a radish. When he discovered a talent for cooking, he persevered for the love of it, but mostly it was about making money and a better life.

Those guys in the kitchen made me see how hard it was to cook really well. They tried, God knows, but they couldn't teach me to do it; I didn't have the patience, but then, maybe that was because I didn't have to.

CHAPTER 17

CHEF

S hane McBride was a man who loved books. Like everybody in a restaurant, he worried about the menu, about ingredients and prices, and he spent hours on the phone fixing things, listening to his bosses; but even while he was doing it, feet on the desk in his office, he might be glancing at the computer to check on the George Orwell. Shane had a passion for first editions of authors he loved: George Orwell, Jim Harrison, Hemingway. He knew he spent too much on modern firsts, but he couldn't help himself. When he spotted a first edition of one of his authors, he wanted it, had to have it.

Having collected several of Salman Rushdie's books, *Midnight's Children* and *Shame* especially, he heard one day that Rushdie, a Balthazar regular, was in for lunch. Shane took the books upstairs and asked Rushdie to sign them. "I was moved," Salman Rushdie told me. "He had collected first editions of these books, and it was just nice."

Shane and I discovered that we shared huge affection for John D. MacDonald, the late mystery writer. Nobody wrote better about Florida, where Shane had grown up. I could see Shane as a character in a MacDonald book, living alongside the writer's hero Travis McGee on his boat, the *Busted Flush*. Living there, cooking, maybe setting up a floating bistro.

Above Shane's desk was a bulletin board with handwritten recipes tacked to it. There were rows of clipboards, schedules, recipes, and while we talked, he took one or the other down and scribbled some notes with a fountain pen in small, neat handwriting, like the Catholic schoolboy he once was.

In the coming week, Shane was putting several new items on the menu, and this required writing out a recipe and making it with the other cooks for a couple of weeks until they got it right. An appetizer of octopus and radishes, sliced thinner than paper, dressed with olive oil, had been added; it was delicious. So was the English pea risotto, a dish I loved.

Over time, Shane's office had silted up with *stuff*: food mixers in need of repair, a broken TV set, a box of hairnets. A couple of copper chafing dishes hung on the wall. Over Shane's head, alongside the blue bike, another bicycle had appeared and was hanging upside down.

From the first, I'd always thought Shane looked like he could have played bass in a pickup band, and as it turned out, he did play a little, but there wasn't much time. He had two kids who came up from Florida on weekends, and charity events he cooked for, and a pop-up barbecue joint in Brooklyn and another one in the works on Bleecker Street.

In his spare time, he competed annually in the epic Memphis barbecue competition with other good old boy cooks who showed up with their pickups, hauling refrigerators, smokers, and the spicy sauces and marinades for various cuts of heart-stopping barbecued meat.

Shane was the only child of a single mother who ran a small business in Florida and did it successfully. She was a terrible cook. When he was eight, he started fooling around with food, messing in the kitchen, looking for spices, hoarding barbecue sauces and other condiments in the hope of fixing up whatever his mother cooked. I had the feeling that he was always a bit of a loner; he gave the impression of a man who had been a solitary kid.

Cooking shows on TV held him transfixed, and he claimed it was Julia Child and *The Galloping Gourmet* that got him hooked. "They would say, 'Here's a chicken, here's an onion, you can make something delicious,'" Shane said. "I inherited a pretty strong work ethic from my mom and my grandfather who raised me." As soon as he started cooking in professional kitchens, he found that he loved the discipline. It fed his ambition. "If you learned the rules and methods, you could get on, you could rise up and do interesting things. I got that even when I was a teenager. It wasn't like the other menial jobs I'd had where none of the guys gave a shit." "Giving a shit" was always high praise around Balthazar.

While he was still a teenager, Shane worked at various local kitchens until, when he was nineteen, he got work at Narcissus in West Palm Beach; he worked his way up there from garde-manger to sous chef.

To get his first job at a good restaurant Shane had gambled with a five-gallon bucket of lychee nuts. Retired for most of Shane's life, his grandfather fancied himself a kind of gentleman farmer and grew lychees and mangoes and other exotica on two acres in South Florida. Shane was nineteen when he saw an ad in the paper from a chef looking for exotic fruits.

"I took the pail of lychee nuts to him and I'm like, 'I'll give you this for free if you let me come in and try to get a job here.' And he was like, 'That's awesome.'"

The job was at the Four Seasons. It turned him on to the glories of good food.

"It was an awesome experience. It was a great restaurant. I think the chef lives in Thailand now, but he was, like, the president of the local agricultural society. He was a big gardener, and we grew tons of stuff on the property of the hotel, so it was a great introduction into farm-to-table type of stuff." As a result, when he arrived at Baltha-zar, Shane was already much more conscious of seasonal dishes and local produce than his predecessors had been.

The Culinary Institute of America in New York's Hudson Val-ley, where Shane got his degree, was probably America's preeminent cooking school. It started in 1947 in Connecticut as a vocational school for returning World War II vets. By the 1970s, it had moved to its present location in Hyde Park, about forty-five minutes north of the city, and in the next couple of decades, as interest in food and cooking exploded, transformed itself into an institution that gives bachelor's and master's degrees. Shane told me that, as much as anything, he had loved the history of food and cooking and the books by the likes of Brillat-Savarin that went with it.

By the time he got to Balthazar, Shane had worked for some of the best chefs in New York—for Charlie Palmer at Aureole and for Tom Colicchio at Craft Restaurants, and most of all for Christian Delouvrier at Lespinasse, whom he considers his mentor.

He also opened—and closed—his own restaurant. In 2010, Shane arrived at Balthazar. He started out working as chef de cuisine under Riad Nasr and Lee Hanson, who had opened Balthazar with Keith McNally and who had invented the menu, or at least adapted the classic brasserie dishes: the brandade, the onion soup, the escargots.

I knew Riad a little. He was dark and handsome, and I used to see him at Bicycle Habitat on Lafayette and we'd make cracks about this or that. With McNally, Nasr and his partner, Hanson, opened Balthazar, Pastis, Schiller's Liquor Bar, and Minetta Tavern; Minetta became virtually their own operation, and the reviews were spectacular.

And then, in 2013, they left. The departure of the two chefs shook the New York food business with the kind of tiny aftershocks that kept everybody guessing what had happened. Had there been dis-sent? Did they want a TV show, more fame? Were they pissed off, or was there a misunderstanding over an air ticket to London? In New York City, these things mattered. The food world—the world of chefs and critics and cookbook writers—was big, it made money, and on this island devoted to commerce, there was plenty of competition for the dough.

The rumors flew around for a little while, but nobody was saying or telling, though when I ran into Riad at the Apple Store in SoHo one afternoon, he was as charming as ever. I asked what he and Lee were up to, but he merely smiled and said, "We have some things in the works."

The challenge for Shane when he took over was keeping as much as 60 percent of the original dishes without going mad from boredom or driving away the regulars who had a taste for something different. The classics had not changed since Balthazar first opened.

Anna Wintour, the Artistic Director of Condé Nast and Editor in Chief of *Vogue*, who was a creature of habit, said, "I always return to the same places." A woman with the choice of any New York restaurant, she went to Balthazar as often as possible. "Balthazar is basically the only restaurant I go to regularly. Keith is so intelligent about the atmosphere he creates at his restaurants—they are comforting and always feel familiar."

"You can't mess around too much," Shane told me. "You can't take off the roast chicken or onion soup, and why would you want to?" So he made them better. Or, as he put it, "I just fool around a little with them. When I got here, some of the techniques of cooking were dubious," he said. "I changed the short ribs. They used to put them into a big pot and simmer them and scoop them out. I changed it. We marinate them for a week and cook them slower in an oven, and we press them so they're all consistently sized and they cut easy. So that was the big advantage to me changing the menu, making the classics better and adding a few new things, like the soft shell crab BLT."

This was a dish I loved the first time Shane put it on the menu.

The crunchy and sweet crabs, the creamy mayo, crisp lettuce, and smoky bacon layered between thick slabs of homemade bread played off each other in a way that was both comforting and sumptuous. It's the transcendent BLT.

In his recipes, in whatever he said, when he talked about it, I heard a man who loved food, who loved eating it and cooking it. To Shane, recipes, dishes, ingredients, these were all invested with their own singular flavors, regions, history. Even though I was no kind of cook, he was patient and funny, too; when I asked him how best to make a soft-boiled egg, he quipped, "First get a hen."

Over time, I got to like Shane a lot. We fell into a friendly relationship. He cracked jokes and looked at me with feigned exasperation when I asked questions about cooking that would have embarrassed an eight-year-old. I played the older sister, reminding him that there was a Tiffany's around the corner where he could easily get a ring for Jen, his marvelous girlfriend.

I admired Shane for his lack of fuss at work, his obsession with certain books, the way he bought art and crammed the walls of his house with the pictures he loved, and his surprising lack of self-importance. This was no celebrity chef who required veneration. Maybe he hid it from me, but I didn't think so.

When I first met him early in the morning, he'd said he was just a "cracker"—said it twice, actually, casting himself as a good old boy redneck. It was just shtick, a way of dismissing any possible pretension. As I got to know him, as I talked to the others about him—his cooks, Erin, some of the waiters, too—I saw that everyone had time for Shane. In his lack of pretense, in his crazy sense of humor, he was simply a good guy. Jen told me that he was a real boy scout, first on the scene if somebody needed help.

There was also the stainless steel professionalism, the way he treated his guys in the kitchen, and his love of food. Jen told me, "On rare days off, he sits in his leather chair reading stacks of cookbooks from his library for inspiration. He will turn and say to me, 'Babe, look at this dish.'

"He's super-serious and focused and yet silly at the same time, like his signature argyle socks. Shane isn't that cocky, celebrity-hungry chef. He wants to make nice food. That's how he shares what he loves, his talent with others," said Jen.

By the time Shane became executive chef at Balthazar, it was a gorgeous, expensive, famous restaurant, listed on *National Geographic*'s "Ten Things to Do in New York City." I felt that somehow Shane's cooking gave the menu a tweak it needed, with more seasonal food and inventive dishes like the soft shell crab BLT. His presence somehow also helped retain the things I had always loved about Balthazar—the robust good French food, the unfussy friendliness of it, the way you were treated well no matter who you were.

I had eaten in hundreds, maybe thousands, of restaurants. Quite a lot had good food. Nice décor. The essence of the really special ones was always the visceral sense that somebody is at home. Like Shane is at Balthazar.

CHAPTER 18

BALTHAZAR INC.

There were times when I was downstairs in the kitchens for a while and hardly aware at all of the outside world. It was a little like being in a Vegas casino where there was no daylight. No TV, no radio, no windows either, everybody downstairs at Balthazar was intent on the work. Duck breasts cooked, oysters shucked, spuds mashed, grapefruit halved; the floors were washed, the chefs and cooks and dishwashers went on with their chores, and the only news I heard was chatter about family or baseball, and it was all in Spanish.

I'd feel as if I had been on the moon—or farther—and then emerge and discover the world had gone nuts. The Brexit vote. Donald Trump. Terror and death in the twenty-four-hour news cycle. Still, when I got out, there was a woman eating a chocolate éclair in front of Balthazar Bakery and a pair of expensive mommies pushing a pair of drooling babies up Spring Street.

Around three in the afternoon, after I'd cooked the gumbo with Shane—watched him cook it—I left Balthazar and walked around the block to 568 Broadway, where Keith McNally had his offices and where the reservations crew worked. A twelve-story terra-cotta and brick building with a gorgeously elaborate front door, it had been designed by George Browne Post, an architect who trained in the Beaux Arts tradition and pushed the boundaries of design around New York City in the late nineteenth and early twentieth centuries. Finished in 1897, 568 Broadway was built for H. O. Havemeyer, a sugar baron and art patron. Those rich guys liked their buildings big, and they wanted innovation, and so New York was built.

I realized I had never paid much attention to the building or its provenance before this.

I went into 568 Broadway, through the marble lobby. The elevator stopped at four. I went in. Inside the McNally offices, I looked out the window to the chaos on Broadway and across the street to the Prada shop, and only then did I get it: this had been my father's office. I knew the lobby when I saw it, but I had never been to Keith McNally's headquarters. So I was here, back where my pop had worked for decades, where his printing business had been.

He had sold up more than twenty-five years ago. No printing presses left, of course, or those first computerized machines that had replaced them, that left him astonished. There were no piles of cream-colored boxes ready for shipping; no guys at the back wiping their hands on dirty rags or stopping for coffee; my father was not at his desk near the front window, puffing on his pipe, trying to decide between the Rouault and the Picasso for the Christmas cards he made every year.

In the main room now was a long table used for conferences or lunch, filing cabinets pushed against the walls where a few French travel posters hung. In a large adjacent area, Vinnie DeFrancesco and several others sat plugged into phones and computers, ordering chickens or anchovies or butter from Vermont. At the far end of the room sat Erin, and on his way out now was Arnold Rossman. Arnold, who shared Erin's duties as deputy director of the company, had been the general manager of Minetta Tavern, gone on to Augustine, and was the most glamorous dresser in the company. His suits, shoes, and waistcoats were gorgeous. Arnold always looked a bit of an Edwardian dandy.

In the back of the offices was the room where the reservationists were at work. It was three in the afternoon and the phones were ringing like crazy, people wanting reservations. At least now the phones were computerized so the operators could look up whoever was calling. But to the surprise of many, most reservations are made over the phone. From time to time, a caller failing to get a table or a friendly enough response ran riot with angry tweets or sulky posts about how dreadful the phone experience had been, which was code for "didn't get what I wanted." Most of the time.

In the beginning, the reservations system had been a problem. Balthazar opened and people got crazy and they called and were told there wasn't a table for a month and some showed up anyway. It was pandemonium.

Judi Wong, the owner of Café Cluny, helped open Balthazar. "Everybody was really knocking down the doors. I remember Naomi Campbell, hers was the first cell phone I ever saw," said Judi. "People lied to get in. As soon as we opened, it was crazy. People would call my personal number. 'I'm so-and-so, I'm friends with so-and-so, I need a reservation for blah blah.' We caught somebody saying they were the Red Hot Chili Peppers one night. And I think Keith called them back, mimicking them, you know his sense of humor is out of this world."

A private number was handed out, to friends and to the famous, who were often the same anyway, and then that became the most desirable thing you could imagine—people were virtually bribing people or threatening them to get hold of it. Thing was, and is, it wasn't enough to get the number; your name had to be on the list as well.

"Do you have it?" "Did you get it?" It was insane, and then insanity grew because somebody—an assistant at *Vogue*, the way I remember it—gave the number to the *Post*. The phone system went into overload and crashed. Four thousand reservations were lost. The private (or secret!) number became legend. The Number! In fact, during the first few years when I only went for breakfast, somebody said to me, "Don't you ever come for dinner?" I said, "How do I get a table?"

I stood for a few minutes and listened to the men and women working the phones. On their screens, they could check if it was a VIP on the phone. VIPs were marked A, AA, AAA, although the last was almost impossible to come by. There were never more than a couple of hundred Triple As.

"Hello, can I help you?" The reservationists always answered the phones with polite interest, *This is Max* or *John-boy* or *Amy*.

"Of course," Amy was saying. "Let me see, four at Balthazar on Friday, what time? Can you do 7:45? Can't promise you a booth, but we'll try." This went on every day from nine in the morning.

"The reservationists are actually the first point of contact," a former Balthazar manager told me. "From this moment when you call up, when you have anything to do with the restaurant, you are held in the palm of Balthazar's hand, or that was always the idea."

A restaurant might tell you there was no such thing as a "bad" table, that all of their tables were the same, all locations marvelous; no New Yorker ever believed this. We were always wary of too good a thing, we always *knew* that there was always something better and somebody else had it. It was in the bloodstream.

Balthazar always looked gorgeous, always served great food, but how much sweeter getting a table had been when it took a certain effort or a good connection, best of all when you could report this to your friends. In New York, bragging rights, the very act of getting a table, a theater ticket, was the addition of some particularly rare spice.

Interestingly, the best piece of advice I had ever been given on this subject was the simplest trick in the book: *Be nice.* If somebody wanted one of those big comfy red booths at the back of Balthazar (numbers 60, 61, 62), charm often helped. A big *Hello* to the voice at the end of the phone, a *How you doing?*

"Demanding, crazed, screaming customers rarely succeed," somebody told me. "If you're pleasant and let the reservationist know you think he or she is a human being, you're a lot more likely to get that table you want."

Balthazar left its imprint on James Weichert, though he had long been in a different business. "You think you're getting special treatment, because they know you here and pull out all the stops," he said. "But the reality is they do this three hundred sixty-five days a year for every customer." He added that, "part of the deal is that no matter if you're in the 60s or one of those tables where you come in the door and you've got people's butts right up against your table, you get the same level of service. Who wants to be sat in Siberia? Or treated as a second-class citizen when you're spending two hundred bucks on dinner—are you kidding me? So you never feel like you're second-class."

I admit that when I first got into the 60s, I was kind of, well, *chuffed*, as the Brits say; no, I was like, *Wow! I'm in the big leagues.* The booth was so comfy. You could throw your coats on the back of it next to the pretty flower-shaped sconces. You had a perfect little nest from which to view the room.

It was always nice, but getting into the 60s was not exactly a means to a Nobel Prize, or even tickets to a hot show, as Rona Middleberg—she never fell for this kind of thing—reminded me a little drily from time to time.

It made me think of the time long ago when I called my mother up, wildly excited, hardly making sense. "You got into what?" she said down the phone. "You got into Harvard?"

"Not exactly," I replied.

"What, then?" she said.

"Studio 54," I said.

She wasn't impressed.

• • •

568 Broadway was the building where McNally Inc. had its headquarters. From here the empire was run: Balthazar; Minetta Tavern;
Schiller's Liquor Bar; Lucky Strike; the new one, Augustine. Pastis had closed when the building was sold, but a new version was
opening on Gansevoort Street. There were also Morandi, McNally's
Italian place in the West Village; the bakery on Spring Street; and
the bakery in New Jersey. All the reservations were handled by the
crew at 568. And at least some of the London operation (or Balthazar
Deux, as I liked to think of it) was also run from these offices.

The space itself had little that was corporate about it. Near the
reservations area, in a small office with a big window and a green
plant, was Roberta Delice, the CEO of the McNally operations. In
2010, when Keith had gone to live in London, Roberta became his
consigliere, the woman who had his ear and his trust. She was in
charge of pretty much everything at all the restaurants. Her energy was daunting, and she was known for running in Prospect Park
with her dogs. Slim, wiry, handsome, she had been born in Italy, had
worked for Keith for decades, and was devoted to him.

Roberta had come to New York when she was a young woman
and she more or less fell into restaurant work. For a while, she
worked as a waiter at Balthazar, commuting from Brooklyn, where
she raised her children. I had heard she was also a phenomenal cook.
Shane told me that Roberta had the best taste memory he had ever
encountered. "She can sample a sauce and a year later remember
exactly how it tasted and probably what has changed if there is a
difference," said Shane. "It's very, very useful."

Talking fluently about the company, Roberta was keen to note
that the main goal was for everybody to work as a team; she was
insistent on the fact that everybody was equal, that nobody was allowed to feel superior. She had a thorough and detailed understanding of all the issues at stake.

Financial issues were a plague on any New York restaurant, and one that was successful was lucky to make 12 to 15 percent profit. Rents in New York City were an enormous problem, as were the skyrocketing food prices Vinnie had mentioned.

From the beginning, Balthazar had been a very profitable baby, a restaurant that defied all the rules, that flew in the face of business school wisdom or those books, and they were legion (I had fallen asleep reading one of them), on how to run a successful restaurant.

A decent run was five years, they said, though most closed sooner. As far as I could find out, Balthazar took in around $20 to $25 million a year, but financial details were hard to get (rather like pulling teeth, no drugs), and these changed constantly. Roughly, it seemed about 24 percent was spent on food, 32 to 35 percent on labor and benefits. Operating expenses ran about 8 to 10 percent, and this included credit card fees, as well as everything from cleaning supplies to bar supplies, fees for music rights to ASCAP and BMI, flowers, transport, little items like blenders, pots and pans, ice machine rentals, parking, garbage removal, gas, water, electrical. Another 8 percent went to administrative costs, 3 percent for repairs and maintenance, 12 to 15 percent for rent, and anything left was profit.

While I was writing, for instance, the whole restaurant business was in an upheaval over tips. Roberta made clear that this was not going to be resolved easily. Some people in the business wanted change in the way front-of-house staff were paid for a long time; to some, the system of tips as the main source of pay made for tremendously unequal opportunity for the kitchen staff.

Apart from a few senior people—the chef, sous chefs, pastry chefs—almost everybody in the back of house (the cooks, dishwashers, porters, etc.) was paid by the hour, forty hours a week, pegged to the minimum wage, which was going up to fifteen dollars an hour in New York state by 2018. Some of the back-of-house staff made close to the minimum; others, depending on how long they'd been around, a bit more. Unlike the front of house, though, there was no basis on which they might make serious money, because only the front of house got tips.

And so, claimed those in favor of changing the system, everybody would be paid wages or salaries. Trouble was, to pay waiters the equivalent of what they made on the tip system, especially at a restaurant like Balthazar, could break the bank. As it was, some waiters were making, on a good night, as much as seventy-five bucks an hour.

All tips were pooled at Balthazar; all the waiters, bussers, runners got a share that had been worked out by points. (Bussers got about half what the waiters did.) Those who made customers happy or had charm got better tips. If a waiter sold a good wine or an extra dessert, the bill was bigger and so, too, the tip. In a sense this made them mini entrepreneurs.

For those who worked at Balthazar, the tip system was, of course, a good thing; you just made more money. If the management had to pay salaries or wages to equal it, they'd have to raise prices yet again.

The European system, by which waiters worked on salary and were not tipped, was, claimed those in favor, more equitable; neither front nor back of house was tipped. Tipping, it was said by many Europeans, was patronizing, insecure, and offensive.

No matter how it all panned out, tipped servers or not, it was going to be, Erin said, "a shit show."

Roberta laid it out in great detail, the percentages of tips earned by each member of staff. Clearly she had a fine grip on the tiniest details.

To some, Roberta was a brilliantly effective, competent, and attentive executive. Staff, waiters, managers, and others whom she had hired were faithful to her and fond of her. Others thought her bossy.

She was the boss, and this was a company with a lot of talented people and big personalities. In a few, she induced fear. And then there were those who adored her.

"I love Roberta," said Massiel Pagan. "She gave me the chance."

Massiel, the morning waitress who had looked after us at breakfast for years, had gone on to work lunch and dinner before moving permanently to Florida. She was visiting her family in New York, though, so we went out for coffee, and she said, "I was born in Brooklyn, but I had been out in California, came back, and I'm working but I want to get into Balthazar where my father, Rene, worked." Rene was one of the longtime bussers. "So I say to Roberta, 'Can you get me in?' and she intervened for me, and says, 'Oh, you're Rene's daughter.' Some of the staff were sassy with me, some would be quick to stab you in the back. Riad, the chef, flipped out when I called the puff pastry 'bread.'"

"I gave my whole thirties to Balthazar," said Massiel. "The stress level was terrible. The wines, the grapes, the pairings, I was known as the bitch, but it taught me good. I'm the lead server now where I work in Florida. Balthazar was a great place to learn. Josh, my son, works in Balthazar Bakery."

I had been happy to see Massi. She was a reminder of all those long-ago breakfasts.

"I remember you guys," she said. "You, Steven, and Rona. Everybody used to be afraid of you guys because you were there with Dick Robinson."

This wasn't just surprising; it shook me up. It made me realize how naïve we had been. We had thought of Massiel as a friend, a charming young woman we liked, whose welfare was our concern, her life of interest to us. To her, though, we had, at least in part, been scary people; worse, we belonged to a different class; we were friends with the top dog. That I had never understood this made me feel rotten.

• • •

I met Kate Pulino downtown at a building site that would become Augustine, the next McNally restaurant. She spent most of her time here in a hard hat, though her office was at 568 Broadway.

Like the other executives, she often dealt with issues across the company, but now she was working as the project manager on the new enterprise, and it was late and this was pressing. That morning we climbed over parts of brown leather banquettes and un-hung chandeliers. Designed and built by the usual McNally cohorts—Ian McPheeley, Richard Lewis, and Kris Spychalski—when Augustine opened in November 2016 it was flawless; a polished jewel box of a restaurant, all pearly ceramic tiles and painted glass panels. It was a classy joint where you might want to doll yourself up for a night. Shane McBride and Daniel Parilla were the co-chefs, and they had cooked up a menu with the tenderest gigot of lamb, a luscious duck, a rich saucisson brioche. "Brasserie Lipp with great food," said my date the first time I went to Augustine. I saw Keith there when it opened, and he knew it was good, and there was a rare relaxed look on his face. Everyone had a lot of wine that night, and when we all said good-bye, Keith peered at me and said, "Are you drunk?"

"A bit," I said. "You're more fun when you're drunk," he said with a gnomic grin, call it short and sweet.

Kate Pulino had been researcher, majordomo, project manager, for most of Keith's creations since she answered an ad in the *New York Times*. This seemed to her an idea out of a simpler time, to look for a job in the newspaper. Even more old-fashioned was the way she actually landed the position.

An art historian, she had spent half a decade in Italy and was back in New York when she saw an ad for a researcher, and it was downtown, and she read it and thought, *Health care? NYU?*

"The interview was at Keith's house in the West Village, and we talked a lot and he never asked what I'd done, just asked what I was reading and if I had a dog." She got the job. Her first job was buying decorative chicken wire for Schiller's, which McNally was opening that year. Eventually she became a fixture in the world of McNally; Kate even had a restaurant named for her. Before it was Cherche Midi, Keith's restaurant on the Bowery and Houston Street had been a pizza place named Pulino's.

Ducking under wooden planks, brushing dust off mahogany siding, Kate showed me around the site. She was effusive and forthcoming, and she knew her stuff. The construction guys seemed perfectly comfortable with her. She worked closely with Polish Kris. "We're a team," Kate said, and pointed out the banquettes—brown leather this time—and the hand-painted Italian tiles. "Mirrors, of course," she added.

We went out for coffee and as soon as we sat down, I realized Kate was staring, a puzzled expression on her face, at some guy. He was wearing a dark blue knitted watch cap pulled low over his forehead, which gave him a sinister air, but suddenly he jumped up and shouted, "Kate Pulino!"

"Dean!" she replied.

There was an exchange of *What are you doing here*s and the collegial, delighted chatter of old mates reunited.

Dean was Dean Jankelowitz, a native of South Africa, who for many years was the general manager at Schiller's in the East Village, the restaurant for which Kate found the chicken wire. His wife, Maya, half American, half Israeli, had been an adored maître d' at Balthazar; the sight of her, drop-dead chic in her wild, sometimes kooky, always fashionable outfits, brought in friends and customers in droves. When the two started going around together, even customers at Balthazar followed the news of it, as well as that of the wedding in Israel and the two little boys that followed soon after. And then there was a restaurant of their own: Jack's Wife Freda— named for Dean's grandparents—opened on Lafayette around the corner from Balthazar.

Dean and Maya were among the many graduates of McNally's

restaurants who had gone on to other restaurants, other lives. Somehow, and perhaps only because Balthazar had been around a long time and had employed a lot of people, it had produced plenty of love affairs, partnerships, marriages.

It was a family in the early days, Kate said. People went out drinking late, and Puck Fair, a bar on Lafayette, became an after-work annex. When it closed in 2016, Kate went for a last drink with her friends and it seemed like the end of an era. "So many relationships," Kate said. Even Keith met his wife, Alina, at Balthazar when she worked there.

In those days, there were always rumors about the young staff, about their affairs, about the possibility that some were having sex in the basement or a cupboard under the stairs—though I could never quite work out how—or doing cocaine in one of the storage rooms. Keith gave enormous staff parties. More marriages, more breakups, more or less everything that came with a tight little community.

More trouble, too. It had not always been so jolly within the McNally empire. Internecine battles took place between employees who were destined never to get along; ambitions were thwarted. There was at least one lawsuit about tips and taxes. I heard tell of an IRS raid that concerned undocumented workers, but I wasn't able to confirm anything.

Still, an astonishing number of people stayed for years, even decades; what's more, plenty left and came back. "Everybody always comes back," an ex-manager told me. "It's a family." Those who left, and those who came back, referred to Balthazar as "the Mother Ship."

I asked Erin if she thought the McNally group had changed over the years.

She did. The health department was ever more demanding and made unannounced visits. The city had begun requiring health grades posted on every restaurant door.

Clearly the days of sex, drugs, and rock and roll were long gone, but that was true of just about everything in the city where money was what mattered. If this was the city that never slept, by 2017, it didn't sleep because it was mostly awake doing deals. Any sort of bohemia had been priced out.

Balthazar, like so many restaurants, was getting more and more expensive, and locals who had once dropped in at will now considered the cost. There was more talk about the bottom line and budgets now, about money and how to organize and systematize. Erin was rueful. "You know, it's funny, when I think of the shit that happens now—there's so much with the labor board and, you know, the taxes and the liquor license, so much having nothing to do with an actual restaurant. So much of it takes precedence over the romance aspect of the restaurant that some of the fun has been taken away," she said.

"The bigger the company got, and with Keith not here, you needed a bigger umbrella," Shane had said. "In the old days, and in every restaurant, not just Balthazar, cooks took a drink during the day, let's say, and things were swept under the carpet. All those Wild West days ended. Things became more formal."

No longer could a chef-owner open and live off a single restaurant unless he owned the building, too. Instead, the big-name chefs opened restaurant after restaurant.

True, Keith had not been Balthazar's chef, or its general manager, but he was much more than the money guy. He *was* the restaurant and he had always been hands on. He had often been in the restaurant or at the offices near by or one of his other places; even at home on 11th Street, he was ten minutes away.

Everyone at Balthazar knew him and saw him, and he knew their names, waiters, cooks, customers. He saw everything that went on and that made Balthazar feel like a bespoke operation, the creation of the guy who had dreamed it up and was constantly worrying about it—were the steps down to the bathrooms too worn?—or tinkering with it.

And though he was frequently in New York, when Keith McNally went to live in London, it had been a kind of watershed, the moment when things for the company changed. He opened the London Balthazar and that, too, required attention.

Run out of the offices at 568 Broadway, the company became increasingly complex. With Keith three thousand miles away, and more restaurants in the offing, the company took on a more corporate aspect. In a sense, the new structure was a replacement—a lousy one, most everybody agreed—for his regular presence. An HR person was hired. Erin said hopefully, "Keith will never do corporate, but the city changes, the neighborhood changes." The onslaught of the corporate ethos, Erin added, was hard to avoid for anyone.

The rent at Balthazar went up about two years ago. Information was hard to come by—there's nothing a company holds as close to the chest as facts about money—but from what I understood, it rose from about $88,000 a month to around $280,000.

Rodney Propp, the landlord, told me he had kept it below market value because of civic pride and his love for the area and his admiration for Balthazar itself, that he had turned down much more lucrative tenants. I was wary of the rhetoric, but Dick Robinson told me he thought Propp really did care and could have charged another tenant more.

"Keith was brilliant about it, though," said Dick, who was always a bit of an optimist, a man who liked good news. "When the rent was to go up and the building's owner mentioned he could give Aritzia bigger area and a frontage on Spring Street if he rented them the Balthazar space, Keith managed to keep the rent at about three-quarters of what Aritzia would have paid. It could have been much worse."

Real estate in New York was everything, and location has, of course, always mattered, but until the 2000s there were still unfashionable little areas on the fringes of town and Keith McNally usually

found them. Not anymore. So much of the city was occupied by chain stores or banks, there wasn't much room for the innovative restaurateur or artist or retailer.

There were no more fringes; Manhattan, which had been all bought up, was done; Brooklyn was going fast.

The terrible sadness was that SoHo had been gobbled up by its own greed; landlords charged anything they could get; there were no regulations to limit the excess. By the spring of 2016, a third of the shops in SoHo were empty, landlords waiting for the tenant who could pay whatever it took, not caring if the shops stood empty for months, even years, which meant the eventual arrival of more chains, of more Nikes, more crazy Japanese sneakers, even a Cadillac headquarters. If this went on, soon there would be no reason for anyone to come to a SoHo completely occupied by big-box stores and branches of designer shops.

When I was feeling really gloomy, I allowed myself a dystopian vision in which Manhattan had become a theme park where only tourists were allowed. Everything had already been flattened by the corporate ethos and the real estate developers, and increasingly there was no room for the little one-off shops or bookstores or galleries, not even the cafés or the bodegas; it reminded me of how the city gentry in the nineteenth century had laid out the grid; flattening hills, tearing down trees, filling in streams, they smashed everything in the way.

Was it only this kind of change that made me feel there had been a little bit of corporate creep at the McNally headquarters? Or was there an obsession with the bottom line, and if there was, wouldn't this change everything? Would the lovely golden goose that was Balthazar lose its shine or eat itself?

Occasionally I had the feeling, just a faint whisper of it, the kind of thing that brushed against your skin, and it was that one day Balthazar would be sold, and then it would be just an overpriced joint for tourists.

• • •

Gloomy, I left the offices and went back to the restaurant. Not a thing was different, of course. The cooks were getting ready to move up to the kitchen for dinner. A few people sat around talking over the remains of their lunches. At a large table, a group of young women was finishing up a birthday party, or maybe it was a shower. The table was heaped with fancy wrapping paper and ribbons, blue, pink, silver. Carol Iseman, their waiter, was taking a picture of them, and the girls laughed and posed. Carol had come to New York years ago to help get her own daughter set up because her daughter had some disabilities. She never left.

After she said good-bye to the birthday party, Carol came over to say hello and to tell me her daughter had just got a wonderful job with Chanel and would be heading for Paris.

Once, Dick Robinson had asked me what I thought it was that kept people coming back to Balthazar over and over. Now, I climbed up on a barstool, thinking about his question. The man next to me was laughing at a joke the bartender had told him. The smell of lilies in a vase at the end of the bar wafted in my direction. I sipped the red wine I had ordered, and it had an amiable taste. José Luis rushed over to find out if I needed anything; he would make me my favorite iced cappuccino in a beer glass if I wanted it. My lousy mood subsided. If I found it hard at times to celebrate New York these days, I could still celebrate Balthazar. There was music coming from the sound system—was it Ella? "We'll turn Manhattan into an isle of joy," she sang.

"The thing about it," one of the regulars at the bar said even before her third whiskey sour, "Balthazar makes people feel good."

and he sometimes called her "Maman Nicole." Sitting with her, he cheered up, and in the few minutes before their shift, they sat and giggled together, like teenagers over a private joke.

The waiters did chores before the dinner shift, and for this Moustapha and Sazzad donned their paper caps—soda jerk–style caps—which they wore with as much panache as possible. The caps were to cover their hair because the chores included pouring mustard and ketchup into little cups.

A little later I found Moustapha—in the tiny area between the back door to the bakery and the dishwashers—spooning ketchup from a huge plastic tub into tiny metal serving cups. In the prep room, Sazzad worked on the mustard and mayo. Everyone was occupied with getting dinner up and running, and in a small room off the prep area, the seven bussers on duty that night were cutting up blocks of yellow butter, putting it into little white china ramekins, smoothing it down with a knife dipped in hot water. Intent on their work, they didn't talk much, but when I walked in with my photographer, they posed happily. These guys looked modestly proud of their precision.

"Soft butter!" said an ex-waiter. "Soft butter is what you want. They do have it down pat."

In his office, Shane was rooting around for his street clothes. Like an actor after the matinee, he was hurrying to change because he was cooking for one of his charities, and then heading home to Astoria.

From everywhere underground at Balthazar, from all parts of the catacombs, kitchens, staff room, wine cellars, everyone was on the move, waiters and bussers upstairs, the cooks from the prep room to the kitchens. It was getting to be dinnertime.

You could feel the buzz, smell the food, hear the voices. Nicole was in stride, making her way to the stairs and then the restaurant for the waiters' meeting. One of the downstairs Josés (there were a couple with the same name) was looking at a slab of beef, wondering if it would be needed and when he should butcher it, if necessary. Mark Mason, the cellar master, was carrying something tenderly in his arms, like a big baby; from his tender ministrations, it was clearly very good, a magnum of some rare, marvelous wine.

"That time before dinner was always exhilarating," said James Weichert. Zouheir Louhaichy, the maître d' that night, had come downstairs to discuss last-minute items with Frank Ortega. Frank was looking at the cooks, who picked up the crates of food that had been prepped and took them up to the kitchen. I asked Frank if I could come by the kitchen. "Sure," he said. "It will be hot, though. Really hot."

COCKTAIL LE BALTHAZAR

*I'd always wanted to know how a cocktail is invented.
For some years now, cocktails have been the property of
the mixologists who make "craft" cocktails. I was after
something simple, delicious, and French. Jimmy Norris,
the bartender, and Rebecca Banks, who is in charge of
spirits and wine, figured this out. Grey Goose is French,
so is Grand Marnier, and the Champagne makes it all
fizz. Add lime juice and a little simple syrup. Voilà. Le
Balthazar. Curiously if unintentionally, the cocktail
came out the color of the restaurant walls—a sort of pale
liquid bathed in gilded light with a fine froth on top.*

INGREDIENTS

1 ounce Grey Goose Vodka

1 ounce Grand Marnier

½ ounce lime juice

½–¾ ounce simple syrup

1½ ounces Brut Champagne, or to taste

Martini glasses

Cocktail shaker (you can get one online for less than ten bucks and it's worth it; shaken not stirred is best for most cocktails)

INSTRUCTIONS:

Chill the glass. Put all the ingredients in the shaker except the Champagne.
Shake vigorously. Strain into the chilled glass. Top with Champagne to taste.
Serve up with a twist of orange peel.

Dinner

SOFT SHELL CRAB BLT

Yield: Serves 4

This is one of Shane's most delicious creations.
It may seem anomalous for a French brasserie,
but a person can't live off just steak frites.

INGREDIENTS

4 soft shell crabs

8 slices of cooked bacon

2 heads of baby gem lettuce (or romaine hearts)

2 green tomatoes

1 frying setup: frying pan, 3 large eggs, 3 cups panko, 3 cups all-purpose flour

1 box falafel mix

1 quart buttermilk

1 quart canola oil, for frying

½ cup Green Goddess dressing (recipe follows)

Green Goddess dressing ingredients:

1 cup parsley leaves

1 bunch chives

1 bunch tarragon

½ cup basil leaves

1 cup mayonnaise

1 pint buttermilk

4 teaspoons lemon juice

1 clove garlic, finely minced

Salt and pepper to taste

1 teaspoon anchovy paste

INSTRUCTIONS:

Clean soft shell crabs: With scissors, cut off the face, then remove the lungs and the apron. Marinate in buttermilk for at least 1 hour. Dredge the cleaned crabs in the falafel mix and set aside.

Set up a standard breading station: Put the whisked eggs, bread crumbs, and flour each into a separate bak-ing dish or a bowl. Slice the green tomatoes into ½-inch-round slices and then bread them, first lightly coating with flour, then the egg mix. Make sure the egg completely cov-ers the tomato. Finally, put into the bread crumbs. Cover the dredged and breaded tomatoes and refrigerate until needed.

Cook the bacon until nice and crispy and put aside. Wash the baby gem lettuce and pull into individual leaves. Fill small saucepan with water about halfway, add 1 tablespoon salt, and bring to a boil. In a medium-size bowl, prepare an ice bath with cold water and ice cubes. Drop the parsley leaves into boiling water for about 30 seconds, remove, and put in ice bath. Repeat with chives and other herbs one at a time. Once all the herbs are blanched and shocked in the ice bath, remove them, squeeze out excess water, and add to an upright high-speed blender—at the restaurant the chef uses a Vita-Prep—and blend until smooth.

In a mixing bowl, add the mayo, buttermilk, anchovy paste, garlic, and lemon juice, whisking until smooth. Add the blended herbs and whisk until nice and green. Taste and adjust seasoning with salt and pepper.

In the skillet, pour about one inch of canola oil, and put on medium-high heat, about 350°F. Set up a draining station of paper towels or newspaper with salt on hand to season. Fry the tomatoes until nice and golden, remove from oil onto draining station, season with salt. Repeat with the crabs. Be careful, as they tend to pop and splash oil. Cook on both sides until golden, about 3 to 4 minutes. Drain on towels, season with salt.

TO PLATE:

Dress the baby gem lettuce with Green Goddess dressing. Cut the crabs and tomatoes in halves. This is like building a sandwich horizontally. Instead of building up, you build out. So, from right to left: tomato, lettuce, crab, bacon. Repeat using the other half of the tomato.

TO DRINK:

For this, something subtle: a white Burgundy, acidic enough to pair with the crab, weighty enough to stand up to the bacon: St Aubin "Les Castets" H Prudhon '11—like a baby Meursault.

GUMBO

Yield: Serves 10

This is a great dish for any party, including brunch. Like most chefs, Shane McBride loves New Orleans, where gumbo is the iconic dish. He also loves every bit of the pig.

INGREDIENTS

2 pounds smoked bacon

1½ pounds each of tasso ham and andouille sausage

½ pound butter

1 pound all-purpose flour

3 cups onions, medium-diced

2 cups green bell peppers, medium-diced

2 cups celery, medium-diced

2 cups okra

1 cup peeled garlic, minced

Hot sauce (Shane likes Crystal hot sauce) to taste

2 tablespoons gumbo filé

2 quarts chicken stock

2 jalapeño peppers, finely chopped

1 pound shrimp

2 pounds chicken, cut in one-inch cubes (dark meat is always better)

INSTRUCTIONS:

Dice the onion, celery, and green pepper into ⅓-inch pieces. Cut the okra into ½-inch rounds. Mince the garlic as well as the jalapeño peppers, removing the seeds and stems. Cut the bacon, tasso ham, and andouille sausage into ½-inch cubes.

Place a 12-quart pot over medium-high heat. Add bacon, tasso ham, and andouille sausage. Cook until golden brown and all of the fat has been rendered. Remove the meat from the pot, leaving rendered fat inside. Set aside the meat.

Add butter to pot, let it fully melt. When the butter is fully melted, add flour. Stir until the color of dark mahogany. When the color is achieved, add the onion, celery, and green bell peppers—known as the Trinity. Cook the vegetables for about 5 minutes, then add the garlic and jalapeño. Cook for about 3 to 4 minutes, then add half of the bacon, ham, and sausage mix.

Add the chicken stock, stirring continuously until fully incorporated and nothing is stuck to the bottom of the pot. Add the chicken, cook for about 15 minutes more. Add the other half of the bacon, ham, and sausage mix, stir in, and then add the gumbo filé. Let simmer 5 minutes more. Add shrimp, cook 5 minutes more.

Adjust heat (spiciness!) with hot sauce and check seasoning (to taste). If it's too thick, add a little water. To serve, spoon the gumbo over fluffy white rice.

TO DRINK:

The chef likes beer with gumbo, a New Orleans beer if you can find one. Also great with a mint julep (keeps the theme), or Balthazar's Petit Cochon cocktail (WhistlePig rye, peach purée, and lemon).

SHORT RIB DAUBE

Yield: Serves 6 to 8

INGREDIENTS

6 pounds boneless short ribs, cut into 2-inch cubes

1 pound smoked bacon, cut into lardons

4 carrots, peeled and diced into medium-size pieces

2 large onions, peeled and diced into medium-size pieces

1 small head of celery root, peeled and diced into medium-size pieces

2 heads of garlic, broken apart and peeled

2 herb bouquets, each containing 6 thyme sprigs, 1 small bay leaf,

2 sprigs parsley, tied with kitchen twine

Zest of 1 orange

½ cup pitted nicoise olives

3 quarts red wine, preferably Syrah

3 quarts veal stock

4 to 6 tablespoons duck fat

1 cup Armagnac

Salt and pepper to taste

SEVEN DAYS BEFORE YOU NEED THE STEW:

Marinate the short ribs in the red wine with one of the herb bouquets, ½ of the orange zest, and one of the heads of garlic, chopped up.

ON THE DAY OF COOKING:

Remove the meat from the marinade, place on a sheet pan, and pat dry. Liberally season the meat and sear with the duck fat or canola oil in a large wide-bottomed pan until golden. Remove from pan and set aside.

Strain the red wine and discard the zest and garlic. Pour the strained liquid into a heavy-bottomed pan and bring to a boil. Skim off all of the foam and impurities that rise to the top, and continue to cook until the liquid is re-

duced by ⅓. Add the veal stock at this point and return to a boil, continuing to skim off impurities.

In the same pan the short ribs were seared, discard all of the rendered fat and salt that has collected and place back over a medium flame. Add 1 tablespoon duck fat and then the bacon lardons. Once the bacon is lightly caramelized, add all the vegetables and the other head of garlic that has been minced, and continue to sweat the vegetables until just tender.

At this point, add the Armagnac to deglaze the pan and allow it to burn off (be careful of the flame). Once the alcohol has flamed out, add the red wine/stock base and bring to a boil. Add the meat pieces, the other herb bouquet, the remaining orange zest, and the olives. Bring back to a simmer, then place in the oven at 350°F for 3 to 4 hours.

Once the meat is tender, remove from oven and let cool slightly. With a slotted spoon, remove as much of the meat and vegetables as possible. Or you can use a strainer.

Place the liquid in a heavy-bottomed pot and bring back to a simmer and reduce by half. As it reduces, skim off any foam or impurities. When it's reduced you can add the meat back and the rest of the fresh garnish. It's now ready to serve.

You can garnish with some fresh olives, fresh grated orange zest, and chopped parsley. I like to serve it with cheesy grits or creamy polenta.

TO DRINK:

Rebecca says, "Gotta go southwest France—Cahors 'Petite Étoile' Mas des Étoiles '11—a medium-bodied, Malbec-based wine."

PART
FIVE

EVENING

WELCOME TO THURSDAY NIGHT

G od, it *was* hot in that kitchen. I went back to the kitchen around five-thirty just as the dinner shift had begun. Frank Ortega was overseeing it. I stood in a corner, trying to stay out of the way, but the kitchen was small, and there were seven men on the line.

To stand on the line for even half an hour was to experience a kind of contained frenzy unlike anything else, or at least anything I had experienced. In truth, there was no frenzy; it just seemed that way to me. But some of the half dozen cooks were not kids; some of them were as old as me, and I was half blind from the sweat running into my eyes.

Starting at five-thirty, the orders came in, and they kept coming. The men who worked as runners kept coming as if in a relay race. Each took finished plates, backed out through the swing doors into the restaurant. Frank Ortega's usually calm expression had changed only a fraction, but he was watchful. He looked over every plate that went out to the restaurant, moving a little bit of frisée lettuce over the skate, wiping an invisible speck of buttery garlic off the rim of the plate of escargots, rearranging the frites on top of the steak in what seemed a more artistic way—more like a Jackson Pollock, it seemed to me.

Rarely did anyone talk, except when Frank picked up the phone to call downstairs to one of the two Josés to send up more potatoes. In the middle of the group of seven men, José Paez was at the meat station. He was, as Shane put it, "the man in the middle. The expediter who makes sure everything is in sync and everybody was doing the right thing and doing it consistently."

Paez barely missed a beat; if he had, the whole operation would slow down, or worse, somebody would make a mistake, somebody would send out the wrong dish or the wrong side, sautéed spinach instead of steamed spinach.

From the time a customer ordered and the waiter typed it into the computer and then hit "Fire," the rule was to get the dish back in fifteen minutes. Frank replated a salad. José Paez tossed a steak on the grill.

Shane looked in. "Looks good," he said, pleased, buttoning his coat. Ostensibly, he said it to me, but the comment was really for the guys, and along the line, though nobody looked up, the men were pleased.

One brandade, an onion soup, one trout with lentils, two salmon, a branzino, three steaks au poivre, roast chicken for two, a duck confit—the orders arrived, and this would go on and on until midnight, or one in the morning on weekends. The steaks sizzled; otherwise there wasn't much noise.

Again a runner appeared and picked up the food and backed out of the kitchen. Frank glanced at the printout of the order and stuck it on a spike with the others.

My feet hurt, I was exhausted, I wanted fresh air, and the men working the line had six hours left or more, and I thought: *Why would anyone do this?*

"It's the adrenaline," William Hackman—a protégé of Shane's—

said. "If it wasn't for that rush you get on the line, the sense of doing it over and over and doing it right and in a rush and not losing track of it all, you wouldn't do it, would you?"

Will is a young chef who has more or less followed McBride around town from one restaurant to another. Shane knew he was good. The guy had a real future. Last I heard he was sous chef at Augustine.

Class in a New York restaurant was not something people often talked about. In Will, a tall, handsome young guy, a guy who had studied physics at the College of William and Mary before he felt the call of the kitchen, it seemed to reveal itself.

One afternoon, I was sitting in Shane's office and Will was there, and we were talking about working in restaurants. They agreed it was hard, dirty, and underpaid, some chefs were real screamers, and the hours were long.

I wondered if for the regular line cooks it really was the adrenaline, as Will had said, or if it was simpler, if it was the work, the paycheck. Maybe this was the key to class in New York City, where so many people, especially the educated young who, in this age of self-obsession, insisted on jobs that were exquisitely satisfying, that fulfilled them completely. For everyone else, it was about work that paid a decent wage, if you could get it.

On my way out of Shane's office, I had overheard a conversation about the employment of a guy for the kitchen or the prep, and somebody said, "Is he on $9.75 or $11?" Clearly this made a difference.

It's not that I had failed to think about the contrasts before this experience: the lovely restaurant upstairs with its miraculously friendly staff, many of whom had other lives as musicians or architects, or who spent days off at the Met. I thought about how much pleasure this place had given me, and then I thought about the workers in the kitchens, the cleaners, the dishwashers on minimum wage or a bit more. This made me uncomfortable.

"They work for the paycheck, and they know here it's good, the money is consistent, we all like to bitch and moan, but your check's not going to bounce. They get paid on time, and it's not up and down," Erin said.

"You love it," Jerry, the Bolivian oyster shucker, told me philosophically for the second time. "You have to love what you do, even if you just love a little piece."

"Welcome to Thursday night," said Erin to the group of waiters and managers who had assembled at a table at the far back of the restaurant for the evening meeting. "Last night we had a good solid night, let's make it even better." She turned it on, cheerleading the group.

Kouider Zioueche, one of the evening managers—they were once known as captains—was born in Roanne, about sixty miles from Lyons. He told me his family house was just on the other side of Troisgros, the great restaurant. "I hope to be having dinner there in a few weeks," he said. He had a humorous face, a French face out of Algeria, where his family came from, and a vivid style to match. Under his breath, he was whistling "La Vie en Rose." He could have been a song and dance man.

I once asked Kouider if he was always so cheerful. "Yes, pretty much so," he said. "What do I have to complain about?" The other floor manager for tonight was Jason, handsome and hirsute, who had lived in London for years.

There were a few specials to taste—a white bean soup (no cream, chicken stock, topped with Parmesan cheese)—and implicit in Nicole's seniority was that she went first. She made a little "hmm" noise that signified she quite liked it. Also around the table were Silvia Karina Fiorina and Paule Aboite.

Erin told the waiters that there were also two new wines on the list for them to "sell": a white Burgundy, the Vocoret Chablis '14, for seventy-three dollars, and a red Bordeaux, a Château Moulin de Tri-

cot Margaux '11, at ninety-nine dollars. She passed around a couple of bottles, the waiters sampled it, Erin continued the predinner rap.

"Keith is back from London, and he will probably sit in the 60s," said Erin. "I'm sure he's going to be excited to see the restaurant. You guys have been doing a fantastic job, everyone is really stepping up. I'm seeing a lot more engagement between customers and staff. People want to show off to Keith, of course, and I think he'll come directly from the airport. He has a Balthazar in London now, but this is really his baby and you should know he's very proud."

There was a generation of waiters who had never met Keith, Erin had told me. "There is something missing without him here, no doubt."

One of the newer waiters looked anxious. His foot was jiggling and he was fussing with his apron when he said, "I served him grapefruit at breakfast, and he never looked up."

Erin said, "Keith is very shy." Then she mentioned that there were two Triple As and a Double A coming in; she thanked the bussers for having done a fabulous job polishing the wood in the restaurant. To me she said, "Balthazar changed how you view a restaurant. It's a bistro, it's a brasserie, it's loud, it's busy, but we give you four-star service. And if the room doesn't have the glow of making everyone absolutely stunning at night, it's totally wrong. This is what makes Balthazar."

"OK, have a great night," said Erin to the waiters, glancing around the room. In her smart black pant suit and pearl earrings, she was ready for the performance. Looked around the room and said, "Nice! Right?" She was pleased. The waiters got up, checked their uniforms, and went off to their stations, where they stood in twos, smiling, waiting for the curtain.

At night, the waiters had all the best lines, the big speeches; they had memorized scores of wine and dozens of oysters and the daily specials.

The bussers, though they were generally silent and had much less overt interaction with the customers, were critical to the action. They kept everything moving, played backup for the waiters. If this had been a theater they would have been the stagehands, the extras, the chorus, even minor character actors.

The lights went down, the mirrors seemed to glitter in the soft light, the brass and glass shone. Bouquets of purple roses and pale green hydrangeas were in vases on the back of the central banquettes—purple roses for enchantment—sometimes impermanent, fleeting enchantment.

CHAPTER 24

CALVIN KLEIN'S UNDERPANTS AND THE USES OF CELEBRITY

C atching a glimpse of himself in the glass pane of the front door, Zouheir tugged his tie, smoothed the jacket of his snappy suit, and went back to his reservation list and his seat plan, both laid out on the little podium inside the front door. He was a handsome man. A faint smile played on his face as he checked the Triple As, those top VIPs who were due in that night. A guest he knew well and liked was coming in at nine. He looked at his watch. It wasn't yet seven, and he was in good shape.

Of all the celebrated customers Zouheir Louhaichy met over the years that he had been Balthazar's maître d', the most famous, he told me, was Joe DiMaggio. When Zouheir had been a kid in Casablanca he had dreamed of a soccer career, but he knew all about Joltin' Joe. Scores of celebrities had passed Zouheir's desk, and he had a good memory and could tell you that Jake Gyllenhaal had been in almost every night when he was doing a play on Broadway and was a real sweetheart.

Although Zouheir and the rest of the staff treated everyone well, the charming celebrity who behaved uncommonly well was clearly to be relished and the staff at Balthazar always remembered them. For Nicole, it was Brooke Shields. "She was a darling," Nicole said. "Humble and lovely." Of the celebs who did not behave, they did not speak; it was against the code. And once in a while, there would be the very, very famous, the mythical figure who dropped by and whom nobody ever forgot, like Joltin' Joe.

Zouheir looked up and saw a friend who had just been at the bar and was leaving. Leaning in close to his friend—he always leaned in close to talk to friends this way—Zouheir inquired about his family, and they chatted and shook hands again. Before the rush, the front desk sometimes resembled the town square of a tiny village and Zouheir felt himself its mayor.

Both watchful and charming, Zouheir had the ease of an athlete and people remembered the days when he ran marathons. When Balthazar got crowded and the crowd at the front was a little too pushy, he handled it with a certain inborn physical cool and the kind of mental agility you got from seating a large room every night as if it were a diplomatic crossword puzzle.

With a wary eye for the unexpected, Zouheir had dealt with even the most demanding, most self-aggrandizing celebrities. Once, he'd told Donald Trump he couldn't have what he wanted.

"It was a Saturday night, and I think he was dating his current wife, they were at a table for two and the people at the next table finished and he wanted their table as well. I said I was so sorry, but it was Saturday night and we just needed it, somebody else had a reservation." Zouheir paused. "He said OK, because what else could he do? Unless he walked out in the middle of dinner, but he didn't. Amazing, right?" said the man who told Donald Trump no.

• • •

"*Renommée*," Rebecca Spang calls it in her book *The Invention of the Restaurant*. In it she writes, "As surely as restaurants relied on fish and fresh vegetables, silverware and champagne, they depended on 'legend.' Fame (*Renommée*) was the first of a restaurant's household gods; Venus [goddess of love, fertility, beauty, prosperity, and sex], the second; and Comus [god of festivities, dalliance, good times, and the son and cupbearer of Bacchus], only the third."

This was as true in an America obsessed with fame and celebrity, where everybody yearned for just a taste; fame was as important in the twenty-first century as it had been in the nineteenth. True, you couldn't keep a New York restaurant going long without good food and service, but fame came first, preferably even before you opened and the news went out in advance on a hundred websites and blogs.

Fame Balthazar had from the first day, and rumors, and lore. And for twenty years, they kept coming. Zouheir recalled the night Michael Jordan came, when he was not just the greatest basketball player but the biggest sports star in the country, and how guests got up on the banquettes to look at him. Dick Robinson remembered that he ate a double portion of roast chicken.

And then there was Jack.

The night Jack Nicholson was there, he got up from his table to go to the bathroom, just across the room to the doorway with the sign that said TOILETTES over it. Out of the blue, the entire restaurant broke into applause, and Nicholson smiled his devilish smile and turned and bowed.

Too many stories to tell: Madonna and Meryl Streep, Michael Bloomberg and Tom Hanks, De Niro and Taylor Swift; and Lauren Bacall, who, having used the ground floor bathroom—usually reserved for the disabled—remarked in her smoky voice, "They let me take a piss where they keep the extra Champagne."

And then: Among my favorite memories of brunches and breakfasts and dinners at Balthazar—and so much about meals you remember was always about those you ate with—were those with the late Alan Rickman, a wonderful friend, a great actor. The obituaries and remembrances revealed how well loved he was. He and Rima Horton, his wife, were in New York a lot, and we had great meals that included good talk, a lot of laughter, and plenty of food and drink. By the time the *Harry Potter* films were out, every kid in America recognized Alan, of course, and he couldn't walk a block in SoHo without being asked for an autograph or a picture. He never refused. He seemed never to refuse anything.

The only problem was Alan would never let you pay. I used to say, "What are you, a Communist? From each according to his means and all that? So what about when I have a best-seller?" Alan would smile his delicious smile and say, "Absolutely. When you have a best-seller."

When Alan died, Erin posted on Facebook: "What a loss. We have taken care of him for years at the restaurant and he was always so so lovely with our staff. A true gentleman. He will be missed."

The cover of Spang's book shows a photograph of the Café Brasserie du Dôme in Paris. Known as *les Dômiers*, the customers included V. I. Lenin and Hemingway, Anaïs Nin and Picasso, Robert Capa, Cartier-Bresson, Modigliani and Man Ray. At Balthazar, instead, there were Tom Stoppard, Anna Wintour, Salman Rushdie, Meg Ryan, and Jerry Seinfeld, who proposed to his wife there. Keith Richards, a vegan and a pal of McNally's, was often around. Derek Jeter and Alex Rodriguez showed up on the same night once and I got to thinking that Jeter was a fair trade for Lenin, though it was said that V. I. actually had quite a bit of charm and knew his way around Western café society. At least it taught him, as he later said, that the foreign radicals who supported his brutal endeavors in the Soviet Union were "useful idiots."

The rumor, the lore, the titillation, Balthazar had all of it, including the secret phone number people had so coveted. But there had never been a velvet rope. In fact, the only time I had ever seen police barricades up outside Balthazar was during Fashion Week when the Beckhams came to brunch.

It happened every year. Balthazar put out metal barricades, some of the men—managers, waiters—locked arms to keep the crowds back, and they came, Victoria and David and their entourage. From the beginning, Balthazar had attracted plenty of celebrities, and the hacks who covered them knew it, so I was always surprised when the Beckhams caused so much chaos. The reason, a former manager told me, was that when they were on their way, one of their people always made it known to the press. True? I'm not sure, but on those occasions, Spring Street was a swamp of paparazzi.

By 1997, celebrity had entered its omnivorous age; it was everywhere; it gobbled up everything in its path. That was the year Princess Diana's death was practically televised live. *Entertainment Tonight* had begun broadcasting in 1981, and it had commodified celebrity in a new way by reporting stuff—a movie star's pregnancy, a singer's face-lift, as well as what they wore and who they were seeing—that had previously mostly appeared in supermarket tabloids. The year before, CNN had started twenty-four-hour news. Not long afterward, the Internet sprang into life, and even the tiniest detail about the lives of the famous and almost famous was made public.

And oh how we got to know them all, all the teeny celebs and huge stars almost as if they were family, except we knew they were having more fun than we were, and their lives more exciting. We wanted it. The places they went, the places they ate, and what they bought. When the Kardashians opened a shop in SoHo, we got in line and were titillated.

And then came reality TV, and we were made to understand, were persuaded that we could have it, be it, buy it, that this wasn't just the stuff of gossip or a magazine you read at the dentist, if only we could get the secret phone number.

Still, best of all was a glimpse of the gods themselves, of Beyoncé or Madonna out at dinner. People were enlarged by the sight of somebody famous. Balthazar, when it opened in 1997, was right up there, a tiny Mount Olympus.

As restaurants became the new form of entertainment in New York—in the 1990s—the uses of celebrity were critical. Wallpaper a room with "faces," people came. Hire a public relations flack, call in favors.

Keith McNally never had a PR person, no restaurant rep, didn't need it. From the time he worked at One Fifth, through to Odeon and then Balthazar, if he barely acknowledged it, he played Pied Piper to a gang of notables, and they followed him from one restaurant to another. A million stories circulated, and in the New York restaurant business this was as good as gold.

Fame, and money, too. Balthazar came into its prime in the boom years. I remember seeing a group of young men, wolves from Wall Street, perhaps, half dozen of them around a table. Their jackets were off, tossed on the backs of chairs. They were big young guys. You could see the muscles under their blue-striped shirts. Each one ordered a bottle of wine that ran to five hundred bucks minimum. They held their knives and forks like weapons, as if they intended to kill the steak. A steady noise like a pack of animals braying rose from their table.

"Before the crash of '07, there was a lot of money around," said Erin. "And you'd have these guys from Wall Street or hedge funds or whatever, and they'd come in and spend a lot of money and they'd think they could do anything, and it was when they figured they could put their hands on the waitresses, on their asses, so you had to tell them off."

● ● ●

But nothing quite conveyed Balthazar's fame as much as the response to one of its mirrors falling off the wall.

In New York, people have always loved an event, a happening, tragic, comic, funny ha-ha, or peculiar. The attention to this small event at Balthazar, even this tiny occurrence, made me understand that it was now an institution, a celebrity itself, that the idea of it had gone into the media bloodstream. Otherwise, who the hell would care so much about a piece of glass coming off a wall, unless maybe it had killed somebody?

And I wasn't there when the mirror fell. I hated that.

"Are you OK?" "Are you hurt?" The e-mails appeared on my screen. A phone call or two followed. The day the mirror fell off the wall at Balthazar, I was sitting at my desk.

Millions of posts went up because, at 10:08 that morning, when it was alleged that Taylor Swift was eating a late breakfast, in a kind of nightmarish slow motion, an enormous mirror seemed to peel away from the wall.

A few customers sitting in its path got up and ran. Others went to help, and the staff was right on it—911 was called, the firefighters came. Everybody else, reportedly, went right on eating their eggs Benedict and their oatmeal scones with blueberry jam. It was rumored that some French diplomat was there, which was true, and had just barely escaped, which was not. Taylor Swift's presence had been only gossip.

Eighteen years after Polish Kris had helped make the mirrors, putting them together like crossword puzzles in the basement, he helped carry one of them away. Eventually he helped put it all back together again.

The story died. It wasn't a ghost in the machine, or a defect in the hanging of the mirror. Head designer Ian McPheely told me that the mirrors, which were very heavy, had been engineered with a steel chassis. "You could hang a bus off those things," said Ian.

As it turned out, the mirror was felled by workers on the other side of the wall. A lot of pounding, intense vibrations, and the mirror came down.

Life went on. Lunch was served. But not before at least seventy thousand items on the Internet and more than thirty-two million tweets whistled into the world.

I was curious about how Zouheir managed to seat the room when there was an overload of VIPs, or unexpected customers; this took some experience.

"When I come in around four in the afternoon, I look at the list," he said. "And then you plan in your head, OK, first seating, second seating. See the tricky periods, see how many large parties you have, how many VIPs, how many requests you have, you know.

"Obviously it depends on the season, there will be some certain periods when there will be a lot more VIPs. Let's say in the fall, and add Fashion Week, and it's like everyone and their cousin, you know," said Zouheir. "This is where all your skills as a maître d' come in. You deal with a lot of people who are in your face. Now you have to talk, you have to charm, you have to schmooze, you have to see what you can do." He grinned. "And sometimes there are ways you can just make someone realize that what they want is not possible, but we have something else that's just as nice. If someone just walks in, and we're not expecting them, I talk to them and I just make them comfortable and say, 'We're just working on something right now. We'll have something coming up very shortly.' And sometimes it just gets screwed up," he added, recalling with mock horror the night Sylvester Stallone arrived and there was nothing on his list. Stallone's assistant had canceled, but nobody had told the actor.

"I had nothing," Zouheir said.

"Nothing?"

"Nothing. The entire dining room was packed. Stallone walked in, and I saw the whole scenario playing in my head, everybody's looking toward the door at him, and his team, they're saying, 'Oh, Sylvester Stallone, party of five.' Again I say, 'We didn't expect you anymore because it was canceled.' Anyway, so they walk out to wait in the limousine, which was idling outside. It was a panic. And I found something eventually," he said, "but it was close."

Zouheir kept an eye on the front door while we talked—it was almost seven and customers were arriving. Growing up in Morocco, he'd had different plans. He wanted to be a soccer star. But when it didn't work out, Zouheir went on to London to try his hand at acting. New York followed. He got some small stuff, he said, and then came a family. "One thing leads to another," Zouheir said. "The next thing you know you have kids and you have a house in Harlem and then the divorce. Life takes over."

Just after seven, a young couple came in without a reservation. Zouheir said, "What can I do for you?"

To me, he said later, "As a Balthazar maître d', it is your ambition to say yes: yes, we have your table ready; yes, we can find something for you; yes, it won't be long, lovely to see you."

Erin had said to me, "What Keith made clear was that the people who were just off the boat from Winnetka, those are the people who are going to matter, so while you wanted to make sure Madonna was taken good care of, it's one thing to be hot for six months, it's another to be successful for a long time. All of this combined with how we treat you at the door—never will you have a snooty host. Never. A few who tried it were gone in a hurry."

As far as I'm concerned, though, the single best lines on celebrity at Balthazar were written by Alan Bennett, the finest, wittiest, and coolest writer in England. Writing in his diary in 1997 soon after Balthazar opened, he quite simply nailed the whole thing:

> Dining at Balthazar, Keith's new restaurant, we are
> across the aisle from Calvin Klein. I have half a mind
> to step across and say: "I don't suppose you'd be in-

terested, Mr. Klein, and I don't want to intrude on your privacy, but we're both wearing your under-pants." Calvin Klein is sitting with Susan Sontag. Actually he isn't, but if he were it would sum up what celebrity means in New York.

CHAPTER 25

DINNER AT BALTHAZAR

In the vestibule at Balthazar, three young women sat on the little bench, chattering, voices high-pitched, like birds. They were waiting for their friends. The main door opened to the celebratory sound of people having a good time. From the bar came some music, and I thought I heard the Beatles singing "I Want to Hold Your Hand" in German; thought I heard something by Ennio Morricone. The theme from *The Good, the Bad and the Ugly*? The girls looked longingly into the restaurant, where there was gridlock around the podium and Zouheir was peering at his reservation list.

A quartet, two men and two women, was fretful about a reservation. "We made it three months ago," said one of them, a tan man with a half-pounder Rolex who also appeared to be wearing Marlon Brando's snakeskin jacket from *The Fugitive Kind*. "We never leave for New York without this," one of the women said. "We are from Florianópolis, in Brazil. Everyone comes to Balthazar."

In spite of the fall of its economy, the Brazilians were faithful customers. I had to believe this particular group had exported their dough before things got bad. They were gorgeously dressed; one of the women wore an immense diamond on her finger, and it was very good, white and clear. Her husband sported a vintage Patek Philippe.

The second man shrugged. To Zouheir he said, "Please, look again."

Zouheir, smiling, nodding, very calm, examined the reservations list as carefully as if he were perusing the Dead Sea Scrolls. "Of course," he said to the snakeskin. "Just give me a minute, please." Then he turned to a tall woman in a black hat and spectacles, a book in her hand. She was on her own.

"Asbury," said Zouheir to the young host, "please take this lady to table 66.

"It's a nice table," he said to her.

It reminded me of something Judi Wong had said. "There'd be a mob at the door. Keith would tell us to keep an eye out for a single person, young, old, because, he'd say, they're coming into your home. They're uncomfortable," Judi said. "I had been working at the Bowery Bar, which was celebs first. If you were a single person somebody'd say, 'Oh, you can sit at the bar.' At Balthazar it was, no, you're going to get a really nice table for one and be made to feel very special and comfortable."

Tourists were already dug in at the bar and were snapping pictures with selfie sticks. They weren't at all self-conscious, and I wasn't sure if, like a good New Yorker, I was irritated by them and their leisure wear, or if I was feeling charitable, a bit of a populist tonight, and happy they were having a good time.

Zouheir handed Asbury another menu, and he led me to 61. Table 61. I had arrived ahead of the others. I pushed my coat and bag up onto the back of the red booth. In the mirror behind it was a reflection of the restaurant in the low rosy light; it looked beautiful. In the corner almost opposite me was the single woman in the black hat, and she was reading her book and sipping a glass of

Champagne. Habitually Balthazar served a glass to a woman who came on her own, something Keith had spotted at a Paris brasserie long ago.

From where I sat, I could see the whole room spread out, all actors in what looked like a beautifully choreographed set piece, or once would have. Now I couldn't look without seeing a thousand separate activities: a busser slicing bread at the bread stand, a waiter putting her orders into the computer, and one of her mates asking her a question at the same time. A runner delivered shrimp cocktail to a man who was talking at his phone and who then began eating the shrimp methodically, one at a time, dipping them in the cocktail sauce until they were finished.

On the dinner shift there were ten waiters, eleven bussers, four runners, a couple of managers, as well as a maître d'—who, in the case of Zouheir, was also an assistant general manager. The bar was a separate dominion where Dave Maher, the head bartender, was running things tonight.

Two guys were working the oysters, one shucking and arranging a dozen Wellfleets, the other putting big langoustines on a platter. Jerry had gone home already. Jerry, who had opened a million oysters in his time and had grown up four thousand miles from the sea.

"How's life?" I said to José Luis, who had hurried over with a pitcher of water and a glass of ice cubes because he knew I'd ask for ice.

He smiled. He said, of course, "Life is good."

"Hello, how are you!?" It was Nicole. She suggested a drink. I accepted, and she went and got a martini for me.

"The way the place is done, it's unbelievable," Eric Ripert, the chef-owner of the great Le Bernardin, had told me. "The flow of energy, the way the energy goes on one side to the other side and the welcoming at the door, and the stress of the people at the door to get in or to get a table or to get the table they want—oh my God, it's like, it's hilarious. But what is special about Balthazar is that they have created a magical menu—forget the ambiance. The ambiance we know is fantastic, it's magical, and when you are regular they take good care of you and you feel at home."

Coming here in the evening made me feel, as it always did, that I had left town, had arrived somewhere else, some Paris of the mind. Paris, but better, because it was my neighborhood brasserie and just down the street from where I live.

When we'd had dinner, Adam Gopnik said, "I think that one of the great fertile comedies of the twentieth century, and conceivably of the twenty-first century as well, is that play of near-understanding, amplified re-creation, and re-appreciation." He was talking about the relationship between France and America, and while we worked our way through the Grand Plateau, the three tiers of seafood, of lobster and oysters, and drank a bottle of Champagne, he had talked about it, about how the French New Wave cinema first brought an intense appreciation of American film noir, and how the French remade the style into their own, and how we fell in love with each other. He might as well have been talking about the relationship of Balthazar to France, to the Parisian brasserie in reverse.

Dinner tonight was a reunion. Steven and Rona and James arrived, friends from all those breakfasts at Balthazar that had begun nearly twenty years ago. We had been through job changes and illnesses, birthdays, love affairs, celebrations, arguments about movies and books and politics, the deaths of family and friends; we had watched George Bush come and go twice, and Obama twice. That night Rona recounted her recent gardening adventures in Maine. Steven told an unprintable joke. Nicole came over, brought my martini, and took the drinks order. Rona ordered a bourbon Manhattan and said, "Should I get extra cherries for you, Reg?"

Cocktails, Trump. Clinton, colonoscopies, real estate. Children, haircuts, Don DeLillo, the death of literature, and whether or not we should share an order of brandade; we talked. We'd hardly sat down before we were talking, all of us at once, and laughing, too. Balthazar had always been a place where we laughed. Other people turned to look.

José Luis, who had worked with James when James was still the breakfast manager, hurried over, a big smile on his face, and they high-fived and man-hugged, and José Luis punched James in the arm as he always did. They had history. There were things they knew about Balthazar only insiders knew; they had shared its family secrets once. After that, he shook Steven's hand for a long time, and Steve asked about José Luis's daughter, who had worked at Balthazar and had just graduated from college. "Life is good?" Steven asked.

Patting his stomach, José Luis smiled. "Sure. Life is good," he said, again.

I thought about Massiel, our breakfast waiter who turned out to have been scared of us without our ever knowing. Were we friends with the staff here? Was it a piece of theater that lasted for a couple of hours and then was over, and was that enough? Were we merely groupies wanting a backstage pass? Was I?

Michael arrived a few minutes later. Tall, fair-haired, English, Mike was a professor at NYU, the only remaining friend I had who had known my parents. He ordered a glass of red wine. He was just back from Singapore via Kyoto. Steven ordered a beer and we all said, *Really?!* Was he now, living in Maine part-time, a man of the people?

"Can I please have a Ketel One martini straight up with lemon peel, Nicole, darling?" said James after they had exchanged kisses.

"Grey Goose is French," I said.

"And?" said James, raising one eyebrow just a fraction.

"Would you like to know the specials?" Nicole asked after we'd ascertained that her mother was well, and that Rona had seen the new exhibit at the Met. "Or shall I get the drinks?"

Drinks, we said.

I saw Michele Oka Doner arrive, tall as ever, with her husband. Nicole saw her, too. "She's lovely, she looks like a Greek goddess, first person I met who had a loft, I love that woman, she's glorious," Nicole said. Another favorite was Philippe Petit, the man who walked a wire from one Twin Tower to the other, whom she described as: "Very humble and naïve, one of my favorite people, and Keith bought him dinner every time he came in." Nicole went to the waiters' station, tapped in the drinks order.

"Nicole has eyes in the back of her head," James said. "She has to. She's a genius at this."

Across from us, a couple of middle-aged, well-dressed guys with expensive briefcases who might or might not have been a couple seemed to be discussing deals, but what kind? Movies? Money?

The restaurant was almost full. It was harder to eavesdrop. At night, Balthazar was noisy. For a while McNally's restaurants had often been reviewed for their decibel level, the blast of noise that hit you like a wall—Keith McNally was, in this way, the Phil Spector of restaurants. Lately, the music had been turned way down when the restaurant filled up. When I mentioned this to Keith, he said, "We're too old now."

At the next table, we became aware, there was a child who was throwing Froot Loops from a plastic bag at a tall blond power couple, presumably the parents. Nicole, without actually turning her head, was already thinking about this and how to avert a disaster in case the child started aiming at other customers. The boy was about four. The woman was wearing skintight white leather pants and four-inch Louboutins. The man had two cell phones, impatience engraved on his handsome but pissed-off and rather dumb face.

Across from us were the four Brazilians I had seen at the door, and they were laughing and eating from the three-tiered platter of seafood, and obviously having a good time, even the man in the snakeskin jacket. The woman with the big diamond saw me looking at it and smiled and waved. Alongside them was a party of six and they looked happy and they were drinking Chablis and eating escargots, toasting each other. On a good night at Balthazar, there was a kind of shared pleasure at being there.

Nicole returned with our drinks, somehow finding a way to stop and drop off Champagne at the Froot Loops' table. The woman said it wasn't bubbly enough, or too bubbly, anyway she was unhappy, and Nicole, who knew instinctively that only a fresh glass would fix it, said she would change it.

Her patience was saintly, but of course it was part of the deal at Balthazar. She would listen and later she would make a note about it, and the note would go into the program that Shane and Erin looked at every morning. Every complaint, every special request, all of it went into that program, and sometimes it caused a certain craziness among the back-of-house people, the people in charge; no customer ever knew.

Rona was cooing into her Manhattan, and I remembered somebody—Eric Ripert, I think—telling me that Balthazar made among the best cocktails in New York. James ordered oysters and steak tartare without hesitation. The rest of us discussed options, and there was steak au poivre for Michael, medium rare but not too rare; I wanted the spinach steamed, not sautéed.

"Why can't you just order what's on the menu?" a British friend always asked me. I explained that New Yorkers never ate items exactly as they appeared on the menu; that, in fact, only fools accepted dishes without a little customizing. New Yorkers want what they want. "Steamed, please," I said. "The spinach."

"Can we have some bread, goddamn it," called the tall blond guy to Sazzad, who was passing his table. "Whatsa matter, you saving money on the bread?" He may have looked Nordic, but his style was more *Goodfellas*.

"Why isn't it on the table?" The woman had stopped eating. The kid was wailing.

"Trouble," James whispered. "Brewing. Trouble, I mean."

We ordered.

"Anything else?" Nicole asked, reciting our orders back to us. She made sure she had it: "One shrimp cocktail, one Balthazar salad for two, six oysters, steak tartare, brandade, steak frites medium rare, skate, goat cheese and mushroom tart, a coq au vin, is that right? Extra portion of frites. Two? Any wine?" Nicole smiled amiably, seemingly unhurried.

Speed mattered; the trick was making it look easy. I suggested Château du Taillan, thinking about the vineyards in Bordeaux. Mike was thoughtful. He liked discussing the finer points of a vintage in detail; it was one of his passions. With Nicole, he discussed Burgundy and Bordeaux, and other more recherché districts in France, while the rest of us looked around; no matter how often you'd been to Balthazar there was a moment when you craned your neck—casually, of course—to see if there were any celebrities.

A new group had been seated at table 60. That guy, he looked famous, right? Wasn't he on TV? A Brit? "Ralph Fiennes," somebody whispered. There was always somebody at Balthazar, and wasn't that Alice Cooper, skinny in black? From a distance, I saw Meg Ryan arrive with her pale hair and dazzling smile.

"New Yorkers want everything that they want, and they want it yesterday," Nicole said. "They want it fast and perfect, and so do the people you work for. So there's all these little things that you need to iron out so that the customer doesn't feel them or experience them.

"You have to get to the table as fast as possible—you have two minutes, and you have to get them drinks and you have to tell the specials. Sometimes you have a few Brazilians"—she smiled at the foursome opposite us—"and you have to figure it out, and get through with the little Spanish or English you both know. It's speed and precision."

Nicole was conscious that, by eight-thirty, several of her other tables had been seated, and another was already on dessert. "You've got this and that, you have a complete juggling act on your hands, and so you juggle. You go to a table and say—somebody's grabbing for you—'Give me one second and I'm going to be right with you,' and you make sure you get to everyone within two minutes. And when you do, when you get to new guests, you say, 'Good evening. Welcome to Balthazar.'"

"You might add something like 'That's a lovely dress' or 'Good to see you.' It's all in the moment," said James, who had spent plenty of time waiting tables here. "This is improv. You're breaking the ice. You know how in second-rate restaurants the waiter comes over and says, 'Hi, my name is James, I'll be taking care of you this evening'? That's how restaurants often think you can break the ice. It's not. You're going to spend a couple of hours together, you want your guests to have a good experience, but you are the actor. You play your part."

Red wine? White? We'd thought to get just a light red.

"Let's get both," said Steven.

"The red could be heavier now, if you're also having white," said Nicole. "My personal favorite is a Cabernet Franc, like a Chinon from the Loire Valley, and it is strong enough to stand up to the chicken and the steak au poivre, it's got enough meat on its bones. But it's a wine that's light enough that you could even pair it with any fish. But if you want a white as well . . ."

Mike was considering some fabulous and rare wine, and I said, "Not too expensive."

"Don't be silly," he said. "This is a celebration." He ordered the wine.

Within fifteen minutes, of course, our appetizers appeared. James perused his oysters with unalloyed greed, ate them, and gazed sorrowfully at the empty plate. "These were exquisite," he said. I thought of Mike Osinski birthing his oysters at Widow's Hole on

Long Island, of Keith McNally shucking them at One Fifth when he first arrived in New York in 1975, and Jerry serving them one day in Bolivia.

A runner went by, his tray loaded with steak frites. "You think that's your Daisy Mae?" Rona asked. "The cow you saw in Kansas?"

What did Rona know about cattle? I thought, but Steven assured me now she had a garden in Maine and was a true rural woman.

Dinner full on now, all the million moving parts that Erin had been dealing with since dawn seemed in place, the gears oiled, the machine invisible. I knew the cooks were in the kitchen, plating the food that had been prepped by the guys downstairs. That the tiniest detail had been attended to, and this made me think, for some reason, of one of the bar guys checking for bugs.

Water bugs love alcohol. Every single morning one of the bar guys shone a light into every single bottle, making sure there were no bugs. Every bug the health department found produced a fine of five hundred bucks. It could add up to hundreds of thousands a year; worse still, one bug meant you were labeled "a restaurant with bugs." Balthazar had no bugs. Our cocktails were pristine.

"You want to taste the mushroom tart?" Steven said. "You should try it." There followed, of course, a certain amount of sampling of one another's dishes. Mike watched us stick our forks into one another's plates with mock British dismay.

"It's how you do it in New York," I said.

You could always tell. Other people did a lot of exchanging of utensils, bites of food placed carefully on other plates. If somebody said, "Have a bite," a New Yorker just stuck the fork in. When the main courses arrived, the skate with brown butter Steve had ordered was delicious.

"You're eating all of Steve's food," Mike said to me.

By nine-thirty, most of the tables had turned over at least once, but we were still sitting and drinking wine, all reaching for the last fries, the little golden brown crispy bits.

Some of the other waiters stopped by. Sazzad, Moustapha, Paule, and the bussers, too; Frank Ortega came out of the kitchen to say hi.

"New York, right?" Steven said. "The microcosm."

José Luis cleared away everything, our plates, our forks and knives, the salt and pepper, bread and butter, too, that practical magic that Eric Ripert loved.

"I think I'll have profiteroles for dessert," Rona said. "Anyone want to share?"

I offered.

By eleven, the Froot Loops were long gone. A kind of satiated delight had crossed the faces of the Brazilians. We had eaten the profiteroles and the lemon mousse tarte, the chocolate pot de crème, and the lovely, light pavlova.

I'd had hundreds of dinners at Balthazar. I had, in fact, lived out much of my life in restaurants, back to when I was that fat, nosy little girl peering through the doors of the pizza joint on Bleecker Street. For the best part of half a century—my God, was it that long?—I'd been eating out at diners, bistros, pubs, at the coffee shop in Delta Junction, Alaska, where there was a prayer breakfast going on the morning I spent there cramming pancakes into my mouth. At Jerry's on Spring Street, where I used to meet my father every day for lunch when he still had his print shop in the space where Keith McNally now ran his empire.

There wasn't a block in SoHo or Greenwich Village that didn't remind me of some meal, some restaurant, some bar or café or dive, where a piece of my life was embedded like a fossil in amber—or chewing gum in a New York sidewalk.

I knew some of the realities of Balthazar now. I knew how hard and hot it was in the kitchen; how difficult the lives of many of the cooks were, of the little disturbances and the mountainous problems that were solved every day; waiters who were waiting for a part in a play, water bugs in the booze, a shortage of the right potatoes for the fries, city bureaucracy, the exploding price of food; and this fickle city that was always looking for the new best thing.

Mike looked at his watch and ordered Armagnac. James gestured toward a couple who had come in late and were sitting down opposite us. They were very young and sat close together and ordered Champagne and never once looked at their phones. Steven set down his glass, looked at the kids. "Balthazar so often seems to me to be a place where everyone's in love," he said. "It's like a little cocoon." Outside the thunder might be rumbling—bad weather, bad politics, troubled times; inside, for a few hours, it was an escape, a little piece of theater.

We sat on a while in a sentimental mood. So much a part of our lives was invested in Balthazar, we were reluctant to leave, as if somehow we might scatter, to Florida and Maine and London, as if it might be too long before we saw each other again. "Don't be silly, Reg," said Rona.

It's just breakfast, Rona had said once, years ago when we were still meeting every morning. "I was wrong," she said now. "It never was just breakfast. It never was."

CHAPTER 26

AFTER MIDNIGHT

J ames and I stayed late. We sat at the bar, and he drank another glass of red wine and I ordered Grand Marnier and espresso; even though we had already had dessert, we shared the banana ricotta tart with the banana ice cream, because the night had been a celebration. We reminisced about the days when he had been the morning manager and that Hawaiian shirt he wore then.

"It was Comme des Garçons," he said, not for the first time. "It wasn't Hawaiian."

On the sound system the Rolling Stones were singing "Brown Sugar," and I thought how, no matter what they sang, it was always a party.

At one, when we got up to leave, there was a lone guy at the bar reading a book. I couldn't see the title, and he didn't look up except to sip his beer.

In a corner, Moustapha and Sazzad were sitting at a table near the window, eating some supper and checking receipts.

Soon the yellow bread truck would pull up at the back door, bringing Paula Oland's beautiful loaves from New Jersey for another day's worth of meals.

• • •

Before Erin had left earlier that night, I asked what she thought gave Balthazar its particular character, if it had one.

"I think that, regardless of what people may hear, there is a loyalty and a care for the way they do it, and for whom they do it, that you will not find anywhere else," she said. "I've worked in NYC, Portland, LA, New Orleans, it's different, it's just different, there is a soul to here. And it comes from the people here, not just from the place.

"Sometimes I can't believe I work here, much less run it," Erin added. "Somewhere along the line, the people who've been at Balthazar forever, we drank the Kool-Aid, we put it into our lives that we're part of the culture of this city, this neighborhood, art, film, theater, we're part of that. I like to think that, anyway."

Outside the front door was the unflappable Nigel; Shane called him "Security" as if it were his name because it was on his badge. Nigel Williams, broad-shouldered, cheerful—nothing got past him, but he never seemed aggressive at all, just a pleasant guy waving you off for the night. He kept an eye on the crowd, the door, the curb, the cars, but he seemed always to be at ease.

"Good night, Mr. Security," we said.

"Good night there," he said. "Be careful how you go."

I turned to look back at the almost empty restaurant. Somewhere I read that *Nighthawks*, Edward Hopper's 1942 painting, was one of America's favorite pictures. For a long time the diner in the painting—it was based on a place in Greenwich Village Hopper had known—had seemed to me an evocation of loneliness. The last time I'd gone to look at it at the old Whitney Museum, I realized something else. In that diner, the lights on, a few regulars drinking coffee, the man and woman talking to the guy behind the counter, another fellow a few seats away. Dark outside, the streets empty, the diner seems a haven, a place where those customers look safe, look OK, look as if they're part of a little community, if only while they drink their coffee.

On Spring Street it was dark and quiet, but the lights inside Balthazar were on, the man with a book still there, at the bar. It reminded me of *Nighthawks*, and it reminded me of a brasserie on some dark corner in Paris, the yellow lights spilling onto the sidewalk.

JUSTINE'S FAVORITE BANANA RICOTTA TART

Yield: 6 tarts

I used to take my goddaughter Justine to Balthazar after school for this dessert, and now, having just had her own little girl, Rosie, she plans to raise her on it. This is a long recipe, but the results are richly worth it.

INGREDIENTS

Cookie ingredients:	Ricotta filling ingredients:	Banana ice cream base ingredients:	Banana cream caramel sauce ingredients:
4 ounces confectioner's sugar	6 ounces ricotta cheese	1 quart heavy cream	½ cup water
2 ounces white sugar	½ cup sugar	2 cups whole milk	1 cup sugar
2 eggs	2 eggs, plus one egg white	1 cup sugar	2 teaspoons lemon juice
2 teaspoons vanilla	2 teaspoons vanilla extract	2 teaspoons vanilla extract	2 cups heavy cream
4 ounces almond flour	½ cup heavy cream	4 ripe bananas	1 banana
10 ounces all-purpose flour	**For plating:**	12 egg yolks	
1 pound butter	6 bananas		

COOKIE INSTRUCTIONS:

Mix butter and all-purpose flour in a mixing bowl. Add the eggs and vanilla, and mix until incorporated. Add the almond flour and the sugars and mix until just incorporated. Do not over-mix.

Once the dough is mixed, put it on some plastic wrap and roll into a tube about 3 inches around.

Preheat oven to 325°F. With the plastic still on, slice the dough into

⅛-inch thick cookies. Throw away plastic. Line half-sheet pan with parchment paper. Put the cookies on top. Bake for 20 minutes or until nice and golden. Set aside to cool.

RICOTTA CHEESE FILLING INSTRUCTIONS:

Mix the cheese together with the sugar until fluffy and creamy. Add the two eggs, egg white, and vanilla extract and mix until incorporated. Add the cream and mix until incorporated so that the mixture is nice and smooth. Place the mixture in a 2-inch-deep 8- x 12-inch baking pan and place the pan in a deeper roasting pan.

Preheat the oven to 325°F.

Add hot water to the roasting pan until the water reaches about ⅓ up the side of the baking pan. Bake for 1 hour or until set. Remove from oven and let cool completely.

COOKIE AND FILLING ASSEMBLY INSTRUCTIONS:

Put cooled almond cookies on a plate. When the cheese mixture has cooled, put it in a pastry bag with a small or medium tip. Pipe from the middle of the cookie to cover it, making a dome-like shape.

BANANA ICE CREAM BASE INSTRUCTIONS:

Mash bananas well. In a large saucepan, mix with heavy cream, milk, sugar, and vanilla. Bring to a boil over medium heat.

Mix the egg yolks in a bowl with a small amount of the milk mixture, about 4 ounces at a time. Stir constantly with a wooden spoon over medium heat until the mixture coats the back of the spoon and is quite thick.

Strain through a fine-mesh strainer. Refrigerate at least 24 hours.

Run mixture in an ice cream machine according to the manufacturer's directions. Spread parchment paper evenly in half-sheet pan, spray with cooking spray.

When the ice cream is almost fully frozen, spread it over parchment paper, about a half-inch thick.

This will become the base of the dessert. It is then frozen solid and cut out with a 2-inch round cookie cutter. See plating on next page.

(This ice cream is so good, I could happily eat it on its own for dessert!)

BANANA CREAM CARAMEL SAUCE INSTRUCTIONS:

Mix water, sugar, and lemon juice and place in a saucepan. Bring to a boil and cook until caramelized, about 10 minutes.

Slowly add the heavy cream and boil until bubbly like gazpacho. Add the banana, mix, and cook for another 4 minutes until thick. Punch with a hand blender, strain, and cool. Pour into a squeeze bottle.

PLATING INSTRUCTIONS:

Slice the 6 bananas into thin coins. Lay coins over each dome-shaped, ricotta cheese–topped cookie. Lightly dust each banana-topped dome with sugar and caramelize with a blow torch.

For each plate you're going to serve each tart on, put a dot of the banana caramel cream sauce in the middle of the plate. Place the ice cream puck on the sauce, then place the caramelized banana cookie dome on top of it.

Squeeze a circle of the banana cream caramel sauce over the whole dish. If you haven't got a squeeze bottle, you can drizzle with a spoon, but it won't look as good. Balthazar puts a little bit of crème anglaise with the caramel sauce, but enough is enough. It's a step too far for me.

LEMON TART

Yield: Makes 2 eight-inch tarts

INGREDIENTS

Sucre dough (sugar pastry) ingredients:

36 ounces pastry flour

8 ounces 10x powdered sugar

24 ounces butter

4 egg yolks

1 ounce heavy cream

Lemon curd ingredients:

16 ounces lemon juice

3 eggs

20 ounces granulated sugar

2 ounces cornstarch

8 ounces butter

Soufflé ingredients:

4 egg whites

2 ounces granulated sugar

For decoration:

blueberries or edible flowers

SUCRE DOUGH INSTRUCTIONS:

Cream butter and sugar together until light and fluffy, then add yolks and cream. Fold in flour. Let rest overnight in the fridge.

LEMON CURD INSTRUCTIONS:

Put all ingredients into a bowl, place over pot of boiling water, and cook (as in a bain-marie) until thick.

Chill overnight.

SOUFFLÉ INSTRUCTIONS:

Whip 4 egg whites and 2 ounces granulated sugar until light and airy. Fold this into 16 ounces of lemon curd as above, using plastic spatula.

You will need 2 8-inch tart rings. Roll out the sucre to ¼-inch thick and 10 inches around. Line the rings with the rolled-out dough.

Fill with the lemon curd soufflé mix, and bake at 300°F for 15–20 minutes. Decorate with a few blueberries or some edible flowers.

TO DRINK:

Beaume-de-Venise dessert wine or a medium-bodied Champagne never disappoints! Duval-Leroy Cru Brut NV.

COCONUT CAKE

Yield: Makes 2 cakes

Mark Tasker is Balthazar's chief sweets man. His cakes are incredible and even to read the recipe feels like drowning in buttercream.

INGREDIENTS

You will need 2 10-inch cake tins and a table-top mixer.

Cake ingredients:

6 ounces butter

6 ounces vegetable shortening

8 ounces desiccated coconut

24 ounces granulated sugar

16 ounces cake flour

¾ ounces baking powder

6 eggs

10 ounces milk

1 vanilla bean pod

Pinch of salt

For decoration:

4 ounces shaved coconut

Pastry cream ingredients:

MIXTURE A

16 ounces whole milk

16 ounces crème fraîche

4 ounces sugar

½ vanilla pod

MIXTURE B

2 whole eggs

2 egg yolks

4 ounces granulated sugar

2 ounces cornstarch

Buttercream ingredients:

8 egg whites

11 ounces granulated sugar

½ vanilla pod

20 ounces soft butter

Rum soak ingredients:

16 ounces stock syrup (boil up a mix of half sugar and half water and cool)

2 ounces rum

CAKE INSTRUCTIONS:

Cream butter and vegetable shortening with sugar. Add seeds from vanilla bean pod. Add coconut and continue to cream. Using stand mixer, beat for 10 minutes, until light and fluffy. Add eggs slowly and continue to mix. Add baking powder and salt to flour, then slowly add flour, alternating with milk, and continue to beat for 10 minutes.

Preheat oven to 325°F. Pour batter into 2 10-inch cake tins. Bake for 70 minutes.

PASTRY CREAM INSTRUCTIONS:

Pour Mixture B ingredients into a bowl and mix with a whisk until combined. Pour ingredients for Mixture A into a large pot and bring to a boil.

Slowly add Mixture A (while still boiling) to Mixture B, whisking constantly. Once both mixes are introduced (and have had conjugal relations), put back on the stove and bring to a further boil, mixing until your arm falls off.

Put the whole mix into the bowl on the stand mixer. Add softened butter. Whisk for ten minutes. Cool and refrigerate overnight or for up to one week.

BUTTERCREAM INSTRUCTIONS:

Cook first three ingredients in bain-marie. (If you haven't got one, just put a bowl on top of a pot of boiling water so the steam does the cooking.) When hot, put on stand mixer. Slowly add the soft butter and whisk with attachment. Mix until creamy and ready for use.

COCONUT CAKE ASSEMBLY INSTRUCTIONS:

Cut 10-inch cake into three layers and soak each layer with rum soak. Lighten pastry cream with whipped heavy cream (32 ounces of pastry cream will need 4 ounces of whipped cream to lighten). Spread approximately 12 ounces of pastry cream on each layer. Alternate cake layers with pastry cream. Beat buttercream until light and coat the cake top and sides with the buttercream. While cream is still soft, cover with toasted coconut shavings.

TO DRINK:

A medium-bodied rosé Champagne like Philippe Gonet Rosé Brut.

Suggested Reading

There were some books I read while I was writing *At Balthazar* that I thought useful, informative, and entertaining with regard to any number of subjects; a few of them I just plain loved and thought I'd share.

Delmonico's: A History by Peter Andrews

Forty Years On, Writing Home, and *Untold Stories* by Alan Bennett

The Physiology of Taste: Or Meditations on Transcendental Gastronomy by Jean Anthelme Brillat-Savarin

The Restaurants of New York, 1979–80, 1988 editions by Seymour Britchky

Heat: An Amateur Cook in a Professional Kitchen by Bill Buford

Alexander Hamilton by Ron Chernow

The Oysters of Locmariaquer by Eleanor Clark

Restaurant Success by the Numbers: A Money-Guy's Guide to Opening the Next New Hot Spot by Roger Fields

Paris to the Moon and *The Table Comes First: Family, France, and the Meaning of Food* by Adam Gopnik

Appetite City: A Culinary History of New York by William Grimes

Downtown: My Manhattan by Pete Hamill

A Moveable Feast by Ernest Hemingway

Behind the Kitchen Door by Saru Jayaraman and Eric Schlosser

SoHo: The Rise and Fall of an Artists' Colony by Richard Kostel-
anetz

The Big Oyster: History on the Half Shell by Mark Kurlansky

Meat: Everything You Need to Know by Pat LaFrieda

On Further Reflection: 60 Years of Writing by Jonathan Miller

The Omnivore's Dilemma: A Natural History of Four Meals by Michael Pollan

*Comfort Me with Apples: Love, Adventure and a Passion for Cook-
ing* and *Tender at the Bone: Growing Up at the Table* by Ruth
Reichl

Low Life: Lures and Snares of Old New York by Luc Sante

*The Invention of the Restaurant: Paris and Modern Gastronomic
Culture* by Rebecca Spang

*It Must've Been Something I Ate: The Return of the Man Who Ate
Everything* by Jeffrey Steingarten

*Banquet at Delmonico's: The Gilded Age and the Triumph of Evolu-
tion in America* by Barry Werth

The AIA Guide to New York City

And a few novels:

The Alienist by Caleb Carr

Bright Lights, Big City by Jay McInerney

Burr by Gore Vidal

The Age of Innocence by Edith Wharton

One book in particular that changed my whole view of New York
City (and which gave me the idea for this book's title) is *The Island
at the Center of the World: The Epic Story of Dutch Manhattan and
the Forgotten Colony That Shaped America* by Russell Shorto. It is
about the best history of the city I can remember reading. It covers
only the brief period when the Dutch ruled Manhattan but it reveals,

in microcosm, exactly how the city became itself—a great port. Those early ships from Amsterdam brought a stunningly diverse crowd of immigrants. In Manhattan money mattered a lot more than religion, tolerance was felt to be good business, the newcomers made friends with the natives—it was also good for trade—and there were more taverns and eating houses than people.

Acknowledgments

C hef Shane McBride and Erin Wendt, the general manager, are both, simply, wonderful in what they do and as people, and they are also very funny. Without them there would certainly be no book. They answered every question, no-holds-barred, and showed me how the place works, and to both, well, thank you.

The whole staff of nearly 250 people at Balthazar made me welcome. So many of the staff have been with Balthazar for so long that they've grown up and raised families, some of whom have worked at the restaurant too. The sweep of all those lives can never be captured in one book but only hinted at. This wildly diverse collection of talented, valuable, hard-working, and often lovely people are a microcosm of the best of New York City, and though many of them are out of sight of the regular customer, they are the reason that, as an institution, Balthazar works so well. I want to thank them all and a few by name: Roberta Delice, Rebecca Banks, Zouheir Louhaichy, Kouider Zioueche, Bruce Rabanit, James (Jimmy) Norris, Paula Oland, Kate Pulino, Mark Tasker, Frank Ortega, Gerardo Alvarez, Cesar Gomez, Nicole Hopson, Sazzad Islam, Moustapha Konte, Asbury Wilkinson, Carol Iseman, Paule Aboite, Silvia Fiorina, José Luis Juarez, Henry Ly, Ante Diopp, and Ranfis Felix. And so many others who have made breakfast (and lunch and dinner) at Balthazar a joy. If I've left anybody out, this is to thank you, too.

Huge thanks, too, to Ian McPheeley, Richard Lewis, and Kris Spychalski.

For the wonderful photographs, I have to thank Peter Nelson.

Thanks, too, to Gili Getz for extra photography and support in the early days of work on this book.

Great input for the "Port of Balthazar" section came from Guillaume Clarke de Dromantin, Armelle Cruse, Pat LaFrieda, Mark Pastore, Nate Stambaugh, and Mike and Isobel Osinski.

For taking the time to talk to me about food and restaurants and France, I owe lavish thanks to Ruth Reichl and Adam Gopnik, and to a couple of chefs who love and really get Balthazar, Eric Ripert and David Chang.

Among the original Balthazar Breakfast gang, Rona Middleberg and Steven Zwerling were essential to all of this, great friends, and still the best company you can have over an oatmeal scone (two blueberry jams), and an espresso.

I want to thank a few of the visiting Brits: the witty and shrewd William Miller, whose input was essential, and his parents, the wonderful Rachel and Jonathan Miller.

Friends, old and new, shared their own stories and much else:

Anthony Andrews, Sally Roy, Salman Rushdie, Shaun Woodward, Luke Redgrave, Judy Wong, and Frank Wynne, as well as old SoHo hands Michele Oka Doner, Lynn Hectman, Art Spiegelman, and Lynne Yu. And many thanks, too, to Allan Jenkins at the London *Observer*.

Finally, I want to thank some people who literally made this book happen, especially everyone at Gallery Books, in particular Jen Bergstrom and Navorn Johnson. Also, Molly Gregory. And Kate Dresser, my editor, who is both young and talented, not a bad combination to encounter when you're a writer; with Kate, I got very, very lucky.

To Matteo Bologna, the talented designer—and a very funny man—who turned the book into a work of art at record speed: *mille grazie.*

William Clark, my agent and friend, a genius with a proposal, is also smart and caring, and he has a Rottweiler and will take on anyone to make sure his writers are properly published. When he says, "Don't worry, we'll make this happen," he will.

I met James Weichert the first day I ate breakfast at Balthazar, and his input on it and the restaurant business were invaluable, the friendship more so.

"Top of the goddamn morning," his greeting at breakfast at Balthazar, has remained over these last twenty years our agreed salutation.

And finally, there is Leslie Woodhead. Friend, editor, co-conspirator in books and films, he read endless revisions of the manuscript, provided reassurance and a stream of good advice, and, though not a natural gourmet, managed to down plenty of escargots, steak frites, and red wine.

Oh, and during the time I was writing this book, Rosie Rodricks made an appearance. She is, naturally, the most gorgeous grandchild ever, and I'm waiting until she's just old enough to go to Balthazar and sample the banana ricotta tart and the profiteroles.

I'm afraid this is her destiny.

Photo Captions

Insert 2

Page 1: Chief Spring Street baker Mark Tasker finishing a glaze on his luscious plum galettes.

Page 2: Chef Shane McBride on Spring Street outside Balthazar.

Page 3: Reflections in a golden glass—the Balthazar bar seen in an interior glass panel.

Page 4: Waiter Amari Williams checking an order at the seafood stall.

Page 5: Investor Dick Robinson drinking Champagne in the early evening.

Page 6: Restaurateur Keith McNally drinking espresso in the morning. Photo courtesy of Keith McNally.

Page 7: One of the caryatids behind the bar at Balthazar.

Page 8: Alejandro Negreros cooks with flame.

Page 9: Sous chef Cesar Gomez and runner Paiga Diego with steak frites.

Pages 10–11: A waiters' meeting and wine tasting at Christmastime: Nicole Hopson in foreground, standing; to her left is Sazzad Islam; Maria Musei is the blond waitress in center; next to her is Silvia Fiorina, then Paule Aboite.

Page 12: José Luis Juarez, Balthazar busser.

Page 13: Dr. Emilia Hermann enjoying a cocktail and a laugh at Balthazar in the early evening.

Pages 14–15: David Maher, head bartender, late at night behind the bar, as seen through Balthazar's front window.

Page 16: The iconic yellow Balthazar Bakery truck, delivering bread to the restaurant at dawn.

About the Author

Reggie Nadelson is a journalist and author who has written for *The Guardian* and *FT* in London and for *Vogue, Departures,* and *Travel + Leisure* in the US. She is the author of the Artie Cohen mysteries published in a score of countries, and she has written and produced documentaries for the BBC. She was born in downtown Manhattan, where she still lives and where she eats at Balthazar as often as she can.